LARS VON TRIER

INTERVIEWS

CONVERSATIONS WITH FILMMAKERS SERIES
PETER BRUNETTE, GENERAL EDITOR

Photo credit: Leif–Erik Nygårds

LARS VON TRIER
TRIER
INTERVIEWS

JAN LUMHOLDT

UNIVERSITY PRESS OF MISSISSIPPI / JACKSON

www.upress.state.ms.us

The University Press of Mississippi is a member of the Association of American
University Presses.

⊗

Library of Congress Cataloging-in-Publication Data

Lumholdt, Jan, 1961–
    Lars von Trier : interviews / Jan Lumholdt.
      p. cm. — (Conversations with filmmakers series)
    Includes index.
    ISBN 1-57806-531-3 (alk. paper) — ISBN 1-57806-532-1 (pbk. :
alk. paper)
    1. Trier, Lars von, 1956– —Interviews. 2. Motion picture
producers and directors—Denmark—Interviews. I. Title. II. Series.
PN1998.3.T747 A5 2003
791.43'0233'092—dc21   2002015751

British Library Cataloging-in-Publication Data available

CONTENTS

Introduction *ix*

Chronology *xxi*

Filmography *xxv*

He'd Rather Watch a Cop Show Than Himself 3
LARS HOFFMANN

Passion Is the Lifeblood of Cinema 5
OLE MICHELSEN

We Need More Intoxicants in Danish Cinema 13
LARS SCHWANDER

Sightseeing with the Holy Ghost 24
THOMAS ALLING

A Conversation between Jan Kornum Larsen and Lars von Trier 32
JAN KORNUM LARSEN

A Conversation with Lars von Trier 47
MARIE BERTHELIUS AND ROGER NARBONNE

A Conversation with Lars von Trier 59
MICHEL CIMENT AND PHILIPPE ROUYER

A Conversation with Lars von Trier, Henning Bendtsen, and Ernst-Hugo
Järegård 64
EVA AF GEIJERSTAM

A Romance in Decomposition   71
MICHAEL TAPPER

Maniacal Iconoclast of Film Convention   81
NIGEL ANDREWS

Euro Paean   84
JONATHAN ROMNEY

Lars von Trier, Director   86
TOBY ROSE

A Stone-Turner from Lyngby   88
LARS K. ANDERSEN

I Am Curious, Film: Lars von Trier   100
STIG BJÖRKMAN AND LENA NYMAN

Edge of Darkness   103
WALLY HAMMOND

Control and Chaos   106
CHRISTIAN BRAAD THOMSEN

The Man Who Would Give Up Control   117
PETER ØVIG KNUDSEN

Tracing the Inner Idiot   125
EBBE IVERSEN

Dogme Is Dead! Long Live Song and Dance!   130
JØRN ROSSING JENSEN

Lars von Trier: The Man Who Would Be Dogme   133
SHARI ROMAN

Dance in the Dark   144
GAVIN SMITH

Lars von Trier Comes Out of the Dark   153
ANTHONY KAUFMAN

There Will Be No Fun-Poking Today   159
JAN LUMHOLDT

9 A.M., Thursday, September 7, 2000: Lars von Trier   170
   KJELD KOPLEV

Lars von Trier in Dogville   205
   MARIT KAPLA

Index   213

INTRODUCTION

''WHAT THE HELL,'' notes Peter Aalbæk Jensen, producer and Lars von Trier's closest colleague for over ten years; "you can say of him what you want, but films of a certain level of quality—he can make those. And then it's unimportant what he says or does or how he is, right?"

It is perfectly true that Lars von Trier sometimes takes matters to the point where von Trier, the showman and manifesto-slinging provocateur, upstages Lars, the director of ambitious, visually distinctive films featuring increasingly interesting character studies. The forty-seven-year-old Dane has on occasion been labeled "confrontational," "self-promoting," "arrogant," and "testy." His willful impishness has even prompted epithets such as "manipulator," "charlatan," and "misogynist," as well as "The Mad Prince of Denmark" and "The Antichrist of Celluloid."

Succulent fodder for tall tales and scandalmongering has certainly been served up at that celestially infernal big top called Cannes; there, Lars von Trier has had films on six occasions. The first time was in 1984, when he showed up in black leather with a shaved head and *The Element of Crime*. He immediately stirred up controversy, not least by being visibly less than thrilled when the film received only a pedestrian technical award. In 1987, he again aroused indignation with *Epidemic*, which the normally shock- and ennui-resistant Cannes-goers literally walked out on. He next gave Roman Polanski's "midget"-led jury of 1991 the figurative finger when *Europa* failed to garner top honors at the award ceremony. Then, with *Breaking the Waves* in 1996, he failed to show up entirely, the result of phobias concerning traveling and public appearances (his phobias include trains, planes, blood, boats, hospitals, crowds, and, occasionally, journalists.)

In 1998, von Trier arrived in Cannes with the 35-mm result of a new cinematic manifesto called Dogme95 and created a stir not only with the manifesto itself, but also by including hardcore porno scenes in his festival entry *The Idiots*. His most recent visit to Cannes was in 2000; he finally won the Palme d'Or for *Dancer in the Dark*, but by then all anyone wanted to talk about was his feud with his leading lady (and nobody had forgotten those porno scenes from 1998). Over the course of eighteen years, he has actually attended the Cannes festival for a total of less than ten days; yet his reputation there constitutes the core of the whole myth of Lars von Trier as most of the world knows it. Those less than ten days (and especially those less than ten seconds of explicit sexual penetration) have certainly shaken the cinema world. At the same time this is a man who has been making films of varying quality for the last thirty-six years—and of a "certain level of quality" for at least the last eighteen.

Lars von Trier: Interviews contains two conversations conducted at Cannes, in 1987 and 1991—long before the infamous hubbubs of 1998 and 2000. Otherwise, we mainly encounter the director at the office, in the studio, on location, or at home. Meeting him on his home turf—be the visitor a foreigner or a compatriot—has allowed for more candid conversation than the turmoil of Cannes, needless to say. (Perhaps there should be a separate volume entitled "Lars von Trier: Cannes Interviews"? It would be entertaining.) And despite the admonition, quoted above, of Albæk Jensen, what von Trier says or does, at least in the context of an interview, has been accorded a great deal of importance.

Not that "The Mad Prince" is entirely absent, but he's not entirely in charge either. Rather, the focus of this volume is on thoughtful, at times passionate and outspoken, conversations on such subjects as cinematic politics, filmmaking philosophies, influences and ideals (predominately Dreyer), groundbreaking technical solutions (like hypnosis), working with or in spite of actors, being or not being Jewish, childhood impressions and the (de-)formative values of von Trier's youth, religion, parenthood, going fishing— these are a few of the crucial themes that should shed some light on a director of "films of a certain level of quality." And, yes, there will also be discussions of both porno and the brawls with that pebble in his shoe called Björk. But much, much more as well.

In all, we span thirty-three years of von Trier's career in cinema, with many of the interviews appearing here for the first time in English translation. The majority of them are, for several reasons, from Scandinavian sources: von Trier was born and lives in Denmark, and a reluctant traveler, he seldom leaves his native Nordic habitat. Danish journalists were of course the first to meet him, and as early as 1968 at that. While doing a piece on the new children's television series *Hemmelig sommer* ("Secret Summer"), *Aktuelt*'s Lars Hoffmann has a brief, yet portentous, encounter with the pre-teen Lars Trier, who has been given the male lead in the series. "I don't know, but I know I'd like to be something in pictures," says the boy. Young Trier will use his wages (3,000 crowns) to buy himself an electric organ, "to make some sounds with when we're making short films," and he's happy to get three weeks off from school thrown into the bargain. Might this cocky kid one day amount to something?

Cut to 1982: "If you ever amount to anything, it's not on account of, but rather *in spite* of something, and in this respect, film school has worked tremendously well." Fresh from the Danish Film School, young Trier has caused controversy with his graduation film, the World War II drama *Images of a Relief*, and also with that defiant "von" added to his name. When Ole Michelsen from *Tusind Øjne* asks about the future, von Trier says that he might have to learn to compromise to stay in the business. . . .

A little later: "Things can *only* get better!" A slap in the face of contemporary Danish cinematic tastes is imminent, as the angry, ruthlessly uncompromising prodigy is about to enter the big scene. While preparing a noir-ish thriller with "a glossy plot," he is interviewed by *Levende Billeder*'s Lars Schwander, the brother of one of von Trier's film-school classmates. An unglossed attack on the Danish film industry permeates this conversation, which leaves few holy cows unmolested. This cocky young man wants things to become "completely different" in the world of cinema. So much for compromising. . . .

Yet a little later: "I regard the plot as some kind of skeleton, a kind of alibi for making the images." The shooting of *The Element of Crime* has begun, and *Levende Billeder*'s Thomas Alling pays a visit to the set. Alling's interview, which takes us on a strange journey through Copenhagen and its environs— from the nighttime gloom of a wooded ground to the stench of underground sewers, to the lofty casemates of a medieval castle—with the music of Wagner, brought along by von Trier for *stimmung*, blasting out over portable loudspeakers, also includes comments from von Trier's two principal co-workers at the time, cameraman Tom Elling and editor Tómas Gislason. The director has evolved and has begun to explore other dimensions of filmmaking. "I have to admit that I initially saw the crime story as a necessary evil," he says; now, however, he admits that the turns the story ended up taking proved to be quite interesting. Actors, though, according to von Trier, are to be treated like puppets, and leading man Michael Elphick (who, von Trier says today, never mentioned *The Element of Crime* in his work résumé) is duly confused.

"It's like not good form to be fascinated, and it's very un-Danish." It is 1984 and the phrase "politically correct" has not yet been popularized; but had it been, then von Trier would surely have been using and abusing it in various contexts. Jan Kornum Larsen's extensive interview for *Kosmorama* from this year finds the serious young filmmaker talking at length about different aspects of his vision in a close reading of *The Element of Crime*. Lars von Trier speaks of his "very mathematical" and "incredibly, almost hysterically, structured" concepts—we're still more than a decade away from the control-shunning filmmaker of the late 1990s. A soon-to-be-popularized phenomenon, later baptized bungy jumping, is anticipated by the "rope-jumping scene" in *The Element of Crime* ("a ritual that's actually being executed in London, I've heard"). Mention is also made of a possible Wagner project in Germany (an idea that rings truer than ever at the time of this writing, since von Trier has recently agreed to direct the "Ring Trilogy" at the 2006 *Festspiele* in Bayreuth).

Although *The Element of Crime* does only modestly well at the Danish box office (37,000 moviegoers, compared to Bille August's *Twist and Shout*, which sells 503,000 tickets the same season) and wins "only" the technical award at Cannes, it is sold to several countries and opens in England in 1985. Lars "I never fly" von Trier drives from Denmark to London and shares his unabashed views on cinema in general and on Danish cinema in particular ("There have been two Danish director—Carl Th. Dreyer and me"[1]) with flabbergasted journalists, who, in accordance with Danish rumors, expect "a wild and wayward skinhead with a tendency to assault interviewers with coleslaw and other foodstuffs."[2] On the other side of the Atlantic (where von Trier, years later, still has never been and still may never go), Steven Spielberg expresses curiosity about the prodigy, but his telexed request for a video copy of the Dane's latest film is ceremoniously ignored. "If Spielberg wants to steal my ideas, he can do it the hard way and see the film in a theater."[3]

However, the precocious swell of the angry young filmmaker soon ebbs—at least temporarily. With the exception of a rambunctious commercial called *Sauna* (1986), the late 1980s are lean years career- and publicity-wise for him. The main reason is the 1987 fiscal fiasco called *Epidemic*.

"You could say that *Epidemic* is a very private film. I like to see private films at the cinema." Too private for most people, it would seem—it comes and goes with little notice (4,929 moviegoers in Denmark) and is seen by small audiences abroad, if by anyone at all. In Sweden—a country that has always appreciated von Trier—the film wouldn't open until late 2000, but even then it failed to benefit from the newfound prestige of its Palme d'Or–winning director (a loss for everyone involved, for it is truly a gem).

Early on, audiences in France take von Trier to their hearts. The Parisians, in particular, give a Jerry Lewis–like welcome, and magazines such as *La Revue du Cinéma* and *Positif* display great interest in the Dane. The *Positif* interview is one of the few published interviews with the director in connection with *Epidemic*. Here, von Trier is grilled by Michel Ciment and Phillippe Royer on such subjects as the alleged "organic substance" of the film, conceding at last that "it was all a joke, if you prefer that."

While von Trier is "not on good terms" with his earlier films, he constantly returns to *Epidemic* (its style anticipates that of both *The Kingdom* and *Breaking the Waves,* as well as the tenets of the Dogme95 movement) in his interviews; it may be a black sheep, but it's certainly one of his favorite offspring.

The same cannot be said of the 1988 TV production *Medea*, based—verbatim—on an original script by Carl Th. Dreyer (in collaboration with Preben Thomsen). Few interviews are available from this period, although many interviewers will later make reference to this project when asking the "new" Great Dane about his relationship to the "old" one.

"With [Dreyer], I have an almost holy relationship," says von Trier to Marie Berthelius and Roger Narbonne, who also perform an in-depth dissection of *Epidemic*, while visiting the director during the making of *Medea* in August 1987. In Stig Björkman's film *I Am Curious, Film,* made in connection with the 1995 centennial anniversary of the birth of cinema, von Trier talks about *Medea* and Dreyer in his characteristically light, yet profound, way with actress Lena Nyman (who asks Björkman's written questions); a transcription from the film/interview appears here. (Stateside, the rarely seen *Medea* is reportedly aired from time to time on the Independent Film Channel, although it's been very hard to find in Europe.)

Three years then pass with no cinematic signs of life from von Trier. In 1991, his next film—"consciously made like a masterpiece. It's something you decide beforehand"[4]—finally hits the big screen. Against all odds, von Trier has managed to get sizeable financial backing from several countries, including France, Sweden, and Germany. He shoots *Europa* (renamed *Zentropa* in America to avoid confusion with Agnieszka Holland's film *Europa, Europa*[5]) in Denmark and Poland and invites journalists to come to the studio and documentary crews to follow the shooting on location. Several enlightening portraits of the artist as a slightly older dog appear here, including Eva af Geijerstam's relaxed on-set sitting with von Trier in the company of cameraman and Dreyer collaborator Henning Bendtsen and the late great Ernst-Hugo Järegård (soon to be immortalized in *The Kingdom*). Here, we also get the full story of Dreyer's tuxedo ("It fit me like a glove!").

Michael Tapper of *Chaplin* drops by the studio for a peek at the *Europa* promo-reel as well as an early career interview; von Trier sums up the score so far, with the aid of longtime script collaborator Niels Vørsel (the two have since separated). In the U.K. (where *Europa* somewhat confusingly retains its original title), *Time Out*'s Jonathan Romney and *Empire*'s Toby Rose get hold of von Trier in time for the British premiere, while he has already met with Nigel Andrews of the *Financial Times* at Cannes, just before setting off to shoot three new minutes of his ongoing project *Dimension* (set to open—God willing—in 2024).

Despite a handsome number of awards (including another technical prize at Cannes), international premieres, and respectful reviews, the commercially inclined *Europa* does not fare well. In Denmark (where it attracts only 31,000 moviegoers) Lars von Trier is still regarded as the offensive, pretentious ne'er-do-well with the big mouth and the shaved head, and many critics complain about his obsession with images, matched in scope only by his reputed neglect of the actors.

When asked, von Trier is more than happy to talk about his technical achievements, and a link to Orson Welles's famous toy-train definition of cinema is very apparent. The euphoria of von Trier's filmmaking is as unmistakable as it must have been when his mother gave him his first 8-mm camera when he was eight. He waxes poetic to Alling about the outrageous locations in *The Element of Crime*; to *Levende Billeder*'s Lars K. Andersen about the handheld camera work in *The Kingdom*; to Peter Øvig Knudsen of *Weekendavisen* about the possibilities provided by the technical limitations of *Dogme #2—The Idiots*; and to *indieWIRE*'s Anthony Kaufman about the somewhat frustrating work with 100 stationary DV cameras in *Dancer in the Dark*. Readers interested in technical aspects of the director's work will greatly appreciate the clarity with which he explains his approach (he would make an excellent lecturer).

And then there's the issue of "von Trier and the actors." It has both posed practical problems on the set and become a topic that scholars continue to debate. "He's a very, very sweet boy," according to actress Kirsten Rolffes. "But he hasn't got the first idea about actors. Sound, light, scenery, technicalities, all that works just fine, but actors! He looks at us as if we were a long hair in the soup!" To af Geijerstam, he unveils the model of his casting philosophy: "If an actor has a back catalogue of work and even a private life that stands for something, then of course he brings it into the film. And you can just as well work with these things, take advantage of them."

The cast of 1994's *The Kingdom* is no exception. It represents different eras of Danish cinema and TV, with links to everything from the 1946 classic *Ditte, Child of Man* to Dreyer (in the form of *Gertrud* co-star Baard Owe, and the voices of the two dishwashers, who certainly recall a Dreyeresque atmosphere); to more contemporary Danish entertainers (including cast members from the legendary Danish television series *Matador*); to soft-erotica icon Birte Tove (from *Bedroom Mazurka*); to the ever-durable Jens Okking ("Denmark's Depardieu," who, incidentally, played the father of twelve-year-old Lars Trier's character in the *Hemmelig sommer*).

And how does he deal with this dream team? "Just rub them the right way," he tells Andersen before the television premiere of *The Kingdom* but after its success at the Venice Film Festival. "I used to argue with the actors, but today I have a wonderful relationship with them. I've become very popular."

Armed with a handheld camera and novel editing techniques, von Trier slowly begins a momentous assault on the actor "problem." And things slowly begin to improve. In the process of making *Breaking the Waves*, von Trier will arguably transform himself into an actor's director. While working on the film, Emily Watson talks at length with von Trier about her character, Bess: "I immediately understood what he meant, and scenes that at first seemed difficult turned out to be no problem whatsoever."[6] From Cannes 1996, Katrin Cartlidge reports: "He did everything in order to form a relationship with the actors. There was a fantastic atmosphere. That was a singular experience." At Cannes 2000, Peter Stormare compares the process of making *Dancer in the Dark* to a ball game: "Being in a von Trier film is like playing soccer on a dream team, but instead of playing in a big arena, he invites us all to play on the beach—barefoot." And finally, one Björk Guðmundsdottír, to whose troubles with the director much ink has been devoted, observed that it took her one year to become herself again, after having been Selma. Be it kid-gloved sparring with a moody pop star or fatherly tutoring of a wide-eyed, shoeless waif conversing with God—von Trier seems to have put some effort into the direction of his players throughout the years.

The domestic success of *The Kingdom* miniseries has made von Trier a household name in Denmark. The completion of *The Kingdom* also marks the end (perhaps) of his highly prolific collaboration with Vørsel, and from *Breaking the Waves* onward, von Trier will compose his scripts alone. Emerging out of all this is the von Trier who will conquer the world; this is the cocky kid who has at last amounted to something, to the great surprise of everyone (save one).

"Lars von Trier—what has happened to you?" asks critic/writer/director Christian Braad Thomsen, who once got annoyed at von Trier while giving a lecture at the Danish Film School—a lecture von Trier attended sporting the hissing headphones of a Sony Walkman. It's 1996, and Lars von Trier relates what has in fact happened to him and candidly discusses his phobias and religion with Braad Thomsen.

In addition to actors and technical logistics, von Trier's private life has at this point begun to offer a large dose of turbulence, which leaves its mark on his creative production. In 1989, at his mother's deathbed, he is told that his father was someone other than the man he has grown up believing was his father. In 1995 he leaves his wife, Cæcilie Holbek Trier, shortly after the birth of their second child, and moves in with his present partner Bente Frøge.

These events are heavily covered in the Danish tabloid press. Initially, von Trier does little to discourage the publicity, but during the mid to late 1990s—ironically at a time when *Breaking the Waves* has won him many new fans—he does only a few interviews, most of them with Stig Björkman, and stays away from Cannes (where *Breaking the Waves* will earn him a Grand Prix du Jury) on account of traveling jitters.

"For me personally, I've reached the point of nausea, and I feel very comfortable no longer talking to anyone." This, the opening statement of the somewhat curious May 1998 interview with *Berlingske Tidene*'s Ebbe Iversen, should in truth be in the past tense, since it's from a man who is about to go to Cannes and lose control—and from a true man of contradiction (the interview even contains a rare compliment to a favorite target of derision, countryman Bille August!). A few days later, while presenting the first fruits of the Dogme95 movement, von Trier starts talking more than ever before—or at least it seems that way (the hundreds of journalists at Cannes certainly help). The Cannes chaos of 1998 and the hardcore sex footage from *The Idiots* turn out to be a terrific purgative for many of von Trier's problems. The titles *The Man Who Would Give Up Control* and *Tracing the Inner Idiot* speak for themselves. This period is one of the best covered of von Trier's career. It's also the most wasted period, as far as the questions asked by journalists are concerned. "When are you going to make a real porno film?" is by far the most commonly asked question during Cannes 98. The showman side of von Trier takes over once again. He never once protests against a confusing, but interesting, side effect of the Dogme95 rules that immediately materializes: journalists begin to draft their own rules regarding what Dogme95 and von Trier are all about. "Breaking the rules" is at first clever pun, but rapidly outstays its welcome. (Although the movement has often been called "Dogma," the correct designation is "Dogme," according to HQ in "Mecca.")

An alarming number of journalists miss one of the major points of the "vow of chastity" of the Dogma Brotherhood—that the vow will be honored for *one* film only (thus, von Trier's decision to make a musical is wrongly seen as "treason" and rule breaking of the worst kind). The interview with Jørn Rossing Jensen, entitled "Dogme Is Dead! Long Live Song and Dance," should set the record straight for all those who still bemoan von Trier's supposed betrayal. Read, and forever hold your peace. (A probable effect of his porno jokes, von Trier is often falsely credited with the "honor" of having directed porno videos for the Zentropa-owned subsidiary Puzzy Power.)

The Palme d'Or-winning musical *Dancer in the Dark* was Lars von Trier's most recently realized project at the time of writing. Several accounts of the clashes between von Trier and Björk appear in the interviews, although some of the interviewers (including myself) try to avoid the subject, due to the excessive exposure it was receiving during the summer of 2000. Most of us fail.

Through cable television, *The Kingdom* gains a cult following in the U.S. (at the time of writing, Stephen King was set to adapt an American version for ABC), but not until *Breaking the Waves* and Emily Watson's Oscar nomination does von Trier expand his American beachhead. After that, however, things seem to fall nicely into place. But since American promotion tours are out of the question, the mountain will have to come to Mohammed. Thus, writer/filmmaker Shari Roman crosses the Atlantic on several occasions and visits von Trier in Denmark, and two more pilgrims, *indieWIRE*'s Anthony Kaufman and *Film Comment*'s Gavin Smith, conduct extensive interviews with the director. Contributions from all three writers are present in this installment of Conversations with Filmmakers (which in itself must be further proof of von Trier's American breakthrough).

For the background rather than the lowdown, Danish radio legend Kjeld Koplev conducts the ultimate "My Dinner With André" interview. It airs on 7 September 2000 on Danish national radio and offers 110 minutes (minus 1 minute of silence) uncut von Trier. He is planning on going fishing in Sweden, is tired of talking about film and Björk and promises not to, yet ends up talking about the latter. The interview provides valuable insight into von Trier's life and world. The traumatic events mentioned above—the revelation concerning the identity of his father and other events with bearing on his relation to his mother and other women and to the portraits of women in his films—turn up in different contexts. His relationship to journalists is also investigated. (Indeed, there is an account of an encounter with the *New York Times* that someone might want to pursue further.) An interesting discussion on religion, which is sure to offend adherents of nearly all faiths found in the Western world, is yet another highlight. And there are still more high jinks to be found in this interview; it is arguably von Trier's most outspoken ever. (It was, incidentally, on Koplev's show that an anonymous caller told the dinner-speech story that served as inspiration for Vinterberg's *Festen/The Celebration*.)

In December 2001, Swedish journalist Marit Kapla collected some thoughts from von Trier before the shooting of *Dogville* commenced in January 2002. Since then, among the sadder events is the untimely death of *Dogville* co-star Katrin Cartlidge in September 2002. (She had already been replaced by Patricia Clarkson at an early stage of production). Other and happier ones include a new manifesto-shaped concept, "Dogumentary" (hinted at in the Koplev interview), and a collaboration with Tomas Vinterberg, *Dear Wendy*, as well as preparations for the forthcoming *Manderley*—these are some of the children of this Dane's tomorrows.

Today—as he would be the first to admit—Lars von Trier is a different filmmaker from the one at the beginning of his career. In this book you will find interviews made when he was honing his craft and stood firmly by his taste—made, in short, when his "aim was true." However, many grains of future ventures can be spotted in these early interviews. Of his yesterdays, he still speaks willingly, but now in a quite different fashion from the way he did back then.

Warmest and sincerest thanks go out to all the many people who have helped me in different ways and made this journey such a delight: first and foremost, to Leif Erik Nygårds and Thomas Masterman, for priceless contributions; to Christian Mongaard Christensen, Kim Foss, Peter Schepelern, Ole Michelsen, Ib Bondebjerg, and Christian Braad Thomsen of the Danish cineaste stronghold; to the Abell, Ettrup, and Ravnsborg families of Lyngby; to Peter Brunette and Gerald Peary for a series of splendidly informal discussions that led straight to this project; to Eva af Geijerstam (true nobility interviewing fake ditto) and Ernst-Hugo Järegård (for starting it all . . . and profoundly missing in action); to Stig Björkman, Michael Tapper, Marie Berthelius, Richard Kelly, Bruno Jacobs, and Ludvig Hertzberg for guidance along the way; to all the writers, who were extremely helpful and generous; to the patient, pleasant people at University Press of Mississippi; to Danish cinema in general, for being such a truly great adventure; and to Lars von Trier in particular, for saying, "I'll gladly assert that everything said or written about me is a lie."

This book is dedicated to *Levende Billeder, Kosmorama, Chaplin, Filmhäftet*, and all other fine cinema publications that struggle, or struggled, in the name of excellent film writing in Scandinavia and elsewhere.

Notes

1. Nigel Matheson, "The Lars Frontier," *New Musical Express*, 22 June 1985.
2. Ibid.
3. Ibid.
4. Nils Ole Qvist and Jens Grund, "Von Trier vil ud til folket," *Morgenavisen Jyllands-Posten*, 3 February 1991.

5. Throughout this volume, the title *Europa* is preferred, since the meaning of that title is discussed on several occasions. It would, for example, seem strange to read that von Trier chose the title *Zentropa* as the third "E" film of the "Europa Trilogy" or as an echo of Kafka's *Amerika*.

6. Thomas Porskjær Christiansen, "Bess & Emily," *Scope*, 6 July 1996.

CHRONOLOGY

1956   Lars Trier is born on 30 April in the Copenhagen suburb of Lyng-
        by. His upper-middle-class parents, Inger Trier (née Høst) and—
        seemingly—Ulf Trier, both have degrees in sociology.

1967   Starts making short films with a super-8 camera given to him by
        his mother. 11 yrs old

1969   Plays the male lead in the children's television series *Hemmelig
        Sommer* (*Secret Summer*).

1976   Registers as a student of cinema history at the University of
        Copenhagen. Remains registered until 1979, but never graduates.

1977   Makes *Orchidégartneren* (*The Orchid Gardener*) together with like-
        minded friends, all fellow members of the Filmgruppe 16 (Film
        Group 16), an amateur nonprofit association.

1979   Makes *Menthe—la bienheureuse* with Filmgruppe 16. Trier is also
        accepted at the National Film School of Denmark as a directing
        student.

1980   Makes the short film *Nocturne* at film school, which receives an
        award at the Europäischer Studienfilmwettbewerb festival in
        Munich.

1981   Makes the short film *Den sidste detalje* (*The Last Detail*).

1982   Graduation film *Befrielsesbillder/Images of Relief* which is shown at Danish cinemas and awarded at international festivals. *age 26* Receives his diploma from the National Film School of Denmark.

1984   *The Element of Crime*, von Trier's feature film debut, wins the technical award at the Cannes Film Festival. *age 28*

1986   Gets a foretaste of wide public exposure through the television commercial "Gå i bad med Ekstra Bladet" ("Take a Bath with Ekstra Bladet"), which gets banned by the newly founded TV2.

1987   *Epidemic*. The film fails miserably at the box office, and von Trier becomes persona non grata in the Danish cinema business. *age 31* At Cannes it is shown in the *Un certain regard* section to general irritation. In the ensuing years, von Trier will make a living shooting commercials. Marries Cæcilia Holbek.

1988   Makes *Medea*, based on an unrealized script by Carl Th. Dreyer, for Danish television. Meets producer Peter Aalbæk Jensen while making a commercial for the French transport company Calberson. His first daughter, Agnes, is born.

1989   Converts to Catholicism. On her deathbed, von Trier's mother reveals the truth about his real father—that he is not Ole Trier *Jew* but rather law expert Frits Michael Hartmann. *age 33* *gERMAN*

1991   *Europa* (U.S. title *Zentropa*). The film is a critical success and wins both the jury prize and the technical award at the Cannes Film Festival. Together, *Europa*, *Epidemic*, and *The Element of Crime* form von Trier's "Europa Trilogy." Starts making *Dimension*, a project planned for release in 2024 (with its premiere planned for 30 April, von Trier's sixty-eighth birthday). *age 35*

1992   Founds the production company Zentropa together with Peter Aalbæk Jensen.

1994   *Riget* (*The Kingdom*), a darkly surreal and at times hilarious hospital-horror miniseries made for DRTV, the Danish Broadcasting Corporation. Domestic success is immediate, and its reception internationally is very positive, when an almost four-hour cinema version is shown at various art-house theaters around the world. Lars von Trier also creates the debate show *Lærerværelset* *age 38*

(*The Teacher's Room*) for the commercial Danish TV station TV2, but the concept is not a success. His second daughter, Selma, is born.

1995   While attending celebrations devoted to the centennial birthday of cinema in Paris, von Trier presents the Dogme 95 manifesto, drafted together with Thomas Vinterberg in February 1995. Divorces Cæcilia Holbek Trier. (1987-1995)

1996   *Breaking the Waves*, von Trier's international breakthrough, wins
age 40   the Grand Prix du Jury in Cannes and leading actress Emily Watson receives an Academy Award nomination. *Psychomobile 1: The World Clock*, a live installation based on a concept by von Trier, is presented in Copenhagen. *Marathon*, another concept for DRTV, is withdrawn after eight episodes.

1997   *Riget II (The Kingdom II)* appears, to renewed accolades. Marries
age 41   Bente Frøge. Twin sons, Ludvig and Benjamin, are born.

1998   *Dogme #2—The Idiots* opens in Cannes to huge controversy, and the Dogme 95 manifesto becomes a hot topic in the world of cinema.

1999–2000   The four original Dogma brethren, von Trier, Vinterberg, Søren Kragh-Jacobsen, and Kristian Levring, create *D Dag (D Day)*, a Dogme-related television experiment shot in Copenhagen on New Year's Eve.

2000   *Dancer in the Dark* wins the Palme d'Or in Cannes, with Björk
age 44   Guðmundsdóttir receiving the Best Actress award. (Björk also receives an Oscar nomination for the song "I've Seen It All.") The film marks the end of the second von Trier trilogy, "The Golden Heart Trilogy," which also includes *Breaking the Waves* and *The Idiots*.

2002   Shoots *Dogville*. The film is presented as the second part of "The America Trilogy" (which actually started with the last part of "The Golden Heart Trilogy," *Dancer in the Dark*.)

2003   *Dogville* opens in Cannes.

2012, age 56

FILMOGRAPHY

Shorts and Student Films

1967 (approx.)
TUREN TIL SQUASHLAND (TRIP TO SQUASHLAND)
Director/Screenplay/Cinematography/Editing: **von Trier**
8mm, animation, color
1–2 minutes

1968 (approx.)
NAT, SKAT (NIGHT, SWEETHEART)
Director/Screenplay/Cinematography/Editing: **von Trier**
8mm, color
1 minute

1969 (approx.)
EN RØVSYG OPLEVELSE (A BUMMER)
Director/Screenplay/Cinematography/Editing: **von Trier**
8mm, color
1 minute

1969 (approx.)
ET SKAKSPIL (A CHESS GAME)
Director/Screenplay/Cinematography/Editing: **von Trier**
8mm, B&W
1 minute (fragments)

1970

HVORFOR FLYGTE FRA DET DU VED DU IKKE KAN FLYGTE FRA? (WHY ESCAPE WHAT YOU KNOW YOU CAN'T ESCAPE?)
Director/Screenplay/Cinematography/Editing: **von Trier**
Cast: Hans Skriver (the refugee), Ole Heberg (the mummy)
8mm, color
7 minutes

1971

EN BLOMST (A FLOWER)
Director/Screenplay/Cinematography/Editing: **von Trier**
Music: "Hallelujah Chorus" from Handel's *Messiah*
Cast: Ole Benzon (the boy)
8mm, B&W
7 minutes

1977

ORCHIDÉGARTNEREN (THE ORCHID GARDENER)
Production Company: Filmgruppe 16
Director/Screenplay/Editing/Producer: **von Trier**
Cinematography: Hartvig Jensen, Mogens Svane, Helge Kaj, Peter Nørgaard, and **von Trier**
Music: Flute solo, performed by Hanne M. Søndergaard
Cast: **von Trier** (Victor Marse), Inger Hvidtfeldt (Eliza), Karen Oksbjerg (Eliza's friend), Brigitte Pelissier (the third girl), Martin Drouzy (the gardener), Yvonne Levy (woman on bicycle), Carl-Henrik Trier (the old Jew), Bente Kopp (the woman in the movie), Jakob Moe (Eliza's child), Jesper Hoffmeyer (narrator), Julie Moestrup (little girl)
16 mm, B&W
Language: Danish
37 minutes

1979

MENTHE—LA BIENHEUREUSE/MYNTE—DEN LYKSALIGE (MENTHE—THE BLISSFUL)
Production Company: Filmgruppe 16
Director/Producer/Editing: **von Trier**

Screenplay: **von Trier** (based on *Histoire d'O/The Story of O* by Pauline Reage/
Dominique Aury)
Cinematography: **von Trier** and Hartvig Jensen
Music: Erik Satie, "Gymnopedie #1"; Claude Debussy, "Des pas sur la neige,"
"La cathédrale englouite"
Cast: Inger Hvidtfeldt (the woman), Annette Linnet (Menthe), Carl-Henrik
Trier (the gardener), Jenni Dick (the old lady), **von Trier** (the driver), Brigitte
Pelissier (Inger Hvidtfeldt's dubbed voice)
16mm, B&W
Language: French
31 minutes

1979
PRODUKTION I (PRODUCTION #I)
"Døden 1—en klinisk oversigt" ("Death 1—A Clinical Survey"); "Døden 2:
Jeg ser mig selv på et par meters afstand" ("Death 2: I Watch Myself from a
Few Meters' Distance"); "Epilog—ringen sluttes" ("Epilogue—Coming to
Full Circle")
Produced by Den Danske Filmskole/The Danish Film School
Director/Screenplay: **von Trier**
Music: Alban Berg, Adagio from "Lyrische Suite" (1926, orchestral edition
from 1929)
Video (VCR), B&W
Language: Danish
5 minutes

1979
PRODUKTION II (PRODUCTION #II)
Produced by Den Danske Filmskole/The Danish Film School
Director/Screenplay: **von Trier**
Music: Thelonious Monk, "Round Midnight," performed by the Miles Davis
Quintet, 1956
Cast: Åke Sandgren (the man)
Video (VCR), B&W
Language: Danish
10 minutes

1979/80
VIDEOØVELSE (MONOLOG) (VIDEO EXERCISE [MONOLOGUE])
Produced by Den Danske Filmskole/The Danish Film School
Director: **von Trier**
Video (VCR), B&W
Language: Danish
4 minutes

1979/80
VIDEOØVELSE (DIALOG) (VIDEO EXERCISE [DIALOGUE])
Produced by Den Danske Filmskole/The Danish Film School
Director: **von Trier**
Video (VCR), B&W
Cast: Claus Strandberg (the man), Lea Brøgger (the woman)
Language: Danish
6 minutes

1979/80
LARS & OLES DANMARKSFILM (LARS & OLE'S DENMARK FILM)
Produced by Den Danske Filmskole/The Danish Film School
Directors: **von Trier** and Ole Schwander
Video (VCR), B&W
Language: Danish
24 minutes (unfinished)

1980
PRODUKTION III: MARSJAS ANDEN REJSE (PRODUCTION #III: THE SEC-
OND JOURNEY OF MARSJA)
Director/Screenplay: **von Trier**
Producer: Den Danske Filmskole/The Danish Film School
Cast: Berrit Kvorning (Marsja), Baard Owe (Consul Mendel)
Video (VCR), B&W
Language: Danish
18 minutes

1980
PRODUKTION IV: HISTORIEN OM DE TO ÆGTEMÆND MED ALT FOR
UNGE KONER (PRODUCTION #IV: THE STORY OF TWO HUSBANDS AND
THEIR FAR TOO YOUNG WIVES)

Produced by Den Danske Filmskole/The Danish Film School
Director/Screenplay: **von Trier**
Cast: Baard Owe (Zeppa), Lars Knutzon (Spinelloccio), Gitte Pelle (Filomena), Natasja (Zeppa's wife), Kim Eduard Jensen (young man in car), Masja Dessau (young woman in car)
Video (VCR), B&W
Language: Danish
12 minutes

1980
DOKUMENTARØVELSEN (LOLITA) (DOCUMENTARY PRACTICE [LOLITA])
Produced by Den Danske Filmskole/The Danish Film School
Director/Screenplay: **von Trier**
Video (VCR), B&W
Language: Danish
4 minutes

1980
NOCTURNE
Produced by Den Danske Filmskole/The Danish Film School
Director/Screenplay: **von Trier**
Screenplay: **von Trier** and Tom Elling
Cinematography: Tom Elling
Editing: Tómas Gislason
Cast: Yvette Weisbacher (the woman), Solbjørg Højfeldt (voice on the telephone), Annelise Gabold (dubbed voice of Yvette Weisbacher)
16mm, B&W and color
Language: Danish
8 minutes

1981
DEN SIDSTE DETALJE (THE LAST DETAIL)
Produced by Den Danske Filmskole/The Danish Film School
Director: **von Trier**
Screenplay: Rumle Hammerich
Cinematography: Tom Elling
Editing: Tómas Gislason

Music: Alban Berg, from the *Lulu Suite*
Cast: Otto Brandenburg (Danny), Torben Zeller (Frank), Gitte Pelle (the
woman), Ib Hansen (Smukke, mobster), Michael Simpson (henchman)
35mm, B&W
Language: Danish
31 minutes

1982
BEFRIELSESBILLEDER (IMAGES OF A RELIEF; a.k.a. LIBERATION PICTURES)
Produced by Den Danske Filmskole/The Danish Film School
Director: **von Trier**
Screenplay: **von Trier**
Shooting Script: Tom Elling and **von Trier**
Cinematography: Tom Elling
Art Direction: Søren Skjær
Editing: Tómas Gislason
Music: Mozart, String Quartet in C Major, K465 (First Movement), performed
by the Copenhagen String Quartet; Pierre De La Rue, Mass, performed by the
Ars Nova vocal group, conducted by Bo Holten
Cast: Edward Fleming (Leo), Kirsten Olesen (Esther), Leif Magnusson (German chaplain trying to make phone call), Niels Vørsel (German soldier in
white cotton-wool uniform)
35mm, color
Language: Danish and German
57 minutes

Feature Films

1984
THE ELEMENT OF CRIME/FORBRYDELSENS ELEMENT (a.k.a. ELEMENT OF
CRIME)
Production Company: Per Holst Filmproduktion in association with the
Danish Film Institute
Producer: Per Holst
Director: **von Trier**
Screenplay: **von Trier** and Niels Vørsel
Shooting Script: **von Trier**, Tom Elling, and Tómas Gislason

Cinematography: Tom Elling
Art Direction: Peter Høimark
Editing: Tómas Gislason
Music: Bo Holten
Cast: Michael Elphick (Fisher), Esmond Knight (Osborne), Me Me Lai (Kim), Jerold Wells (Police Chief Kramer), Ahmed El Shenawai (therapist), Astrid Henning-Jensen (Osborne's housekeeper), Janos Hersko (coroner), Stig Larsson (coroner's assistant), Harry Harper (receptionist #1), Roman Moszkowicz (receptionist #2), Frederik Casby (white policeman), Duke Addabayo (black policeman), **von Trier** (receptionist, "Schmuck of Ages"), Preben Lerdorff Rye (the little girl's grandfather), Camilla Overby (little girl #1), Maria Behrendt (little girl #2), Mogens Rukov (librarian), Jon Bang Carlsen (angry policeman), Leif Magnusson (hotel guest), Gotha Andersen (judge firing gun at hearing), Niels Vørsel (man at hearing), Per Holst (railway man)
35mm, widescreen, tinted B&W, sodium-lit color
Language: English
103 minutes

1987
EPIDEMIC
Production Company: Element Film I/S in association with the Danish Film Institute
Producer: Jakob Eriksen
Director: **von Trier**
Screenplay: **von Trier** and Niels Vørsel
Shooting Script: **von Trier**, Tom Elling, and Tómas Gislason
Cinematography: Henning Bendtsen (35mm), **von Trier**, Niels Vørsel, Kristoffer Nyholm, Cæcilia Holbek Trier, Susanne Ottesen, and Alexander Gruszynski (16mm)
Art Direction: Peter Grant
Editing: **von Trier** and Thomas Krag
Music: Richard Wagner: *Tannhäuser* Overture, also the song "Epidemic, We All Fall Down" by Peter Bach, based on a variation of *Tannhäuser* with lyrics by **von Trier** and Vørsel, vocals by Pia Cohn
Cast: **von Trier** (Lars/Dr. Mesmer), Niels Vørsel (Niels), Claes Kastholm Hansen (the film commissioner), Susanne Ottesen (Susanne), Allan de Waal (narrator), Ole Ernst (doctor in the Mesmer episode), Olaf Ussing (another doctor

in the Mesmer episode), Cæcilia Holbek Trier (nurse in the Mesmer episode), Ib Hansen (yet another doctor in the Mesmer episode), Michael Gelting (archivist), Svend Ali Hamann (the hypnotist), Gitte Lind (the hypnotized girl), Udo Kier (Udo), Jørgen Christian Krüff (wine specialist), Jan Kornum Larsen (customs officer), Leif Magnusson (ratman in the Mesmer episode), Gert Holbek (voice), Anja Hemmingsen (the girl from Atlantic City), Kirsten Hemmingsen (the aunt from Atlantic City), Leif Sabro (helicopter pilot), Michael Simpson (black driver and vicar), Mik Skov (corpse), Thorkild Tønnesen (man in helicopter), Colin Gilder (Ole Ernst's dubbed voice), Tony Shine (Ib Hansen's dubbed voice)
16 mm and 35 mm, widescreen (1:1,66) B&W with monocolor
Language: Danish and English
106 minutes

1991
EUROPA (ZENTROPA; American title only)
Production Companies: Nordisk Film in co-production with Gunnar Obel, Gérard Mital Productions, PPC, Telefilm GMBH, WMG, the Swedish Film Institute, the Danish Film Institute, with the support of Eurimages, Sofinergie, Sofinergie 2, Antenne 2, Canal+ (France)
Producers: Peter Aalbæk Jensen and Bo Christensen
Director: **von Trier**
Screenplay: **von Trier** and Niels Vørsel
Shooting Script: **von Trier** and Tómas Gislason
Cinematography: Henning Bendtsen (Denmark), Edward Klosinski (Poland), and Jean-Paul Meurisse
Art Direction: Henning Bahs
Editing: Hervé Schneid
Music: Joachim Holbek
Cast: Jean-Marc Barr (Leo Kessler), Barbara Sukowa (Katharina Hartmann), Ernst-Hugo Järegård (Uncle Kessler), Jørgen Reenberg (Max Hartmann), Udo Kier (Larry Hartmann), Eddie Constantine (Colonel Harris), Erik Mørk (the padre), Henning Jensen (Siggy), Leif Magnusson (Doctor Magnus), Vera Gebuhr (depot assistant), Else Petersen (old assistant), Dietrich Kuhlbrodt (railway inspector), Holger Perfort (Mayor Ravenstein), Anne Werner Thomsen (Mrs. Ravenstein), **von Trier** (the Jew), Cæcilia Holbek Trier (the maid), Janos Hersko (Jewish man), Talia (Jewish woman), Claus Flygare (father of the

young assassins), Erno Müller (Seifert), Benny Poulsen (Stelemann), Hardy
Rafn (man in morning robe), Peter Haugstrup (bellboy), Ben Zimet, Thadee
Lokcinski (old men), Baard Owe (man with papers), Michael Simpson, Jon
Ledin (American soldiers), Jesper Birch (Colonel Harris's batman), Max von
Sydow (the narrator)
35 mm, B&W and color (anamorphic scope)
Language: English and German
113 minutes

1996
BREAKING THE WAVES
Production Companies: Zentropa Entertainments ApS and Danish Broad-
casting Corporation in association with Trust Film Svenska AB, Liberator Pro-
ductions S.a.r.l., Argus Film Produktie, Nordern Lights A/S in co-production
with La Sept Cinéma, Sveriges Television, Media Investment Club, VPRO
Television, with the support of Nordic Film and Television Fund, the Danish
Film Institute, the Swedish Film Institute, the Norwegian Film Institute,
Dutch Film Fund, Dutch CoBo Fund, Finnish Film Foundation, in collabora-
tion with Canal + (France), DR-TV, Icelandic Film Corporation, Lucky Red,
October Films, Philippe Bober, TV1000, Villialfa Filmproductions OY, Yleis
Radio Tv-1, ZDF/ARTE
Producers: Wibeke Windeløv and Peter Aalbæk Jensen
Executive Producer: Lars Jönsson
Director: **von Trier**
Assistant Director: Morten Arnfred
Screenplay: **von Trier**
Screenplay Consultant: Tómas Gislason
Cinematography: Robby Müller
Editing: Anders Refn
Music: "All the Way from Memphis" (Mott the Hoople/Ian Hunter),
"Blowin' in the Wind" (Tom Harboe, Jan Harboe, and Ulrik Corlin/Bob
Dylan), "Pipe Major Donald MacLean" (Peter Roderick MacLeod), "In a Bro-
ken Dream" (Python Lee Jackson), "Cross Eyed Mary" (Jethro Tull/Ian An-
derson), "Virginia Plain" (Roxy Music), "Whiter Shade of Pale" (Procul Harum/
Keith Reid and Gary Brooker), "Hot Love" (T Rex/Marc Bolan), "Suzanne"
(Leonard Cohen), "Love Lies Bleeding" ((Elton John/Elton John & Bernie
Taupin), "Whisky in the Jar" (Thin Lizzy/Phil Lynott, Eric Bell, and Brian

Downey), "Time" (Deep Purple/John Lord, Richie Blackmore, Ian Gillan, Roger Glover, and Ian Paice), "Life on Mars" (David Bowie), "Your Song" (Elton John), "Gay Gordons" (Tom Harboe, Jan Harboe, and Ulrik Corlin), "Happy Landing" (P. Harman), with "Siciliana" by J. S. Bach from Sonata BWW 1031, arr. Joachim Holbek

Chapter Images: Per Kirkeby (digital video, transferred on film)

Cast: Emily Watson (Bess), Stellan Skarsgård (Jan), Katrin Cartlidge (Dodo), Adrian Rawlins (Dr. Richardson), Jonathan Hackett (the vicar), Sandra Voe (the mother), Jean-Marc Barr (Terry), Udo Kier (the man on the trawler) Mikkel Gaup (Pits), Roef Ragas (Pim), Phil McCall (grandfather)

35mm Cinemascope with additional digital video images, transferred on film, color

Language: English

158 minutes

1998

DOGME #2—IDIOTERNE (DOGME #2—THE IDIOTS) a.k.a. IDIOTERNE (THE IDIOTS)

Production Companies: Zentropa Entertainments2 ApS and Danish Broadcasting Corporation in co-production with Liberator Productions S.a.r.l., La Sept Cinéma, Argus Film Produktie, VPRO Television, ZDF/ARTE, with the support of Nordic Film and Television Fund, Dutch CoBo Fund, Helsinki, in collaboration with SVT Drama, Canal+ (France), RAI Cinema Fiction, 3 Emme Cinematografica

Producer: Wibeke Windeløv

Executive Producer: Peter Aalbæk Jensen

Director/Screenplay/Cinematography: **von Trier**

Editing: Molly Marlene Steensgaard

Music: Camille Saint-Saëns, "La cygne"/"The Swan," performed by Kim Kristensen, harmonica, "Vi er dem de andre ikke må lege med" (Kim Larsen & Erik Clausen)

Cast: Bodil Jørgensen (Karen), Jens Albinus (Stoffer), Anne Louise Hassing (Susanne), Troels Lyby (Henrik), Nikolaj Lie Kaas (Jeppe), Henrik Prip (Ped), Luis Mesonero (Miguel), Louise Mieritz (Josephine), Knud Romer Jørgensen (Axel), Trine Michelsen (Nana), Anne-Grethe Bjarup Riis (Katrine), Paprika Steen (Vibeke, the high-class lady who wants to buy the house), Albert Wickman (Finn, the husband of the high-class lady), Erik Wedersøe (Stoffer's

uncle who owns the house), Michael Moritzen (man from municipality), Anders Hove (Josephine's father), Jan Elle (waiter), Claus Strandberg (guide at factory), Jens Jørn Spottag (boss at advertising agency), John Martinus (man in morning jacket), Lars Bjarke (biker #1), Ewald Larsen (biker #2), Christian Friis (biker #3), Hans Henrik Clemensen (Anders, Karen's husband), Lone Lindorff (Karen's mother), Erno Müller (Karen's grandfather), Regitze Estrup (Karen's sister Louise), Lotte Munk (Karen's sister Britta), Marina Bouras (Axel's wife), Julie Wieth (woman with two kids), Kirsten Vaupel (art class lady #1), Lillian Tillegren (art class lady #2), Birgit Conradi (art class lady #2), Peter Frøge (man in swimming pool), Bent Sørensen (taxi driver), Jesper Sønderaas (Svendsen at advertising agency), Ditlev Weddelsborg (Severin at advertising agency), Svend Erik Plannthin, Torben Meyrowitsch, Lis Bente Petersen, Palle Lorentz Emiliussen, Axel Schmidt (mongoloids), Iris Albøge (qualified carer), **von Trier** (offscreen interviewer), Kim Kristensen (offscreen harmonica player)
35mm transferred from video, color
Language: Danish
111 minutes

2000
DANCER IN THE DARK
Production Companies: Zentropa Entertainments4 ApS in association with Trust Film Svenska AB, Film i Väst, Liberator Productions S.a.r.l., Pain Unlimited, Cinematograph, What Else?, Icelandic Film Corporation, Arte France Cinema and France 3 Cinema, Danish Broadcasting Corporation & SVT Drama, Arte Germany, FilmFour, VPRO, WDR, Angel Scandinavia, Canal+ (France), Filmek, Constantin Film, Lantia, TV1000, YLE, TV-1, with the support of the Danish Film Institute, the Swedish Film Institute, the Norwegian Film Institute, Icelandic Film Fund, Finnish Film Foundation, Filmstiftung Nord Nordrhein-Westfalen, Nordic Film and Television Fund, AV-fund, Dutch Film Fund, CoBo Fund, Eurimages, Media Programme of the European Union
Producer: Wibeke Windeløv
Executive Producer: Peter Aalbæk Jensen
Director/Screenplay/Operator: **von Trier**
Assistant Director and Second Unit Director: Anders Refn
Cinematography: Robby Müller

Art Direction: Karl Juliussen
Editing: Molly Malene Steensgaard and François Gedigier
Music: Björk Guðmundsdóttir
Lyrics: **von Trier** and Sigurjon B. "Sjón" Sigurdsson
Choreography: Vincent Paterson
100-Camera Consultant: Tómas Gislason
Paintings for overture sequence (U.S. version and VHS): Per Kirkeby
Cast: Björk Guðmundsdóttir (Selma), Catherine Deneuve (Kathy), Peter
Stormare (Jeff), David Morse (Bill), Cara Seymour (Linda), Vincent Paterson
(Samuel), Joel Grey (Oldrich Novy), Vladan Kostic (Gene), Jean-Marc Barr
(Norman, the foreman), Siobhan Fallon (Brenda, the guard), Udo Kier (Dr.
Pokorny), Zeljko Ivanek (D.A.), Stellan Skarsgård (doctor), Paprika Steen
(woman on night shift), Jens Albinus (Morty, the hairpin supplier), TJ Rizzo
(Boris, "Captain von Trapp"), Katrine Falkenberg (Suzan), Lars Michael
Dinesen (incompetent defense counsel), Michael Flessas (angry man in cin-
ema), Reathel Bean (Judge A. D. Mantle), Luke Reilly (new defense counsel),
Anders Refn (man at Pokorny's practice), Al Agami (dancer), Paola Ciliberto,
Teresa Fabik (lovely girls in cinema)
35mm, color, Cinemascope shot on video
Language: English
139 minutes

2002
DOGVILLE
Production Company: Zentropa Entertainments
Co-Financed by: Danish Film Institute, DR, Slot Machine, Arte France Cin-
ema, France 3 Cinema, Canal+, Euroimages, Isabella Films, CoBo Fund, NPS,
4 & 1/2, Egmont Entertainment, Memfis, Film i Väst, Nordic Film & TV Fund,
Swedish Film Institute, SVT-Drama, Sigma Films, Edith Films, Finnish Film
Foundation, YLE, Pain Unlimited, WDR, Filmstiftung NRW & Zentropa Pro-
ductions
Producer: Vibeke Windeløv
Executive Producer: Peter Aalbæk Jensen
Director/Screenplay: **von Trier**
Assistant Director: Anders Refn
Cinematography: Anthony Dod Mantle
Art Direction: Peter Grant

Editing: Molly Malene Steensgaard
Cast: Nicole Kidman (Grace), Paul Bettany (Tom Jr.), Phllip Baker Hall
(Thomas Sr.), Stellan Skarsgård (Chuck), Patricia Clarkson (Vera), Zeljko Iva-
nek (Ben), Siobhan Fallon (Martha), Ben Gazzara (Jack McKay), Jeremy
Davies (Bill Henson), Chloë Sevigny (Liz Henson), Blair Brown (Mrs. Hen-
son), Bill Raymond (Mr. Henson), Lauren Bacall (Ma Ginger), Harriet Andersson (Gloria), Cleo King (Olivia), Shauna Shim (June), Miles Purinton (Jason),
Helga Olofsson (Dahlia), Evelina Lundqvist (Diana), Tilde Lindgren (Pan-
dora), Evelina Brinkemo (Athena), Anna Brobeck (Olympia), Therese Hogan
(Achilles), James Caan (The Big Man), Jean-Marc Barr (the man with the hat),
Udo Kier (the man with the coat), Kent Vikmo (driver), John Randolph Jones
(police officer #1), Erik Voge (police officer #2), Ingvar Örner (FBI man in
suit), Thom Hoffman (Mr D.), Ulf Andersson (man in dark suit #1), Erich
Silva (man in dark suit #2), Jan Coster (man in dark suit #3), Niklas Henriks-
son (man in dark suit #4), Hans Karlsson (man in dark suit #5), Andreas
Galle (man in dark suit #6), Barry Grant (man in dark suit #7), Ove Wolf
(man in dark suit #8), László Hágó (man in dark suit #9), Mattias Fredriksson
(man in dark suit #10), Oskar Kirkbakk (man in dark suit #11), Lee R. King
(man in dark suit #12), Mikael Johansson (man in dark suit #13)
Shot on HD-24 P blown to 35mm/Cinemascope
Language: English
165 minutes

Television

1988
MEDEA
Production Company: Danish Broadcasting Corporation (TV-Teaterafdel-
ningen)
Producer: Bo Leck Fischer
Director: **von Trier**
Screenplay: **von Trier**, based on the screenplay by Carl Th. Dreyer and Pre-
ben Thomsen
Cinematography: Sejr Brockmann
Production Design: Ves Harper
Editing: Finn Nord Svendsen
Music: Joachim Holbek

Cast: Kirsten Olesen (Medea), Udo Kier (Jason), Ludmila Glinska (Glauke), Henning Jensen (King Kreon), Baard Owe (King Aigeus), Solbjørg Højfeldt (the wet-nurse), Preben Lerdorff Rye (the tutor), Johnny Kilde, Richard Kilde (the children)
Shot on video, transferred to film, transferred back to video, color
Language: Danish
75 minutes
Made for Danish television

1994
LÆRERVÆRELSET (THE TEACHERS' ROOM)
Production Company: Zentropa Entertainment ApS for TV2
Producers: Ib Tardini and Peter Aalbæk Jensen
Director/Concept: **von Trier**

1994
RIGET (THE KINGDOM)
Episode #1: "Den hvide flok" ("The White Herd"); Episode #2: "Alliancen kalder" ("The Alliance Is Calling"); Episode #3: "Et fremmed legeme" ("A Foreign Body-part"); Episode #4: "De levende døde" ("The Living Dead")
Production Companies: Zentropa Entertainment ApS and Danish Broadcasting Corporation in co-production with Sveriges Television (Malmö), WDR, ARTE, the Coproduction Office with the support of GRECO within the MEDIA Programme of the European Union, Nordic Film and Television Fund, Nordic Collaboration Fund
Producer: Ole Reim
Executive Producers: Peter Aalbæk Jensen and Ib Tardini
Director: **von Trier**
Assistant Director: Morten Arnfred
Screenplay: **von Trier** and Niels Vørsel
Shooting Script: **von Trier** and Tómas Gislason
Cinematography: Eric Kress and Henrik Harpelund (steadicam)
Editing: Jacob Thuesen and Molly Malene Stensgaard
Music: Joachim Holbek
Cast: Ernst-Hugo Järegård (Stig Helmer), Kirsten Rolffes (Mrs. Sigrid Drusse), Holger Juul Hansen (Einar Moesgaard), Søren Pilmark (Jørgen Krogshøj, a.k.a. "Krogen"/"The Hook"), Ghita Nørby (Rigmor Mortensen), Jens Okk-

ing (Bulder), Birgitte Raabjerg (Judith), Baard Owe (Professor Bondo), Solb-
jørg Højfeldt (Camilla), Peter Mygind (Mogge), Udo Kier (Aage Krüger),
Morten Rotne Leffers (dishwasher #1), Vita Jensen (dishwasher #2), Henning
Jensen (hospital manager), Annevig Schelde Ebbe (Mary), Helle Virkner (Mrs.
Emma Mogensen), Paul Hüttel (Dr. Steenbæk), Ole Boisen (Christian), Louise
Fribo (Sanne), Otto Brandenburg (porter Hansen), Laura Christensen
(Mona), Mette Munk Plum (Mona's mother), Lea Brøgger (Mary's mother),
Dick Kaysøe (supervising guard), Henrik Koefoed (X-ray physician), Michael
Moritzen (ear specialist), Søren Elung Jensen (man in top hat), Holger Perfort
(Professor Ulrich), Benny Poulsen (head substitute doctor), Lars Lunøe (Min-
ister of Health), Lene Vasegaard (gynecologist), Bente Eskesen (night nurse),
Julie Wieth (pediatric nurse), Annette Ketscher, Birte Tove, Lise Schrøder,
Mette Marckmann (nurses), Tomas Stender (student), Søren Haus-Fausbøll
(orderly), Søren Steen (janitor), Michael Simpson (Haitian guy), Gordon Ken-
nedy (lab attendant), Niels Bank-Mikkelsen (hospital pastor), Søren Len-
ander (young man), Finn Nielsen (Madsen), Claus Nissen (Jensen), Solveig
Sundborg (Miss Krüger), Else Petersen (little old lady), Claus Strandberg (hypnotized patient), Svend Ali Hamann, (hypnotist), Tove Maës (Mrs. Zakariasen), Kurt Ravn (Zakariasen's son), Morten Eisner (mechanic), Erik Wedersøe
(Udo Kier's dubbed voice), Peter Gilfort (Morten Rotne Leffer's dubbed
voice), Ruth Junker (Vita Jensen's dubbed voice), Ulrik Cold (narrator), **von
Trier** (Lars von Trier)
16mm blown to 35mm, color (manipulated)
Language: Danish
272 minutes (63 + 65 + 69 + 75)
A slightly altered export version was cut for theatrical release abroad

1996
MARATHON
Concept: **von Trier**

1997
RIGET II (THE KINGDOM II)
Episode #5: "Mors in Tabula"; Episode #6: "Trækfuglene" ("The Migratory
Birds"); Episode #7: "Gargantua"; Episode #8: "Pandæmonium"
Production Companies: Zentropa Entertainment ApS and Danish Broadcast-
ing Corporation TV-Drama in co-production with Liberator Productions

S.a.r.l., with the support of Norsk Rikskringkastning, Sveriges Television
(Malmö), La Sept ARTE Unité de Programmes Fictions, RAI Cinema Fiction,
the Media Programme of the European Union
Producers: Vibeke Windeløv and Svend Abrahamsen
Associate Producers: Peter Aalbæk Jensen and Marianne Slot
Directors: **von Trier** and Morten Arnfred
Screenplay: **von Trier** and Niels Vørsel
Cinematography: Eric Kress and Henrik Harpelund (steadicam)
Art Direction: Jette Lehmann and Hans Chr. Lindholm
Editing: Molly Malene Stensgaard and Pernille Bech Christensen
Music: Joachim Holbek
Cast: Ernst-Hugo Järegård (Stig Helmer), Kirsten Rolffes (Mrs. Sigrid Drusse),
Holger Juul Hansen (Einar Moesgaard), Søren Pilmark (Jørgen Krogshøj,
"Krogen"), Ghita Nørby (Rigmor Mortensen), Jens Okking (Bulder), Birgitte
Raabjerg (Judith), Baard Owe (Professor Bondo), Solbjørg Højfeldt (Camilla),
Peter Mygind (Mogge), Udo Kier (Aage Krüger and "Lillebror," "Little
Brother"), Morten Rotne Leffers (dishwasher #1), Vita Jensen (dishwasher
#2), Birthe Neumann (Mrs. Svendsen, secretary), Henning Jensen (hospital
manager), Annevig Schelde Ebbe (Mary), John Hahn-Petersen (Nivesen), Erik
Wedersøe (Ole), Helle Virkner (Mrs. Emma Mogensen), Paul Hüttel (Dr.
Steenbæk), Ole Boisen (Christian), Louise Fribo (Sanne), Otto Brandenburg
(porter Hansen), Laura Christensen (Mona), Mette Munk Plum (Mona's
mother), Stellan Skarsgård (Swedish lawyer), Klaus Pagh (bailiff carrying sub-
poena), Søren Elung Jensen (man in top hat), Holger Perfort (Professor
Ulrich), Benny Poulsen (head substitute doctor), Lars Lunøe (Minister of
Health), Klaus Wegener (doctor, casualty), Annette Ketscher (nurse, casu-
alty), Timm Mehrens (doctor, operating theater), Tine Miehe-Renard (night
nurse), Michelle Bjørn-Andersen (pediatrician), Julie Wieth (pediatric nurse),
Birte Tove, Lise Schrøder (nurses), Dorrit Stender-Petersen (assisting nurse),
Michael Simpson (man from Haiti), Niels Bank-Mikkelsen (hospital pastor),
Steen Svarre (man in overalls), Peter Hartmann (3x34 removal man), Torben
Zeller (crematorium funtionary), Mette Hald (cross girl), Claus Nissen (Mad-
sen), Philip Zandén (Jönsson from Lund), Kim Janson (Detective Jensen),
Claus Flygare (Detective Nielsen), Henrik Fiig (car crash victim), Birger Jensen
(superintendent), Cecilie Brask (young woman in therapy), Jens Jørn Spottag
(Attorney Bisgaard), Jannie Farschou (orthopedist), Vera Gebuhr (Gerda),

Bjarne G. Nielsen (hospital pastor, new), Ingolf David (Death), Britta Lillesøe (woman in bed), Fash Shodeinde (Philip Marco), Thomas Bo Larsen ("The Falcon"), Thomas Stender (student), Anders Hove (devil-worshipping celebrant), Erik Wedersøe (dubbed Udo Kier's voice in the part of Aage Krüger), Evald Krog (dubbed Udo Kier's voice in the part of "Lillebror"), Peter Gilfort (dubbed Morten Rotne Leffer's voice), Ruth Junker (dubbed Vita Jensen's voice), Ulrik Cold (narrator), **von Trier** (Lars von Trier)
16mm, blown to 35mm, color (manipulated)
Language: Danish
296 minutes (63 + 79 + 76 + 78)
A slightly altered export version was cut for theatrical release abroad

1998–1999 STILLEBÆKKEN (STILL BROOK), a.k.a. MORTEN KORCH
Directors: Henrik Sartou, Finn Henriksen, and Lone Scherfig
Executive Producer: **von Trier**

1999/2000
D-DAG (D-DAY)
Production Companies: Nimbus Film Productions ApS in association with Zentropa Entertainments ApS, DR, TV2, TV3, TV Danmark, and with the support of the Danish Film Institute
Producer: Bo Erhardt
Directors: Thomas Vinterberg (Niels Henning—TV2), **von Trier** (Lise—TvDanmark 1), Søren Kragh-Jacobsen (Boris—DR1), and Kristian Levring (Carl—TV3)
Music: Flemming Nordkrog
Episode: Lise
Director/Screenplay: **von Trier**
Cinematography: Anthony Dod Mantle
Cast: Charlotte Sachs Bostrup (Lise), Stellan Skarsgård (Ulf), Louise Mieritz (Lise's sister, Dorte), Dejan Cukic (Boris), Nikolaj Kopernikus (Niels Henning), Bjarne Henriksen (Carl), Alexander Skarsgård (Lise's stepson)
Digital Video, color
Language: Danish
70 minutes

Music Videos

1983
ELEVATOR BOY
Production: Jeff Varab and Jacob Stegelmann for Laid Back
Directors: Vladimir Oravsky and **von Trier**
Artists: Laid Back

1990
BAKERMAN
Production: Fortunafilm (Peter Aalbæk Jensen) for Laid Back and BMS-Ariola
Director: **von Trier**
Artists: Laid Back

1990
HIGHWAY OF LOVE
Production: Fortunafilm (Peter Aalbæk Jensen) for Laid Back and BMS-Ariola
Concept: **von Trier**
Director: Åke Sandgren
Artists: Laid Back

1990
BET IT ON YOU
Production: Fortunafilm (Peter Aalbæk Jensen) for Laid Back and BMS-Ariola
Director: **von Trier**
Artists: Laid Back

1992
CHANGE
Production: for Manu Katche
Director: **von Trier**
Artist: Manu Katche

1992
DANAS HAVE (DANA'S GARDEN)
Production: for Kim Larsen
Director: **von Trier**
Artist: Kim Larsen

1992
LENINGRAD
Production: for Kim Larsen
Director: **von Trier**
Artist: Kim Larsen

1994
THE SHIVER
Production: Zentropa
Director: **von Trier**
Music: Joachim Holbek
With **von Trier** and scenes from *The Kingdom*

1998
YOU'RE A LADY
Production: Jesper Jargil
Director: **von Trier**
Music: You're a Lady (Peter Skellern)
Artist: Lars von Trier and the Idiot All Stars (principal actors from *The Idiots*)

Miscellaneous Work

Actor:
1968 HEMMELIG SOMMER (SECRET SUMMER), television series; director:
Thomas Winding

1980 KAPTAJN KLYDE OG HANS VENNER VENDER TILBAGE (THE RETURN
OF CAPTAIN KLYDE), feature film; directors: Jesper Klein and Per Holst

1989 EN VERDEN TIL FORSKEL (A WORLD OF DIFFERENCE), feature film;
director: Leif Magnusson

1999 KOPISTEN (THE COPIER), short film; director: Christian Tafdrup

Singer:
1998 YOU'RE A LADY, Limited edition single

Work in Progress

1991–2024?
DIMENSION
Production Companies: The Dimension Foundation, Zentropa, SFC, the
Danish Film Institute

Producer: Peter Aalbæk Jensen
Director: **von Trier**
Synopsis: **von Trier** and Niels Vørsel
Cast: Eddie Constantine, Jean-Marc Barr, Udo Kier, Jens Okking, Baard Owe, Stellan Skarsgård, Katrin Cartlidge, etc.

LARS VON TRIER

INTERVIEWS

He'd Rather Watch a Cop Show Than Himself

LARS HOFFMANN / 1968

HE'LL BE ON TELEVISION for the next six Saturdays, but he would rather watch a crime story than himself. "A strange mix," says Lars Trier of *Hemmelig sommer* [*Secret Summer*]. "We can't possibly live up to everyone's expectations. We'll get a good whacking after the first episode," says director Thomas Winding of the series, which starts today.

"The first episode is downright boring," Winding continues, "because there we have to introduce all the characters. Things don't really begin to happen until the second episode, and then it gets more and more exciting as events progress. I'd really like to edit the whole thing down to two hours and show the whole thing all at once."

Hemmelig sommer—filmed in color—is a million-crown project made by the Danish film company Laterna, with Winding as director, in collaboration with the other Nordic countries. Lulu Gauguin, the Danish consultant of children's television, and Swede Barbro Boman have written the script together.

Hemmelig sommer is the story of the friendship between the Danish boy Lars and the Swedish girl Sara. They're both eleven years old, but they have different backgrounds. It's also a story about being eleven. At this age, one starts to liberate oneself from one's parents, while still needing them, thus the rebellion takes the form of "impoliteness."

It's also a story of a girl who constantly tells lies and gets away with it. And of a boy who's sticking to the truth, but doesn't like it very much.

From *Aktuelt*, 4 January 1969. Reprinted by permission of the author.

The boy who plays Lars in the film is also called Lars in real life. His surname is Trier and he is twelve years old. He attends the Lundtofte School in Kgs. Lyngby, and his schoolmates make fun of him for being a "movie star."

"But I couldn't care less," says Lars. "I'm the one who made some money and I got three weeks off from school while we were shooting."

Lars was paid 3000 crowns for his participation and he has used it to buy himself an electric organ.

"But I'm not very musical. More than anything, I'll probably use it to make some sounds with when we're making short films."

For Lars Trier has been bitten by a mad movie dog. He shoots away for all he's worth together with a couple of friends. Would he like to be an actor?

"I don't know, but I know I'd like to be something in pictures."

What do you think of *Hemmelig sommer*?

"It's both fun and serious. A strange mix, as most children's films are. No, give me a good cop show instead—any day."

Passion Is the Lifeblood of Cinema

OLE MICHELSEN (1982)

OLE MICHELSEN: *You have chosen to call your film Images of a Relief. It takes place at the end of World War II. Why are you so fascinated by this theme—a theme that you could not possibly have first-hand knowledge of, due to your age?*
LARS von TRIER: When I chose this theme, it was because I needed to have an excuse to create some images. The first thing I look at when I choose my milieus and my historical epoch, is whether there's a possibility to create the images I desire.

OM: *And what are the images you wish to create? Because you work with images and colors that we normally don't see in what could be called ordinary Danish naturalistic cinema. You don't work with courses of events that are logical in relation to what we could refer to as naturalism in feature films.*
LvT: What I would like to see as my forte and my mission is to elevate the ugly and to show that beauty can be found everywhere. This mission nearly becomes religious in this film, as you have seen.

OM: *Beauty and ugliness. But why, then, the war theme? Why this remarkable story of a German soldier, played by Edward Fleming, who in a strange environment contemplates or actually tries to commit suicide together with renegades and German soldiers? A collective, almost ritual suicide.*
LvT: I believe that passion is the lifeblood of cinema, and it can assume many different forms. It can be the personal passion of a particular character.

From *Tusind Øjne*, #54, August 1982. Reprinted by permission of the author.

It can be the passion inherent in the subject matter. This is the case in this film. It's an unbelievable passion that is portrayed here, that I use in a totally unabashed way in my film, and that, of course, might raise some moral questions. But I believe that film always should feed off of a passion of some kind.

O M: *But the passion in this case is from the point of view of the German, and quite literally so, since there's a lot of focus on his eyes. It's about a dream he has had in his childhood, perhaps a source of anxiety—he speaks German and it's not always easy to understand, since you haven't provided any subtitles. Is this because you couldn't afford to, or is it a stylistic trick on your part?*

L v T: Well, you can say many things in German in a Danish cinema, things you cannot say in Danish, because I have to admit that I'm still a student, and there are some things I just can't cope with in Danish and that's why I'm doing it in German. It's a very cheap trick, I agree. And besides, it's also an attempt to work my way away from the notion of the text as what's essential. I have devoted some of my time at school to working my way from the text towards the image.

O M: *Going back to the subject of telling the story from his point of view. The main character is the German, part of the occupation forces. He represents evil, or maybe your fascination with evil. You just spoke of your fascination with ugliness, but you also portray evil to a such degree that we almost feel sympathy for those who are "evil."*

L v T: I'd have to say that it's always the losers that interest me, while the victors are one-sided. The losers in this case—the Germans at the time of their fall, if I may call it that—are the interesting ones, as is evident in the film.

O M: *On one hand there's a continuous story, one that you have made up, and on the other, you also use some documentary footage. Where did you find that?*

L v T: I got that from the archives of the Danish Broadcasting Corporation. And I've gotten permission to use it from various places. Most of it is unseen material. It turned up quite recently. There are some very bizarre images in several of the sequences.

O M: *Try to explain why you decided to include them.*

L v T: What we wanted with the images was to display the losers in documentary sequences. But we didn't want to link them with the film in such a way that you wouldn't notice the transitions between documentary and fiction. They are meant to be a critical commentary on the fiction part, and here I have, once again quite unabashedly, used a melancholy theme: images of Germans being chased down the streets, being jeered and beaten, as well as images of Danish traitors being locked up—on the whole, images that you cannot create, since they have something immediate and truthful to them.

O M : *Perhaps we should give a brief summary of the story in the film: this German, who tries to commit suicide, survives and looks up a Danish woman. We encounter her in some kind of festive situation, a garden party, a very grim garden party at that—there's nothing idyllic to be found in your images, or if there is then it's very Wagnerian, very violent, very decadent, if one would be allowed to use the word "idyllic" at all.* Images of a Relief *seems to have been made with a certain measure of irony on your part! But this man looks up this girl and meets his fate through her when he is offered refuge somewhere in the countryside, where he is ambushed and executed by a couple of Danish resistance fighters. That's the story, right?*
L v T : Very well put.

O M : *From where does your approach to images originate? Who have you been inspired by? Tarkovsky comes to mind.*
L v T : As I see it, the great masters cannot be plagiarized. There's no doubt that Tarkovsky is the master of them all. But I'd like to say something concerning "resemblance." When you go deeper into a subject and look for the images you might use, some parallel things will occur, like when fire and water meet. It's a classic idea. It creates an image, an atmosphere, a tension, et cetera, et cetera. Thus, I create some images that are parallel to Tarkovsky's, but also to those of some of the other older image-makers. It's an old truth, you see, that these elements create an image—in other words, you'll understand the Tarkovsky connotation, or you'll think of Bertolucci, there are plenty. Herzog, for example, he's right in there. But I don't think that it's a loan from them so much as it's the inevitable occurrence of parallels because of everyone agreeing on the basic elements.

O M : *And I never meant that there was anything objectionable in being inspired or influenced by other directors or to having a cinematic standpoint that comes from other filmmakers, because films are related to other films by a long chain of* events. *Cinema inspires cinema more than reality inspires cinema. But we can at least agree on the fact that your film has very few naturalistic elements, which makes it very "un-Danish," if we compare it to what generally is being made in Denmark right now.*

LvT: It would please me, if it were very "un-Danish." I happen to have the opinion that Danish cinema is refined to the point of being unintelligible. In other words the films have gradually become so boring, so insipid and so watered down, because in Denmark there's some kind of great fear, not only on the part of the consultants and the directors, but apparently—I don't know—in most of our society: the fear of fascination, of the miracle. It's called the fear of effects. As a result, the films turn into dull little mini-dramas with so few thoughts in them that they actually cannot be spotted. This style of cinema does not interest me one bit, and I don't understand the fact that there's as much money spent on it as there actually is.

OM: *Don't you think that it might be related to the contented Danish disposition and to a certain anxiety toward the violent expressions and the German heavy-handedness that are quite apparent in your film?*

LvT: Well, yes. But I don't believe in cultivating narrow-mindedness.

OM: *Tell me more about the genesis of the film and about your collaboration with Tom Elling, the cinematographer. How did you come up with the color schemes and the images you have produced?*

LvT: During our three years at the film school, we spend a lot of time trying to experiment our way towards certain things, but it's perfectly clear that we're based in the films of the '30s and the '40s. The idea is to elevate—here I go again with that word, it's very religious-sounding—elevate the effect to the point of the effect becoming the main point of the film. Then they immediately tell you that you're "straining for effect," but for us, the manu-facturing of the effect . . . the effect is the essential. You could say that there's a story—and whether one should be in there is always open to discussion—but what we have desired is to create some moods and some images, meant to live their own lives. We have spent three years in order to move towards something. It's, of course, by no means completed.

OM: *You chose to use professional actors, at least in the leading roles.*

LvT: Yes, and I really don't know if I want to continue doing that, if I'm *allowed* to continue at all. You get so many other things from working with amateurs. I've been very happy in my work with amateurs.

O M : *How would you evaluate the film school, now that you've graduated?*
L v T : Well, you can easily say that if you ever amount to anything, it's not on account of, but rather *in spite* of something, and in this respect, film school has worked tremendously well.

O M : *But don't you have any suggestions on how it might be done instead?*
L v T : Well, yes—my idea is that they should employ the workshop principle to a much higher degree. They've had this idea of banging some culture into the heads of people. If they don't have it already when they come there, then I don't understand why they come at all. It really should be about making a film, putting some sound on it and then watching it, so in my opinion the money from both the film school and the film institute should go to the workshop, instead of . . . all the other crap. As I see it, it's important to develop some fertile ideas, and the institutions we have right now, they just get stiffer as we speak—that's very apparent.

O M : *You say that there's no use in banging culture into the heads of people, if they don't have it in them already. What kind of culture have you got in your luggage?*
L v T : I don't know if you could call it culture, but the things I cultivate could be called a childish fascination. I don't know if you could call it culture, but it's at least one less inhibition. It's about keeping an open mind, and that I claim to be able to do.

O M : *You say that Lars von Trier is your stage name. Where does this "von" enter the picture?*
L v T : Well, aristocracy comes in many shapes and sizes, and when we think of "von," then it's in relation to the aristocracy. You could call it a provocation on my part. But I would very much like to see it as an inner aristocracy, one that I radiate, and besides, it's of course a no-no in Danish cinema and in Denmark in general to radiate anything whatsoever. But I'd really like to give Gert Fredholm credit for the name. You see, I argued with him on countless occasions at film school, and it ended with him actually baptizing me Lars *von* Trier, and I'm very happy with that, so I've kept it.

OM: *The provocation must lie in the fact that a discussion about aristocracy is not exactly called for in our times. Since we live in a time of democracy and equality, the timing might be a little off?*

LvT: Well, true, but this process of democratization has also been the reason for all this watering down of things that I've talked about. That's pretty clear, I think.

OM: *What are your comments on the reactions the film has brought?*

LvT: Well, they've hardly been good enough, because people haven't gotten really mad. That annoys me. But we'll just have to hope that that happens a little later.

OM: *What in the film did you hope that people would get mad at?*

LvT: Our emphasis on images and moods. That usually works, but the critics have obviously been able to find some other positive qualities in it that I myself haven't seen . . . at least when we're talking Danish normality cinema.

OM: *It must be an expression of acknowledgment that it's being shown in a real cinema [Delta]. Most graduation films wind up directly on the shelf.*

LvT: I just have to say, that what's important to me with a film is that you use an impeccable technique to tell people a story they don't want to be told. This is in my opinion the definition of true art. And this is what we succeeded a little bit in doing. Just read the reviews. But no one really cares about things they've heard.

OM: *Explain to me, if you would, the ending with the molehill.*

LvT: The idea of the ending is that we've lifted Edward Fleming 28 meters [approx. 92 feet] up over Gripskov Forest.

OM: *And he has just been blinded by Kirsten Olesen. . . .*

LvT: . . . and there's some form of nature poetry in that ending, I think. We could call it the moral of the story, if we want, in that no matter how bad things go in certain situations, there's always life underneath. I myself regard this as a profoundly positive and humanistic ending, but not everyone has interpreted it like this.

OM: *But it's a handsome ending—the blind man ascends into the sky and the mole starts to dig up the ground simultaneously.*

LvT: I generally think there's far too few moles working inside of Danish cinema, I'd like to add.

OM: *How did you create that scene?*
LvT: Our special effects guy just pumped up some dirt.

OM: *You mention nature poetry. The birds play a crucial part in the film. Why?*
LvT: I'm still stuck in traditional dramaturgy, so I let the film end the way it begins. I thought it would be an excellent idea to have him be fascinated by the birds of his childhood and end up as a bird himself. It's pretty beautiful. That it happens to be a Nazi officer might be seen as a provocation on my part. But again, this is the moral: everywhere there is beauty and life to be found, even within the soul of a Nazi officer.

OM: *Who himself has helped poke out the eye of a young boy, we're told.*
LvT: I see him some kind of voyeur. It's really a self-critical image. Cinema is very much about living off the passion of others, which we've already discussed.

OM: *He's a voyeur, who gets punished by having his eyes poked out?*
LvT: Yes—classic reasoning. Let the punishment fit the crime.

OM: *Lars, what would you like to do now?*
LvT: Well, I'd very much like to explore these cinematic extremes further, but I do realize that I will have to throw some other things into the bargain, in order to get funding.

OM: *In other words, you're already ready to start compromising?*
LvT: Yes, if you want to call it that, but as long as the goal remains clear . . . I do believe that some hustling has to be done. I don't know if hustling is the same as compromising? To a certain extent, I guess, but as such pretty entertaining. I'm very interested in religious films and would like to make a religious film in the traditional sense of the word, but this is obviously not the country to make a film about Jesus in, we've seen that. Those thoughts are too big for the cubicles of the Danish Film Institute. But I just might find some little insignificant thought to make a film from.

OM: *Are you religious yourself?*

LvT: Hard to say. Religiosity is a lot about being able to seek out the essentials in life, some basic elements. I can't come any closer than that.

OM: *But is it a religiosity that approaches the classic forms of religion?*

LvT: All the classic forms of religion also contain the basic elements that I would like to see within films as well, in that they are emotionally moving. I'd rather not label the direction in which I'm heading, but I just might reach my destination one day.

OM: *More specifically—what period and what kind of people will be featured in your next film?*

LvT: I'll leave that up to the Danish Film Institute—let's see what they can come up with. But I assume that it's going to be about someone who lives in the year 1982 in a one-and-a-half-bedroom apartment.

OM: *Have you sent them anything yet?*

LvT: No, but it's very hard to be an idealist. . . .

We Need More Intoxicants in Danish Cinema

LARS SCHWANDER/1983

Element of Crime: genre film [handwritten annotation]

MOST DANISH FILM PEOPLE are charlatans, and the consultants of the Danish Film Institute are so hostile towards culture that they easily could be replaced with businessmen. At least this is the opinion of film director Lars von Trier who neither celebrates the prevailing taste nor acquiesces to the powers that be in order to be able to do what he wants to do.

Last year Lars von Trier caused quite a bit of a rhubarb with his graduation film *Images of a Relief*, an unusual piece of Danish cinema with its expressive imagery, and now he and his crew have been granted financial support from the Danish Film Institute to make the film *The Element of Crime*. The script is written, the shooting is under preparation, and the press conference after the news of the grant gave von Trier an opportunity to give Danish cinema in general, as well as filmmaker Erik Clausen in particular, a swift kick in the butt.

Just as *Images of a Relief* was a kind of war film, set during the last days of World War II, *The Element of Crime* is a genre film—a crime film with a sci-fi bent.

"It's exciting," says von Trier, "to get your hands on a 'glossy plot' and then explore the genre to the limit—embellish it so that it will venture into places genre films generally don't venture. I see the plot as a book cover, and of course we want to have a glossy cover for our film."

The Element of Crime takes place in a future where nature has literally grown into and over civilization. The complicated and far from unambigu-

From *Levende Billeder*, June 1983. Reprinted by permission of the author.

ous story line deals with a police commissioner who takes over a case from his teacher from the police academy, who not only is controversial and untraditional in his methods, but who also has gone insane and is therefore unable to continue his work.

The commissioner follows the leads collected by his predecessor and uses his methods to solve the case: he tries to identify with criminals and understand what makes them tick—"the element of crime," which also is the title of the film. In the society in which the film takes place, there's unrest between the citizens and the police—the latter having curtailed their crime-solving activities. Now they only show up to flex some muscle.

"A little like the way the riot police work at the moment," von Trier observes, "cruising the streets to prove that they exist.

"What I want to do that's exciting is to create great canvases of narrative images. What you can do with a story is for example what Hitchcock did so well when he had a boy sitting on a bus with a bomb. You can allow yourself to show almost anything and for as long as you wish—you have carte blanche to show any image you can think of—as long as you cut back to the boy and the bomb at regular intervals. *The Element of Crime* is a great piece of storytelling with countless pretexts for the many images I want to create. The whole script has its origin in moods and images."

LARS SCHWANDER: *Take for example [Bille August's] Zappa—the people behind that film will promote the story of it. The story gives that film its drive, moves it forward.*

LARS von TRIER: Yes, and in my opinion the importance of the story is wildly exaggerated—both at the Film Institute and among critics. The story line is the pretext of the film, but the other elements don't necessarily have to point in the same direction. But, of course, you have to respect the prevailing tradition—you're forced to package your film inside a story line in order to reach a wider audience.

LS: *Isn't there a fundamental problem in the fact that people who want to express themselves with pictures also are "forced to" express themselves in words, for example by writing a script?*

LvT: No, there isn't—it's just a question of technique. But there is a problem, however, in the fact that cinema has become so similar to the novel. Poetry would be a better form to work with, but you rarely see a poetic film.

It's important to create alternatives, at least in relation to television, where they come up with all these series with plots and thrills and spills as the foundation.

As a moviegoer, you are completely captivated when you're sitting in the theater, and the better the film, the more you're taken for a ride. You aren't given the opportunity to experience something that the guy sitting next to you doesn't experience as well. These are the criteria of a good film, but I definitely think that they're the wrong criteria. We have to make some "counter-films," films that give you the opportunity to experience something broader than this plot-bound thing, which is so damn hackneyed—and only exciting from a craftsmanship point of view, like when a carpenter has made a table. It's important to free yourself from this way of thinking and reach further out.The story line has become a kind of holy cow, especially on television—that's what everyone talks about. Very significantly, there's always been a discussion of morality rather than quality when I have delivered my scripts: "Can you really allow yourself to show these gory crimes?" for example. I happen to be of the opinion that if things exist, then you're not only allowed to show them, you *have* to show them! And life is so richly faceted—it's just a question of going out there and picking things up.

I really don't know anything about people, but I have the sense that, with time, experiences mean less and less, and that people become more and more one-dimensional. The childish fascination with the everyday miracle is a very good place to start when you make a film—the miracle connected with life, the phenomena of nature that you gradually explore. The mole hills in the last scenes of *Images of a Relief* are an example. Herzog had that fascination once upon a time, but to a lesser extent today: the shooting of *Fitzcarraldo* was disastrous. He's entirely caught up in the commercial system, just like Bergman with *Fanny and Alexander*. Throughout his career, he has been saying that he wants to quit because he makes bad films, and it's only been going downhill ever since. None of the "old boys" remain. Pasolini died while he still was a great artist. International cinema is experiencing a very bad spring—it has kind of been infected with social realism.

It may very well be that you get more afraid with age, maybe more morally inclined—should we put an age limit of thirty-five on who's allowed to make films? No, I don't know.

Many films are also insults to the intellect of the viewer. The dramaturgy experts keep on saying, "Yes, but are they able to follow this?" and "Do they understand?" and "Have we made it perfectly clear that this piece is related to the overall story?" and things like that. It's become a golden rule, in that everything has to come together in the end for the great solution of the problems of the film. One grand question that all the other questions of the film are mere parts of. Complete harmony. And, what, may you ask, has that got to do with real life? Nothing. And with art? Even less.

I have this idea that the art of cinema should be like a supermarket, where you go around with your little cart and pick things up.

But it's funny—the critics really jump at the first sign of something outside the pale of the typically Danish. *Thorvald and Linda*, by Lene and Sven Grønlykke, is a good example. Unfortunately I've only seen a clip on television, but it was brilliant. They were sitting there singing and there was atmosphere—now that's worth a whole movie. Jørgen Leth, too, will probably get some wind in his sails with his new film, but he's already holding a few trump cards—he simply cannot make an uninteresting film, even though the quality can vary. I have the greatest respect for him. He's been a part of the avant-garde since the '60s and he's still at it. But most of those who tried their hands at something in those days are all dried up today—they're afraid, they've become big-shots, they're in charge of everything everywhere— while Leth keeps on trying new things. He works intuitively—in my opinion he's such a great supervisor, which is a great advantage. He knows how to benefit maximally from his collaborators. And Dreyer was good at that, too. Simply by being present, combined with the expectations of the actors and technicians, he created great films. Leth has proven himself, and thanks to everyone's positive expectations, he continues to work—that's a dimension of his method, just as his curiosity is his tool. It has produced some great results.

L S : *There's a tradition of social realism in Danish cinema, and Danish films often embrace a radical standpoint that supports the underprivileged in society. Isn't that great?*

L v T : Basically, there cannot be any such thing as a film that everyone agrees on—we can for example all agree that the mentally retarded should be treated better, despite the fact that no one wants to pay for it. Yet, no one disagrees with the basic standpoint. Films should be made to bring something up for discussion and if you were to make one about the retarded, which I myself wouldn't mind doing, then it would have to have a completely different angle. You could for example do a love story, or you could put them in a crime story—that would be beautiful. . . . We had one, by the way, in *Images of a Relief*. I've heard that they have a theater group for the mentally retarded in France. Currently, the interesting thing on the subject of the retarded is the problem of care, as if the only way to approach the topic was with a sense of guilt.

But there's a tension in portraying marginalized groups in order to describe how society reflects upon itself.

Typically, you never see a Danish film where you're basically in disagreement—personally, I'm afraid of social democratism or whatever it's called. Time and time again, wherever you turn in the art circles, the big shots are there to put a stop to all life forms. In Denmark it's enough to mention the word "art" to give someone constipation. And when it comes to film, the drama department at the Danish Film Institute is beneath contempt, because there you're met with an animosity toward art that exceeds your wildest imagination. In my opinion it's totally unjustifiable that they haven't forced Mogens Rukov [lecturer at the National Film School of Denmark, later scriptwriter on Thomas Vinterberg's *Festen/The Celebration*] to take the job as head of that department—he's their biggest talent and the person best suited for the job, but he's always passed over.

The big shots in charge are first and foremost very impolite, but apart from that, they put a stop to creativity by being quite simply hostile towards art. And this is why I'd rather see some businessmen in charge: things could *only* get better! I'd rather have businessmen than moralists. One of our approaches to *The Element of Crime* is that it must be commercial, without a doubt—this isn't some kind of hobby. But apart from that it will hopefully also be much more. . . .

In this country there's no such thing as support for the director—all you get is unemployment compensation! And this is also the reason that they don't cut back on the budget—just like any budget item it fits perfectly into the government's bureaucracy. And the use of the words "cultural funding" is nothing but a joke!

But I also should mention the fact that the Film Institute, together with my producer, has been unbelievably accommodating towards me—among other things, they let the whole crew of *Images of a Relief* stay on. I'm happy about that, it's an unusual privilege. Just like the fact that there are a lot of possibilities for me personally inside the Danish film business, because of the desire to include all sorts of personalities. You become a "hostage" and you have to pay penance, in relation to the rest of the business. Because it's one thing how I would like things to be in the film business and another thing how even the films that I make are necessary for the Danish film business.

LS: *Do the producers normally put any demands on the directors about the casting?*

LvT: I'd like to put it like this: actors are a safe bet, and primarily it's the producers who want to use the big names. You can never go wrong if you use Ole Ernst, because he's got this kind of radiance that always shows, whatever he's in, almost. But in my opinion, this is a boring way of thinking and apart from that in Denmark there are only stage actors, no film actors!

At the moment we're casting our film, and my original idea was to use only nonprofessionals. For me, the problem with actors is that they want to create their character, and this film has no room for that kind of creativity. Of course I like to hear suggestions from the actor—that's the whole point of choosing a certain person for a part—but I will not offer any psychological explanation of the part. I will not commit to that—it's a lot of nonsense and vanity on the part of the actors. As we speak, we are negotiating with some foreign people for the parts, which is OK, because *The Element of Crime* will be in English. . . .

Then I have Bo Holten to compose the music, which is very nice—I finally can afford to have an original score for my film. But again, people warn me, "Not too much music"—just like I've for example met some resistance in relation to using inner monologue. There's a great Danish fear of the commonplace, the familiar. Now, if I want to compress a part of the story into three sentences, instead of using thirty minutes to show it, then that's my prerogative. And music: it's been used a lot before, right now it isn't used very much—it's all a question of fashion. But how I yearn for musical scoring, something that affects the subconscious—well, I should be allowed to do what I want. It's not a question of delicacy! The idea of using the resources at hand has been regarded as quite criminal in this country—the Puritanism, which is so widespread, is something our crew would like to challenge.

LS: *Are you of the opinion that there's a lack of passion in Danish cinema?*

LvT: Yes, and it's a subject for a thesis—how do films come to look the way they do? I'm sure of the fact that there's some great Danish anxiety for the distinctive, the magnificent. If the subject grows too big, then people lack the courage to make the film. It's a form of Jante law—and here we have a great lack of the pioneer spirit. . . .

LS: *"Thou shalt not believe that thou art somebody".* . . .

LvT: Yes, and I totally disagree. It also has to do with the role of the artist as a part of the work of art, like with the lives of Fassbinder and Pasolini. Cinema isn't something you pack up at four o'clock—the ideal thing would be to make films together with a group of tonsured people in sackcloth and ashes, in penance outfits. Art does not come out of an industry. It's important that art arises from an inner urge, and to this some people will surely say, 'Yes, sure, but we all have to live." *But, for God's sake, in that case you have to live from something else!* Cinema is so close to me that I can't stand to see it getting a bad reputation, you know, on account of all these dumbasses.

LS: *And Denmark isn't allowed to make her own Jesus film either. First Dreyer, then Thorsen—*

LvT: Simply because the idea is too grand. It's pretty grand of [Jens Jørgen] Thorsen to want to do this great blasphemous film, and it's definitely a case of wanting to take up the gauntlet, of wanting to accept a challenge. Of course it should be done, and if I became a film consultant tomorrow, it would be the first thing on the agenda. We must have powerful proposals, so that we can make powerful films.

And with respect to Thorsen, it's a mistake to believe that cinema is supposed to please. There are some religious people who think that this film mustn't be made, but for the sake of general spiritual soundness, we need the media—and cinema is one of them—to provoke. It can only be beneficial for everyone involved—religious people will hate it so they will be strengthened in their belief, but blasphemers will be strengthened in theirs, too. What I believe in is a rich variety of conceptions and opinions, and that of course can easily lead to one or two fights. But not everyone should be pleased by a film.

LS: *You can also please smaller groups. Images of a Relief, for example, was very beautiful in its aesthetics.*

LvT: Yes, maybe, but I'm a little sorry about that, too—there was supposed to be a balance there, between the beautiful and the grim, and even that film was a proposal. But in my opinion it should have pushed the envelope even further but I've only just begun.

L S : *You have also said that you would like to uncover the beauty in ugliness. Why?*

L v T : Because I think that the ugliness possesses some dynamics in itself, while beauty has a tendency to fade away with time. Traditional "prettiness" often becomes quite lame. But all I demand of a film is the strength of creativity and love.

L S : *Are there too few chances taken in Danish films, as far as creativity and love go?*

L v T : Well, there's a definite fear of making something bad—give us some great fiascoes, where are they? But I have great admiration for Jytte Rex and her stuff—it also represents a proposal of something alternative—but it's unbelievable that you should have to go over to the spinner's cottage in order to find someone with balls in Danish cinema.

At this juncture, one could pose a general question: is this sorry situation the fault of the Film Institute or is it that the directors lack all imagination? Originally I thought that it was the Film Institute, but I've gradually come to the frightening conclusion that the directors lack capacity. And then the question is whether we should give less money to Danish cinema—there's simply no reason whatsoever to make the films that they're making right now. There's no sense in giving artificial respiration to a business that makes *those* things, and my suggestion is of course to let all the money go— undivided—to the workshop, and then see what can come out of that.

Someone said that in order to create an abstract painting, you first have to be able to draw your subject the way it really looks. But why is that? Why do you have to work your way through a tradition that doesn't have anything at all to do with the final expression? Of course a study of muscles can make an abstraction look like real muscles. But who's to say that these real muscles have, or should have, any influence on the final product? It's really nothing but a great burden.

And this is what you're confronted with in Danish film—when you want to make a film, you're asked the question, "But do you know how it's done?" No, you don't. If I were a film consultant I'd say, "That's great!" A lot of creative people really devote themselves to the medium of film—they produce the worst sort of banalities, whereas in other media they would have been able to create a great work of art. They have a great respect for the film medium, which is probably the most dangerous attitude of all to have. You should devote yourself to your work without respect for techniques and traditions. Cinema is close to dreaming and we all have dreams.

When you have a work of art inside your head, then it's simply a question of stubbornness to get it out! I don't believe much in education and not much in the film school either, despite the fact that it's been good to me. I've been allowed to do some things, but then you have to pay your penance in that you have to do them within a certain framework.

I'm not saying that there's a lack of the love of cinema in the business, but at the top, among the powers that be, there's no love to be found. You'll never get me to believe that it was love that created the films we've seen in Denmark—that I refuse to believe! If you have a love for a certain type of film, then you'll of course try to avoid reproducing what's already been seen. Our film emanates from the *cinéma noir* [sic] style, but we'd like to think that we're working creatively with the genre. That we expand the language, renew it. The majority of the Danish film people are nothing but charlatans—they'd be just as happy doing something else. A true love of the medium is rare.

L S : *Is it typical for Danish cinema—that one often repeats the formula, once it has proven itself?*

L v T : Yes, it is. I have nothing against popularity, but if the only yardstick for whether a film is good or not is the box office numbers, then you're really barking up the wrong tree. If you only gave the people what they wanted, then they'd still be eating sugar because it's sweet. But it's empty calories. It's good to have pioneers who have dared to serve us something bitter, which then turns out to be one of those great experiences—like alcohol, something intoxicating. We need more intoxicants in Danish cinema. Just a few people who dare to serve us something bitter.

L S : *At a press conference, you attacked Erik Clausen[1]—can you comment on that?*

L v T : I'm an idealist and I can be a little difficult at times. The reason I've

---

1. Born in 1942. Danish director of popular comedies with a social conscience. Active in the left-wing political cultural movement of the 1970s. Raised some havoc in 2000, after having been included in the Danish *Who's Who*, on account of his thorough displeasure with this "bourgeois" honor.

been standing up to him is simply my desire to help him to do something better. Filmmaking is a huge undertaking and it seems to do nothing but paralyze Clausen. He should just transform his personality into film—I've heard, for example, that he's a good street jester. And if he has some kind of political message, then he should just let it out instead of hiding it behind some common comedy tradition—there's no reason whatsoever to keep such traditions alive, for God's sake.

L S :   *Why not?*

L v T :   Of course you can make popular films, and that's all good and well, but no one ever said that things have to look alike. There's no reason at all to keep on mass-producing all these identical films, like they've done with those popular comedies.

Cinema should be in constant evolution. Clausen has the charm and all, and I'm sure that he can make better things than he's done so far—it's just a question of putting some pressure on him to do it. But this whole discussion came up when I read that someone had suggested that he receive a yearly stipend, written into the state budget—that he should do one film per year, which would be a disaster for any image-maker. At least you should have to prove yourself, in order to be considered for such a costly protection—in a situation like that, you should really have to prove that you're prepared to work creatively. Mass-production is a bad thing.

L S :   *You said you were an idealist?*

L v T :   And I can't say anything else—my love of the medium has made me myopic. I'm idealistic in the way that I think films should look. The question is then how to reach that ideal. But the work has to progress through a number of phases—I can't exactly make that film tomorrow!

L S :   *Is there a parallel between artistic and political idealism?*

L v T :   That's hard to answer. I've had some terrible problems in that my films are seen as radically right-wing wherever I go. Maybe it can be blamed on the fact that I have such great respect for the right of the individual, which you very well could call a political standpoint.

At one film festival, where I went with *Images of a Relief*—in Germany at that—they called it a fascist film. You have to risk such things when you're striving to convey the extreme Fassbinder was called everything under the sun, right?

Their very single-minded interpretation of the film was that it glorified a Nazi officer. It's a totally idiotic interpretation, of course. And still I insist on the unalienable right of the individual to shape his own life.

LS: *Do you regard* Images of a Relief *as a subversive—dangerous if you will—film?*
LvT: Yes, but not dangerous enough.

LS: *If we compare you to Erik Clausen, who is, or has been, affiliated with the Danish communist party, DKP—he can easily claim that he's much more of a threat to the bourgeoisie.*
LvT: But he isn't at all—he's just what they want him to be and perfectly harmless. Go ahead, do *An Oppressed People Is Always Right*, just don't do *Circus Casablanca*!

LS: *In other words you mean that with an experimental film, you can commit more "dangerous acts" than DKP people like Clausen and [performer] Petersen, or [author] Dea Trier Mørch, or [musicians] Røde Mor and Troels Trier, who all use conventional methods?*
LvT: Yes, and I mean that if you make a film that is reactionary in its form, then the contents are insignificant. This is the way it is: you can't have rebellious or reformist content without adapting the form at the same time. You can't separate the one from the other.

LS: *You aren't afraid of the possibility that your films will become part of the wave of reaction we're experiencing in society today?*
LvT: No, I'm not afraid of that. On the whole, I'm not afraid of how my films will be received—that's something of a starting point for me. Fear is important in the creative process, but fear of the finished product is decidedly counterproductive.

Sightseeing with the Holy Ghost

THOMAS ALLING / 1984

''IF YOU USED A CERTAIN LENS on the camera, you'd get some amazing takes of the insect and animal life that is here. . . . On the other hand all this light will scare a lot of other animals away. But they'll hopefully return once you're finished with . . . yes, what is it that you're actually *doing*?''

The middle-aged gentleman crouches and pulls his collar up over his ears while his peering eyes seek a friendly soul who will answer him. But apparently no one has acknowledged the presence of this lover of wildlife, so he swiftly disappears as quietly as he came. The badger couple who usually resides here will hopefully show up again somewhere. Neither insects nor badgers are of any interest to film director Lars von Trier and his crew on this bitingly cold October night. The dark of night, the trees, and the moss-like wooded area on the banks of the Mølleån creek, north of Copenhagen, serve merely as a suitable backdrop to a scene in Lars von Trier's film *The Element of Crime.*

A prop master is creating a layer of smoke over the wooded grounds, and the lighting crew sets up the projectors. The rest of the crew waits, silent and slightly chilled. The nocturnal takes have entered their third week, and the reversed rhythm of day and night has begun to take its toll on everyone.

"Everyone has accumulated an enormous need for sleep, and when you finally get a chance to get some sleep you rarely get more than three hours—then you jump straight up and shake all over," says script supervisor Stine

From *Levende Billeder*, April 1984. Reprinted by permission of the author.

Monty. "And there's three more weeks of night shoots, so sleeping will just have to wait.

Family life, as well. Nevertheless, almost everyone involved seems very engaged in the project. Understandably so, since it's not exactly an ordinary film that von Trier has thought out. The unusualness lies not only in the style and content of the film, but also in the way that the whole thing has come into being.

The Element of Crime is a "futuristic crime story with religious undertones." This was the original outline at least, when von Trier once upon a time explained his idea to writer Niels Vørsel. Together, they have written the script, and they did agree, already in the initial stages, to remove the religious undertones. But as time went by the undertones managed to sneak their way back into the story line.

Lars von Trier himself explains that archetypes—in this case the Father, the Son and the Holy Ghost—will quite simply always be the elements you can and should build a story around. *Must* build a story around, if you want to talk about true art.

In *The Element of Crime*, the Son is represented by the character of police commissioner Fisher. The story takes place at an undefined time in the near future somewhere in Europe. It's a Europe in heavy decay, where only the ruins are left as reminders of once great cities and their civilization. Here, people live in underground caves and the powers that be control everyone in an unending reign of terror, with Kramer, the despotic chief of police, acting as its evil incarnation.

Fisher, who has been stationed in Cairo for the last thirteen years, is deeply shocked when he returns to this degenerated Europe. He is put on a case, one that his former mentor and idol from the days at the police academy, Osborne, has been working on but has apparently left unsolved, something that leaves Fisher even more puzzled. At the same time, his desire to settle the murder case once and for all increases, and he sets about to solve it using the methods provided by father-figure Osborne in the manual "The Element of Crime." The terms laid out in the manual dictate that one has to gain complete comprehension of the cause and the background of the crime, and in order to reach that state, one has to get into the mind of the criminal, thereby becoming one with the element of the crime itself. Meanwhile, Osborne has gone insane and Fisher ignores his warning not to pursue the case further. Instead, he sets off on a fateful odyssey—a journey into the soul of the presumed killer Harry Grey. Incidentally, Harry Grey's initials might just stand for "Holy Ghost"—omnipresent, yet nowhere to be seen.

Whether Fisher lives up to the legacy passed down to him by Osborne will not be revealed here; nor will any theory be presented on the true essence of that legacy. Fisher is a voyeur in a future society, about which one might ask the question whether the decay is a nightmarish vision, or whether the conquest of mankind by primitive forces might not be regarded as a positive development—a return to where we once came from.

Technically, Lars von Trier makes use of countless effects—dissolves, crosscuts, and other forms of advanced framing. Most of the film takes place at night, in a yellowish glow that emphasizes the nightmarish atmosphere of the flashbacks Fisher recounts for a hypnotist-cum-psychologist—flashbacks that serve as the framework of the film.

The very peculiar *physical* surroundings of von Trier's vision of the future are, as has already been mentioned, not those of studio sets. On the contrary, von Trier has sought out some highly unusual locations in and around Copenhagen: underground sewer systems, a disused limestone quarry, the Tre Kroner fortress, and the casemates of Kronborg Castle are some of the locations on which shooting has taken place. Lars von Trier does not hide the fact that *The Element of Crime* can be seen as homage to the classic film noir genre, in which dramatic intrigue is combined with bloodshed. British actor Michael Elphick, who plays the leading part of Fisher, describes the film: "Despite its sophisticated nature, it can immediately be perceived as a thriller—a kind of cross between *A Clockwork Orange* and *The Third Man*."

In our part of the world, the thirty-seven-year-old Elphick is probably best known as Private Schultz from the television series with the same name. Some might also recognize him as the sadistic hospital orderly in *The Elephant Man*.

Lars von Trier has cast the main leads of *The Element of Crime* with British actors. Partly because he wants to reach an international audience, and partly because Danish actors would render the film "too Danish." And finally, England has a far larger pool of actors, which is an advantage, since von Trier required some rather peculiar characters.

There were no actual sound recordings made during takes—to the benefit of the director, who could direct while the camera rolled. The music of Wagner blasted at full volume from loudspeakers on the set, in order to

infuse cast and crew with the right spirit of things. This meant that the soundtrack of the film was to be created afterwards in the sound studio.

Shortly before Christmas, Michael Elphick visited Copenhagen to record his lines. He said that this way of acting in front of the camera was entirely new to him, since all the lines "disappeared into the deaf ears of the night."

"It's actually extremely unusual to do it this way, and it's also difficult to give your all in front of the camera when you already know that the lines aren't particularly important. Then there's the problem of re-creating what you did in front of the camera when you're in the sound studio. But—and here's the difference—von Trier does not want you to do this. While I might have an impression of how a scene should be acted, I will be asked to add something entirely new here in the sound studio, as I do my lines."

On the whole, there are many of the scenes in the film that Elphick has not understood the meaning of until this stage—after having seen the rough cut of the film in relation to post-synchronization. During shooting there were sometimes difficulties understanding the thoughts and intentions of von Trier. Continues Elphick: "Before the shooting starts, Trier has a very clear sense of what he wants, and he sticks to it. And I think that the finished product will turn out exactly the way he envisioned. But as an actor it can at times be a little frustrating because he sometimes treats you like a puppet on a string, in that he almost cajoles you into expressing your self in a certain way. I'm just not used to that sort of thing. And you never really know why he asks you to do one thing or another. It's not that he's unclear in his direction, he just chooses not to explain himself in the situation. On the other hand I've had a great deal of trust in Trier from the start—and I still do."

The Element of Crime is Lars von Trier's fourth film. The three earlier ones [*Nocturne, Den sidste detalje (The Last Detail), Images of a Relief*] were short films, made at the National Film School of Denmark. *Images of a Relief*, his graduation film, has been shown at festivals all over Europe, where it has received several awards, and this fall it was shown on Danish television. Now is the first time he's tried his hand at a feature film, but as on the three previous films, he collaborates closely with cinematographer Tom Elling and editor Tómas Gislason. This core group has gradually grown to include other collaborators. Thus, the crew on *The Element of Crime* is almost identical to that of *Images of a Relief*, to the great delight of the original trio. It is this trio who play the most important part in the creation of the film, when it comes to the big picture—from the original idea to the final stage, when the film is mixed, mastered and made ready for the copy lab. It's an evening in January and for the first time in a long time the three are seated around a table, not in order to solve practical problems, but rather to put their thoughts on their lengthy collaboration into words. A collaboration that for the most part—like an old marriage—runs on perception and intuitive understanding of each other's point of view.

Lars von Trier explains the nature of their collaboration during the project: "Whereas I usually write the script alone, I have worked together with Niels Vørsel this time around. We met during the making of *Images of a Relief*, where he was an extra. Then, in the fall of '82, we started to write, and last fall there was a finished script, which was the basis of the grant of 3.4 million crowns that we received from the Danish Film Institute. Then producer Per Holst added 1 million to that, and then I started scouting for locations together with Tom Elling. But despite the fact that Tom entered the project at this late juncture, he and Tómas Gislason put their mark on the project from the start. Our experiences together in the previous film are integral to all our new thoughts. Thus we exchange ideas and consult each other on a running basis.

"Like, if we suddenly come upon an awesome location, then we're quick to write it into the story, maybe even change the story to get it to fit in. There was for example this love scene in the script, which originally took place in a hotel room. Then we found some amazing sewer channels—an underground system of channels—so we moved the scene to that place. The last rewrite of the script wasn't done until we had found all the right locations.

"The thing that separates our working method from that of many other people is that the three of us work out a storyboard together. It's a kind of expanded script, where every camera angle, setup, and scene in the film is drawn, described, and timed. In that way the whole film is actually edited beforehand. So Tómas is not just the editor, he's also there to suggest other scenes and takes. In other words, the three of us are all very involved in this very concrete phase—the birth of the actual film."

Elphick felt a little frustrated during the shooting, being treated like a puppet. Why don't you want to explain to the actors what they're actually doing?
LARS von TRIER: Well, there's a reason why the actors are actors and the director is the director. I don't believe in walking around explaining psychological approaches—and I happen to think that actors are at their best when

they know nothing. If you regard the actors as a kind of tool for the director in his quest for certain expressions, it's actually to his advantage if they're unsure of themselves—he can use that.

None of the sound production is performed until after the shooting has been done, which opens up further possibilities for the creation of certain expressions. This affects the acting, in that we at the stage of the post-synchronization are able to *work against* the acting in the images. We have worked like this through the whole process and this is why Elphick must not know of the finished product. Apart from this there's also some inner monologue that Niels Vørsel and I wrote first after the shooting was completed. At the end of the day people have to overcome their vanity. The things we work with here are, in spite of everything else, so much bigger than one person's vanity.

An expression that constantly resurfaces when discussing cinema with Trier & Co. is *images.* In an earlier interview in this magazine, von Trier referred to the plot in a film as a pretext for the essential: the images. And now, at the point when this film is almost finished he says: "I have to admit that I initially saw the crime story as a necessary evil. But although I have become increasingly fond of the genre, I still have to say that I regard the plot as a kind of skeleton, an alibi for making the images. While our crime story is admittedly very exciting, we have set out to do a crime story in a different way. A crime story with some other things thrown in—things that might even be more important than the actual plot. I myself believe that we have made a very original contribution to the genre."

TOM ELLING: Now we're sitting here and talking about how special this film is supposed to be. But the traditional crime films, the ones we're fond of, they, too, have another message than the story they set out to tell. And this is why they still breathe, no doubt about that, and this is why they are classics. There, too, the plot has served as an alibi in order to project the underlying story. An advantage of the crime genre as alibi is that the alibi complements the true aim—the one of creating images.

Could you try to explain exactly what you mean by images?

TE: An image is good if it contains certain elements. It's about atmospheres being created from what you see and hear and feel and experience . . . (he explains, with great animation, but gets interrupted by von Trier).

LvT: Images aren't only what you see. It's also about everything *outside* the image—the plot and the sound and the cliché and everything. Images aren't only images *of* something, but also *on* something.

Of course it's true that people might have an easier time relating to the story than the image. Okay, we've done like this in *The Element of Crime*: we've taken people on a narrative journey, which we will manage to take their minds off of, by way of the mesmerizing effect of the film medium. They're along for the ride, but there's no clear destination. It becomes a sightseeing tour of this universe, the one that we'd really like to show them. And you can call that an alibi, but that's what the narrative journey is there for.

Several reviewers accused Images of a Relief *of being cryptic and distant. Who do you make your films for?*

TE: For us, ourselves, definitely. You can only make a film for yourself. When you make a film, you can't ask anyone but yourself if it's something good you're making. If people find *Images of a Relief* distant, then I think the problem is that they're prejudiced, and thus they block out an immediate experience of what they see.

TÓMAS GISLASON: I love films like *Star Wars* and some other science fiction films tremendously. The thing that makes them so appealing is that they have created novel universes with a lot of things that you've never seen before. But I never worry about whether people will understand what they see. People can have dreams night after night and really get some heavy experiences through that. When similar things occur in our film, then something gets going inside your head—and, mind you, something that's much more useful to you in your everyday life than social realism with its ready-made solutions.

LvT: We're doing some serious refining of the morbid in our film. We do this because there is a beauty in it, a beauty you shouldn't forget—there are for example a lot of dead horses in this film. . . .

TE: While that isn't morbid in itself, it's the fascination for such things that dictates what we do.

LvT: All right, but then I'd like to illustrate it like this: if you on one hand have a family with children and mortgage problems and on the other hand a mass grave for foot-and-mouth disease . . . well, just make your own choice about what you'd like to see on celluloid. To me, for the moment, it's definitely the mass grave that holds the biggest fascination. That thing with the mortgage is about as uninteresting as anything could ever be.

Social realist cinema—as in the film with the family with children, et cetera—is in reality a very intellectual form of cinema. Instead of that, we try to use elements that penetrate directly into the subconscious. In that respect, our film is very anti-intellectual and accessible. It's all about opening your mind to what's being shown on the screen. People might not immediately understand what they see, but there might be some images created inside of them that give rise to certain experiences—things they might not immediately be able to put into words.

TE: The way we make cinema is an expression of how we look at things today—and as such it's a kind of provocation. This is not to say that we look at the world today as it's portrayed in *The Element of Crime*. But the way we've made it is related to the fact that we're here right now. And as such it's a reflection of how we perceive our surroundings.

Trier, you have earlier said that it's uninteresting to deal with the contemporary when making films.
LvT: And I abide by that, if we're talking about consciously dealing with an analysis of society. But the reflection will always be relevant, since we live in the present. On the whole I find analysis a very boring phenomenon. So in that respect, *The Element of Crime* is clearly an anti-analytical film.

A Conversation between Jan Kornum Larsen and Lars von Trier

JAN KORNUM LARSEN / 1984

JAN KORNUM LARSEN: *You recently said that you've been working with a very strange crew. Who are the people in it?*
LARS von TRIER: Well, first of all there's me, then there's Tom Elling, the cinematographer who is also a painter, which in itself is unusual, and finally there's Tómas Gislason who is the editor. The three of us went to film school together. We've also made *Images of a Relief* and a little film called *Nocturne* together. They're a couple of strange characters. Very sensitive and because of that also a little difficult to deal with.

JKL: *How did* The Element of Crime *start out?*
LvT: Well, it was something with Niels Vørsel. He was an extra on *Images of a relief.* Then I found out that he also was a writer and we tried to create the outline for this story together. It was probably also related to some of Vørsel's projects. Among other things, he had a big Wagner project for television. Something to do with a *Percival* performance that was supposed to be performed in the Ruhr district and broadcast on television all over the world. It was supposed be shot from the freeway with moving cameras.

JKL: *An ambitious project!*
LvT: Yes, it was a fantastic project, which I at one point presented to Jørgen Leth, who was also very enthusiastic.

From *Kosmorama*, #167, April 1984. Reprinted by permission of *Kosmorama* and Peter Schepelern.

JKL: *But he wouldn't do it?*

LvT: Well, yes, I'm sure he would have liked to, very much. And I would have, too, but . . . well, anyway I thought that it might be a good idea to add the madness of Mr. Vørsel to that of the others and it certainly has proved to be just that. Vørsel had furthermore written a couple of radio plays. One of them was based on Hammett's *Red Harvest*, and he advised me to read Hammett, which I of course did. Originally the idea was to do something Hammett-like. We then agreed that I should do a draft of a story, but that turned out to be extremely complicated. The first synopsis we presented to the Film Institute included not only the ingredients of the film, but also some mystical things like a principle of nature and some blueprints . . . hypothetical blueprints and something about the pyramids in Egypt—on how you calculate the top angle of the pyramid by using some kind of square root . . . a very mathematical point of view. But that's characteristic of the things I've done. *Images of a Relief*, for example, is incredibly, almost hysterically, structured. It's divided in three parts where each camera setup refers to another camera setup in the next part. The things I've done at film school have also been very painstakingly structured.

JKL: *Is it because of the pyramids that* The Element of Crime *begins in Cairo?*

LvT: No, I think that the main reason for starting out in Cairo probably is that we needed a principal character who came home to Europe. The film is about Europe, and a Europe that's half under water, and he was supposed to come home from a place that wasn't America—I didn't want America to enter into the story—and that's why we chose Cairo.

JKL: *And it's almost buried in sand.*

LvT: Yes, that was the idea, we would go from the sand to the water. Cairo's buried in sand, so no European can remain there. The basis for the story consisted of three scenes that I presented to Niels Vørsel. I said that we'd have to have these in the film, and then we'd have to try to spin a story around these scenes.

JKL: *Which three were they?*

LvT: They are three scenes with Kramer in them. The first time it's in the harbor where the corpse of the little girl is found, the second time is when the second corpse is found in the foot-and-mouth disease pit, and the third one is where the youth gang performs their forbidden initiation rites by throwing themselves off a building crane with a rope tied to their feet. A ritual that's actually being performed in London, I'm told.

J K L : *Authentic, then?*

L v T : Yes, but I didn't know that at the time. I only knew that the Indians had done it for many years in Latin America. In London they jump off the bridge with an elastic rope, thus avoiding more severe types of injuries.

J K L : *The rope was measured, then, so they would just barely miss hitting?*

L v T : Of course. The main thing about the whole ritual is that the closer you get the ground, the higher status you get.

J K L : *Is that what your film is about, taking chances?*

L v T : You could say that, yes. I strongly believe that film is about making film. The films I've made have to a large extent been about making cinema. *Images of a Relief* is very much about voyeurism—about how many dreadful things the protagonist had to go through, before he had his eyes put out.

J K L : *Is it the challenge as well as the ritual that fascinates you? There's something about having to abide by strict rules and patterns, with all the repetition and references that implies. It's even insinuated by the title of your film,* The Element of Crime.

L v T : The killings and the film are structured in the same way.

J K L : *There's a lot about repetitions.*

L v T : But the killings *are* repetitions!

J K L : *In the film, Harry Grey turns into Osborne in a way, and then he turns back into Fisher. The identities of the three people seem to merge.*

L v T : The funny thing that happened when I had some conversations with actors Michael Elphick and Esmond Knight to give them some practical instructions was that they accepted my point of view. My principle for personal direction is to tell the actors as little as possible, just give them practical instructions—take the glass, smile, walk—thus taking advantage of the actors' professionalism for executing the directions without giving them the opportunity to build a character. I build them up like this, in a puppet-like way. It demands a lot of professionalism of the actors.

JKL: *It that why you have used English actors?*

LvT: That is why. That and the fact that we wanted it to be nothing like a Danish film. The Europe we wanted to paint a picture of was not going to become Denmark. I also felt that since the film was going to be a crime drama, it should also make use of the international language of the crime genre, which is English.

JKL: *It's also a kind of cliché.*

LvT: Yes, but things sound different in Danish. Then we would have gotten a lot of meanings and undertones that we didn't have any interest in. It's also quite clear that the performances delivered by Michael Elphick and Esmond Knight, performances that the film depends on, possess qualities that I never would have been able to get out of any Danish actors.

The Actors

JKL: *How did you find the actors?*

LvT: In England you can't get by without a casting director who knows the actors and knows how to draw up contracts. The one we found was Liz Cassidy and she happened to have gone to school together with Michael Elphick, whom I already knew about from the TV series *Private Schultz*. He was fundamentally out of our price range, but as luck would have it, our shooting schedule fit perfectly into a break Michael had between assignments. He's incredibly busy with both films and television, but he wanted to do the film and visit Denmark. So we got him for less than half his usual fee. Very lucky. It's been a great experience working with Mike, who has had to endure some of the worst imaginable things: sewers, phony rain every day—things that I would be very cautious about subjecting a Danish actor to.

JKL: *And Esmond Knight?*

LvT: He's been great, too. He's seventy-seven years old and has been blind since he went down with a warship at the start of World War II. At that time he was an officer aboard the *Prince of Wales*, which was hit by a grenade from the *Bismarck*. Esmond lay in the North Atlantic for twenty-four hours, clinging to some wreckage, before he was saved. He still performs a lot on British stages and is a true cultural and cinematic legend. He has worked with Hitchcock, Renoir, and Laurence Olivier. He is also an old Shakespearean actor. Tremendously experienced.

JKL: *How do you go about shooting a blind man? He certainly moves around a lot.*

LvT: Well, it wasn't always easy, but we worked out a couple of systems where we shouted. During the shootings he sometimes had to climb around on a high ladder. Esmond Knight has an amazing amount of trust in himself as well as in other people. Originally, Liz Cassidy just thought she'd show us Esmond, because she thought he was the right type. Of course she didn't think we'd be able to use a blind man. But that's typical for our working methods, in that we throw ourselves in and make use of the opposite. The way that Esmond gropes about to get hold of things is something that would have taken us a long time to direct an actor to do the right way, and we would never have gotten the same good result.

JKL: *What about the guy who plays Kramer?*

LvT: Yes, he's also a case of typecasting. The actor's name is Jerald Harris, he's a former wrestler and miner. Australian, by the way. Esmond Knight is a very conservative English gentleman, very *British*. Jerald is a communist and a fighter. Michael Elphick is a self-destructor. Their characters aren't that far removed from their own personalities.

Locations

JKL: *You have some formidable locations in the film.*

LvT: The ground rule has been that those locations that were fascinating to look at in real life also would be fascinating to have in the film. Tom Elling and I went out to get good places, and when we found some exciting ones, we reworked our screenplay so it would fit the locations. We called people up and told them we were making a crime film. If there's something people can relate to, it's crime films and thrillers. If we had said any other genre, they would just have shrugged their shoulders, but when we asked them if they knew of any scary places, they went, "Yeah, sure, man, we have one of those scary places just around the bend, and we hardly dare go there at night." "Great," we said. "Let's go out there and have a look." And if they then said that the place was so run down and dangerous that we had to sign a paper to insure them that we went there at our own risk, then we really knew it was good and that we had to see it.

We went down to the free port and said that we were doing this crime film and that we had heard about this really scary place. The man we talked to immediately said, "You must be talking about the underground channel system!" And we of course went, "Yes, Yes! Exactly! Is it possible to go down there?" to which he answered, "Yes, but there hasn't been anyone there in over forty years. I'm afraid you'll find it quite unpleasant." We then tried to climb down an iron ladder, which immediately turned to dust under our weight. It's a very nice place and it turned out to be a very beautiful scene, a love scene, where the lovers float around in a rubber boat in the channel although it looks more like a sewer. There's dripstone everywhere. In the original screenplay this first love scene took place in a hotel room, but we soon found out that that would be incredibly boring. We then got the idea of having it happen in a "Tunnel of Love" instead. Why don't we create our own "Tunnel of Love," we thought, and it turned out to be this channel. The lovers get into a rubber boat, which takes them through the sewers—a boundless system of sewers, in fact.

The Therapist

J K L : *It's all some kind of therapeutic session. The film begins in Cairo where the Arabic therapist listens to what Fisher has to say. That would mean that the film is a flashback, that Fisher has left Europe for the second time.*

L v T : The story is that he returns. Like the therapist says, "You seem to return to Cairo and me whenever you have a problem." The therapist has the function of keeping the story rolling. He starts by saying, "Fantasy can be OK, but my job is to keep you on the right track." And then the film starts from that point, first with some incredible shots of Cairo. We constantly rely on the therapist every time Fisher starts getting carried away with reflections on the beauty of the European chaos. Then the therapist will say, "What's the story, what's the story?" Just like a consultant at the Film Institute might have asked.

J K L : *Those pictures from Cairo, where did you get them?*

L v T : They're from a few 8-mm films made by an architect, a painter, and some others. They were then blown up to 35 mm—very beautiful!

JKL: *The painter is Niels Nedergård, who actually lives in Cairo, right?*

LvT: Yes.

JKL: The Element of Crime *is a kind of battle between the quest for heaven and the attraction of the earth. There are a lot of goings-on in the sewers and abysses, but certainly also a lot up in the air, be it in towers, cranes or helicopters.*

LvT: That's right, it becomes very vertical. You could say that the film catches up with the dream.

JKL: *It is a kind of psychoanalysis.*

LvT: Yes, as it happens in the film, it's a kind of psychoanalysis under hypnosis.

JKL: *Your visual aesthetics have already been very praised and very criticized.* Images of a Relief *brought on its share of fury. Lots of things happen in the images. You present many layers of the story at one time.*

LvT: It's all about trying to convey the fact that the world is so much more than a trite little story that's inside the head of the film's protagonist.

JKL: *The film is a kind of reaction against the therapist's orders about sticking to the story. It's a ritual experience of something else, an attempt to overcome all of it.*

LvT: Yes, it's a rebellion against authority.

JKL: *A line in the film goes, "Do you believe in good and bad? Can you make the bad good again?"*

LvT: Yes, whereupon the therapist very sarcastically breaks in and mocks the statement. There are only a few things that don't fit in with an Arabic therapist with a monkey on his shoulder. We had, by the way, a very funny experience with the Arabic actor who played the therapist. I asked him to remove his watch, and he reacted by saying, "No, no. You're all wrong. You've got a false idea about doctors in Cairo. They *do* have watches and they *don't* have monkeys on their shoulders!"

JKL: *So what's your relation to reality?*

LvT: I think it's very nice with a little monkey like that. In a way it's like the primitive man sitting on the shoulder of this spiritual guide. It's very fitting.

J K L : *Fisher is a somewhat special person. He has apparently fled Europe earlier.*

L v T : Yes, he has a problem—that he's a humanist. It gets him into all this trouble. And things go very wrong for him. He's not only the last tourist, he's the also the last humanist in Europe.

J K L : *In a way, he's also the last European in Africa.*

L v T : Yes, he has the undeniable tendency to finish last.

J K L : *Why does Fisher kill little girls if he's a humanist?*

L v T : That's a good question that not even Osborne can answer. From a dramaturgic point of view it's interesting to let a person arrive in Europe with the best intentions and to end up having him commit the worst imaginable crime. And killing little girls, that *is* the worst imaginable crime.

J K L : *It's a little similar to Fritz Lang's M.*

L v T : Fair enough: this film has many forerunners. It's based on expressionism and is the bastard child of a mating between American and European cinema.

J K L : *And it's the bastard complex that haunts the whole film when you're using all these nationalities in your film. You use actors from Egypt, Poland, Great Britain, Denmark, Sweden, and even Hungary.*

L v T : You can say that again. I thought it was fun to make the film seem un-Danish.

The Consultants

J K L : *Right now there's been a lot of putting down of consultants going on. How have you been treated?*

L v T : We very quickly got support for the film. In fact it went incredibly fast after school and *Images of a Relief*. It's been very pleasant not having to drag synopses back and forth. You could say that the consultant has been very bright, but on the other hand you could maintain that the product we showed them—*Images of a Relief*—couldn't be neglected. And I dare to say that. At the same time it's a little funny that the people we have worked for—the consultants, the producer and so forth—have extorted a solemn vow on my behalf not to do a remake of *Images of a Relief*. You must never do that," they said. Nevertheless it's been the film that opened the doors to this project. Out of consideration for *The Element of Crime*, I would already now like to say that it has some undeniably fine qualities. Regardless of what you think of it as a whole, it breaks with some things and takes a stand for some other things.

JKL: *Christian Braad Thomsen has accused the consultants of not understanding what they are presented with and thus being unable to judge the quality of artistically advanced projects. Is this why you have used the crime genre as a starting point?*

LvT: As I see it, you should use a consultant the way you use an actor. You should be careful not to tell them too much. You wouldn't want them to contribute the wrong thing, now would you? In regard to the consultants, I might be a little disappointed over the fact that they apparently look upon filmmaking as some kind of sardine-canning process. They'd rather not have any increases in the price of the raw material that would cause the price of the finished product to go up. My point is that filmmaking is a very unpredictable thing. The film itself should be allowed, if it wants to, to grow and mature. On this matter the consultants could play a part and I think that the current consultants would agree on that. The product should be followed up in such a way that it gets safely home. If you have started something then you should, as a consultant, follow its evolution and support it as much as possible. I very much feel that I've lacked that support along the way.

JKL: *How has your producer been?*

LvT: I certainly want to give Per Holst his due. He has certainly been a bit difficult to deal with at times, but he has also been a great help. He's a person with a sense of what's above average. No doubt about that.

JKL: *It's become a relatively inexpensive film.*

LvT: It's expensive in the sense that we went over the original amount. It will probably cost more than the 4.4 million crowns of the original budget. But in my opinion it has developed into something worth so much more, and even a consultant from the Royal Danish Film Institute should be able to see that. And in a situation like that it's very good to have a producer like Per Holst. In connection with this I would like to mention the fact that the

Film Institute hasn't allowed us to use stereo sound in the film, despite the need for it.

J K L : *Have Danish films become too inexpensive?*
L v T : No, I'm more inclined to think that they are too expensive. We have been talking to international film people and they simply refuse to believe that the film has a budget under 5 million, and it's as far as I know the second-cheapest Danish film this year—and for a film this size! I'm certain that if you compare the production values of different films, then our film would do amazingly well.

The Fascination

J K L : *The worship of the beauty of decay has with time come to be regarded as pro-Nazi. Your films have also been accused of something similar.*
L v T : I find it hard to believe. I would very much like to use the expression that, for the pure, everything is pure. The only thing we ask of people is that they have a certain naive openness—some receptiveness for what we present on the screen. I really think it's like this: this thing about getting fascinated by something morally upsets people. I think it's there the problem lies. It's like not good form to be fascinated, and it's very un-Danish to let yourself become fascinated.

J K L : *Maybe that's why it doesn't seem very Danish? You're letting yourself get carried away by big subjects.*
L v T : Yes, I allow myself to become fascinated by the things that always have been fascinating people—death and other unpleasant things, for example. Exactly the type of moralizing that says, "We are not allowed to be fascinated by the war," et cetera—that I see as a kind of jail. You mustn't ever put a lid on your fantasies and your fascination. If I have a message to convey, it's definitely that you shouldn't impose restraints upon yourself.

J K L : *And that's typical for your whole career.*
L v T : Yes, but people really have a difficulty in understanding something like that. We just mentioned the fascination with Nazism. It's like people think that when Nazis have been involved in something, then you should really keep away from it out of fear that you will be connected with it if you

don't. But the Nazis have had an instrumental influence on the European culture that they, too, come from.

JKL: *You have been playing Wagner during the filming.*

LvT: I've been using the method, which also was used during the silent film era, of playing music for the actors. We've almost created a kind of happening. It's been very beneficial to the atmosphere, and I think it can be seen in the finished product.

JKL: *The atmosphere is in any case very domineering.*

LvT: It's a Wagnerian milieu.

JKL: *Yes, it's all about big gestures. No quiet smiles here.*

LvT: It's funny, now that we're mentioning "the quiet smile." At one point, Osborne says, "The most important thing is the family and the cheerful smile." It probably has to do with the fact that these guys long for the days of the cheerful smile. Fate, however, had other plans for them.

JKL: *In any case, they don't have much luck in their family life.*

LvT: You can say that again. According to our calculations, Osborne's marriage lasted no longer than a fortnight at the most.

JKL: *Will Fisher find his way back to his "cheerful smile"?*

LvT: It's more likely that he in some way or another will remain in his Europe. At least mentally.

JKL: *So Cairo is some kind of exile, then?*

LvT: Yes, definitely.

JKL: *How do you imagine Europe looks, after Fisher has left it for the second time? Will there be nothing left but ritual and crime?*

LvT: It will probably be the same. It all depends on the forces involved. But you could easily say that both Fisher and I leave Europe this time around.

JKL: *Are you thinking of leaving Europe for real?*

LvT: It depends on whether I get the chance to. I don't have a special relation to Denmark, so if I'm presented with the opportunity to make films abroad, then absolutely.

Clichés and Quotes

J K L : *Your film makes good use of clichés and references.*
L v T : It relates to and makes use of certain film noir clichés. The film is aware of these clichés to the extent that if for example Fisher finds Osborne unconscious on the floor, he will later find Kim on the floor in the same position. We've only avoided the so-called "where am I?" cliché. There are also several more or less hidden film quotes. *The Element of Crime* is a film about film.

J K L : *Why is this so interesting and why does one feel so much joy in quoting and relating to a tradition?*
L v T : Regardless of what you're doing, you're laying a foundation for something or other and it's standard practice to refer to the sources. And the exciting thing within all forms of art is to evolve. That's why it's exciting to take an old cliché and use it in a new context, thus making manifest your relation to it.

J K L : *It's the basis of all forms of art, to take something and then put it in a new context.*
L v T : Yes, and the most direct way of doing it is to quote. I've only quoted things I felt related to in spirit. It's quite clear that the moment you quote something, for example a great work, then you suddenly remember the whole thing, the atmosphere and the contents of the great work. You then feed off the entirety of the other work. In a way it's being conjured up, you conjure up its universe.

The Child

L v T : The monkey in the film is immensely interested in his own sexual organ—he sits there and plays with it quite violently while the therapist discusses the facts Fisher's been instructed to report. The therapist is only interested in the lead that Fisher has to follow. He's less interested in the inner child of Fisher.

JKL: *Is this why Fisher turns into a child-killer?*

LvT: I haven't thought of that. Probably. He kills the female psyche. But I'd like to mention something that has had a great influence on me. At film school, Mogens Rukov gave a series of lectures on humorous cinema and his definition of it was something like this: A humorous film occupies the middleground between the epic film and the dramatic film. He presented a number of typical features of this type of film, among them that it takes time to become fascinated by it. The word "humorous" comes from "humor"—a flowing quality or something like that—and those lectures were incredibly good. Rukov used an example of a car that wouldn't start. If this happens in a dramatic film, it's because someone has tampered with it. In a humorous film, however, the characteristic thing about it is that the event itself opposes the actor. The world acts in opposition to the rational. The humorous film recalls the child, the unspoiled.

JKL: *It's also typical for directors like Wim Wenders, Werner Herzog, and John Cassavetes, and all of them could be said to represent this type of cinema, in that they are fascinated with the childish, the naive universe. Kaspar Hauser and Fitzcarraldo are both two sides of this universe. . . . Are you a voyeur?*

LvT: Yes. Hitchcock for example called himself a voyeur. It depends on what it's about.

JKL: *Do you feel related to Hitchcock?*

LvT: I guess I do, yes. I just pulled myself together and read the interview book by Truffaut.

JKL: *He, too, was definitely one of those children who refused to grow up.*

LvT: Absolutely. That he eventually wasted his talent is another thing. But then again, they've all done that. When Bergman and the others can't make films anymore, it's because they've lost their childishness. And then the world of childhood and fascination is closed. And once closed, it's no longer possible to return through those doors. At least, that's what's become evident.

JKL: *Is it because of this child thing that the women are the way they are in your films?*

LvT: Well . . . I recently went out to the university to talk to some film students and one of them asked me if the film was about love. To that I answered that I definitely thought so. But not so much love between the sexes. It's more like love in the form of a separate, isolated, half-hearted attempt. It never really amounts to anything.

JKL: *That applies to Hitchcock as well, doesn't it?*

LvT: No, but he was such a pig. I admire that tremendously.

JKL: *It that your aesthetic attitude talking again? Your anti-aesthetics?*

LvT: Yes, you could say that. The ugly is a great source of beauty. And much more interesting than the beautiful. You start out with the un-pretty and then you work your way out of that in order to create something pretty. But the un-pretty was there first.

JKL: *It probably relates to the fact that one often perceives good people as rather boring, while evil people are different and exciting.*

LvT: Yes, it's a richer source of fascination. Not everyone agrees that the pretty can be interesting, but in one way or another we can all agree that the really ugly and unpleasant is interesting. If you put a classic work of art some-where in Copenhagen and then beside that have two cars collide, and have the corpses lie there with their intestines showing, then people, no matter how civilized they consider themselves to be, will look at the car crash before anything else.

JKL: *A little frightening, isn't it?*

LvT: Well, I don't know about that. It's all about civilization. I don't con-sider nature that frightening.

JKL: *Is that what you're trying to regress back to, the Stone Age? Are you trying to "fuck yourself back to the Stone Age"?*

LvT: No, I just think that the monkey is more interesting than the film con-sultant on whose shoulder it sits.

JKL: *Poor, poor Fisher.*

LvT: Well—poor, poor human beings. They're all to be pitied.

JKL: *Would you prefer to be a monkey?*

LvT: Well, monkeys are to be pitied, too, but I do think that human beings are to be pitied even more.

JKL: *In that they're not allowed to sit around in public places playing with their sexual organs.*

LvT: That's exactly what they're not allowed to do.

A Conversation with Lars von Trier

MARIE BERTHELIUS AND ROGER
NARBONNE/1987

Q: *You're currently preparing* Medea, *right?*
A: That's absolutely right.

Q: *The classic drama or a modern version?*
A: It's from a script by Carl Th. Dreyer. He wrote it before he died, or rather, after *Gertrud*. It was supposed to be his first film in color—he wanted to practice that process before realizing his great dream, the Jesus film. But he never got to make either film. Interestingly enough, he wanted Maria Callas as Medea, the same Callas that later played Medea in Pasolini's version. I've never heard of any credit being given to Dreyer for that idea, because he's the one who came up with it, not Pasolini.

Q: *Have you seen Pasolini's* Medea?
A: Yes, I have, but I don't really remember much of it. I really like Pasolini's last trilogy of more robust films, *Canterbury Tales, Arabian Nights*, and *Salo*, and also *Theorem*. But *Oedipus Rex* and *Medea* are a little muddled, I think.

Q: *So your* Medea *is a feature film made for television?*
A: Yes. It's an hour and 15 minutes and it will only be shown on television—it won't be shown in the Danish cinemas. And it will be made on

Transcript from a taped conversation made in Copenhagen (in the canteen of Danmarks Radio) 3 August 1987. Printed by permission of Marie Berthelius.

video—I thought it might be interesting to explore the possibilities of that format—combined with film, however, to get a certain effect.

Q : *Have you ever worked with video before?*
A : Only at film school.

Q : *Is* Medea *shot in the studio?*
A : No, on location, in Southern Jutland. It's totally flat there, and there are coastal areas where the water is very shallow.

Q : *I better start asking you about* Epidemic. *I have some questions written down here that I hope we have time to go through.*
A : No problem, as long as they're not as long as some that I recently got in Hamburg, where I met some young Germans who had their own little film magazine. Each question covered one page. I couldn't remember what the question was when they finally had stopped talking. And the French are a little like that, too—some of those cineaste magazine people are unbelievable! But I really don't have that big a problem with that—they're certainly very devoted. I, too, have been a cineaste and studied film science and all, so I'm glad they're still around out there.

Q : *What about Denmark? Do you have them here as well?*
A : Well, a couple of years ago we had some kind of boom, but right now it's a little dead.

Q : *Are there any other interesting young Danes out there at the moment? Because you are the only one we get to hear about at the international level.*
A : I don't know. They aren't really that young—*I'm* not that young anymore.

Q : *Around thirty isn't that old in these contexts, is it?*
A : No, you're right. But it would be much more interesting if they were around seventeen or eighteen. But that's the nature of cinema, I guess.

Q : *Is there a young, new school to be found in the Danish cinema today?*
A : I think the young generation is getting into the safe stuff very quickly over here. That's my opinion.

Q: *Apart from film school, are there any other watershed experiences in your creative life, any rites of passage, so to speak?*

A: Well, when I was eight, my mother gave me an 8-mm camera. And when I was ten, I wanted an editing table more than anything else in the world.

Q: *To edit the things you had made?*

A: Not really—I just liked the concept of an editing table.

Q: *Where did your interest in cinema come from?*

A: I have an uncle who is a filmmaker—Børge Høst—who has done some well-received documentary films. He turned me on to some things.

Q: *And your real name is Trier—not von Trier.*

A: Correct.

Q: *As an homage to Stroheim and Sternberg, perhaps? Since neither of them were inborn nobility.*

A: Maybe. I generally feel that the inborn is less interesting than the "licensed," if you will. And there are several real *von*'s out there who are ashamed to use their *von* names today. No, this was my own initiative, and I strongly believe in the force of initiative. It's all about a nobility of the spirit.

Q: *When you presented* The Element of Crime *at Cannes, you had shaved off all your hair.*

A: Yes, you may be right. I had a little part in the film where I looked like that.

Q: *But this was the first look the international audience got at you. Don't you think they were a bit unsettled?*

A: Well, what can I say? My hair is longer now. But that hairstyle felt right at the time, together with that film. It's important for me to personally connect to the film I'm making at the moment. It might sound a little romantic, but there is a connection between the filmmaker and the film he's doing. And there is a connection between different films in cinema history. I don't think it's silly to connect to things like that, and that hairstyle felt right back then.

Q: *Your films are also connected to one another*—The Element of Crime *and* Epidemic *will eventually form a trilogy together with the forthcoming* Europa. *Had you already planned the trilogy when you made* The Element of Crime?
A: No. We decided on the trilogy idea right after *The Element of Crime*.

Q: *So* The Element of Crime *was at first an "isolated" film?*
A: Yes, it was.

Q: *How do the three relate to each other? Will we get an "a-ha!" experience at the end of* Europa?
A: No you won't. I don't like "a-ha!" experiences—that's almost a sin in my book. If you have an epic with a monumental title like *Europa*, and then it just finishes with a little "a-ha!" it's quite wasted. There will be no logical summing up, but I wish to make a panorama with some recurrent elements to it, and together those elements will create the trilogy. There will be logical reasoning, because I'm very interested in that, but no "a-ha!'s."

Q: *Have you written the script for* Europa?
A: We're writing it at the moment.

Q: *When will you start to shoot it?*
A: I don't know. There's a lot of uncertainty in Denmark right now. We're getting a new film law soon. And a Danish film consultant will surely look at the film as an isolated phenomenon rather than as a part of a trilogy. He won't really care about the fact that I've already made two thirds of my trilogy.

Q: *Do you follow your scripts very closely when you shoot?*
A: It varies. With *The Element of Crime* the shooting was unbelievably meticulously planned, but with *Epidemic*—at least for the documentary-style footage—it wasn't at all.

Q: *Did you improvise it all?*
A: What we did was to do it from memory, because we made it as a kind of drama-documentary and had decided what was going to happen beforehand. Nothing was written down, however.

Q: *But the other part, the 35-mm fiction film, is more planned?*
A: Yes, but not to the degree of *The Element of Crime*, where I got a little tired of all the minutiae of the preparations. But I think I'm getting back into that again right now.

Q: *How did you and Niels Vørsel go about playing your scenes, then? Did you just roll the camera and start the action.*
A: Well, we had this little recollection of something or another, and then we took it from there.

Q: *Did you shoot a lot of material that you later cut out?*
A: No, we didn't. The film is very economical in that respect. We haven't thrown much away. That was part of the idea, that the budget should be one million crowns—that was the format. And there might be some things in the final cut that should have been removed, but that was part of the "rules" of that film, as Jørgen Leth would have called it.

Q: *You don't even use a cinematographer in those scenes—you have shot them yourself. Was that part of the economical decision?*
A: Not solely, because we got a much more intimate situation this way. And I like to just set up a camera and just turn it on and see what happens. And of course it's cheaper that way. I have shot and lighted most of the film.

Q: *I like the idea with the dissection of the toothpaste. How did you come up with that?*
A: In connection with another film that we were about to make, *The Grand Mal*. It was supposed to be shot in Berlin, and Niels and I went there to do some research. And we did it, the dissection, in a hotel room. In *Epidemic* we did it in Cologne instead of Berlin.

Q: *Just one of those ideas one gets in one's head all of a sudden? And something one always wanted to do as a child?*
A: Yes, Niels asked the question: "Have you ever wondered how striped toothpaste looks inside the tube, and how it becomes striped when it comes out of it?" And I said, "Well, we can easily find out." And then we started to cut. And that's very typical of our working process: Niels asks the questions and I come with the answers and then we just cut away. A tube of toothpaste

costs next to nothing, while the curiosity is enormous. And the experience of cutting it up—you can't get that much excitement for ten crowns anywhere else!

Q: *Another thing that has caught my attention is that strange game in* The Element of Crime, *where these people with shaved heads jump off a bridge with a rope tied to them that stops them from getting killed. Where did you pick that up?*
A: Well, it's a ritual that is being performed in Latin America. And people have done it in London, too. And someone did it from the Eiffel Tower recently.

Q: *What is it? Some kind of male test of courage for skinheads?*
A: I don't know.

Q: *In* Rebel Without a Cause, *they jumped out of speeding cars.*
A: That's a really good film. Yes, I'm a little fond of habits and rites like that.

Q: *You have said that you like to start a film with some "pictures" that you'd like to include in the film, like the "rope-jumping" scene in* The Element of Crime. *Are they pictures like paintings, or are they scenes?*
A: Something in between the two, because paintings wouldn't really cover it, while scenes would have to be more elaborate. Yes, I like to start out like that. In *Epidemic* we started out with the taxi scene with the Negro.

Q: *Yes, what's that about?*
A: Yes, well . . . does everything have to be logical?

Q: *There is a little red "Epidemic" logo up in the left corner of the screen for most of the otherwise black-and-white film. Why?*
A: Now we have to get logical. The plot is that we're sitting there, writing a story. In some books, the title appears in the left-hand corner of each page, and we're almost writing a book, right? I also drew a little from my experience while making commercials. In modern, classy, exclusive commercials, you don't know what the product is until you see the name of the brand. You can take the same image, for example a picture of some young people. Then you can put Levi's on it, or Coca-Cola—anything, IBM. And the picture

gets a new meaning with every name. And you wonder what these young people have to do with IBM?

Similarly, I wanted to get something out of the brand name "Epidemic." I managed to link that word together with every scene in the film.

Q: *How did you solve it from a technical point of view?*
A: We did it in the lab. Interestingly, the title changes in intensity during the film—if it's a dark scene, it gets darker, and vice versa. So the logo ending up having certain dynamic qualities, too. And in certain scenes you really notice it more.

Q: *I'm very curious about your protagonists—idealistic people who really don't stand a chance to succeed. It was like that in* The Element of Crime. *In* Epidemic, *when you draw the story line on the wall of Niels's apartment, we immediately see that this protagonist will meet a similar fate.*
A: And it will probably be like that in my next film, or next few films, as well. Fatalistic stories with characters who take a totally slavish approach to their missions. What can I say? Of course, you could make a story where they abandon the sinking ship at the last minute, but to me that really makes the film less interesting. It's a very classic device, that they get saved at the last minute, but it's nothing for me and not a film I would like to make. I can't answer that question, but we have at least established the fact that this is the case. Also, in some of the great works of cinema and literature, at least the ones that I appreciate, there's a similar atmosphere.

Q: *Classical tragedy. From scene one, we all know that the hero will suffer. Is this your only way of dealing with the hero from a personal point of view?*
A: Maybe, but unconsciously. Stories have a tendency to take on a life of their own. *Epidemic*, for example, moved in many strange directions of its own choosing. True, we had an idea about things, like the hypnosis scene at the end, but never that it would get as heavy as it did.

Q: *So you never know how a script will turn out when you sit down to write it?*
A: No, because we work from these visual ideas. In *Europa*, for example, there will be a scene where a coffin is dug up and the corpse will be carried around in a chair in some kind of procession. We wrote this for another film, but it will turn up in *Europa* somewhere. It's a good exercise: how do we

reach this point, where he's dug up and carried around? It has to rain, too, by the way, and there will be these huge power pylons making shrdsh!!! sounds hovering over the cemetery. That will be nice.

Q: *A little like James Whale's Frankenstein films. Did you grow up with films like that, or ghost stories or comic books?*
A: There is kind of a comic book aesthetic here, yes. Well, yes, but not that much. It's more a sign of my culturally radical upbringing and my rebellion against it. One of the main rules of my upbringing was that there is no such thing as good or evil—they don't exist. But they do exist. Not necessarily in the things I do, but they are important. There was also a lack of mythology in my childhood, which I'm trying to make up for.

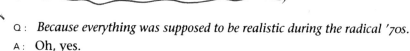

Q: *Because everything was supposed to be realistic during the radical '70s.*
A: Oh, yes.

Q: *Where you ever involved in politics yourself?*
A: I've been a communist. But I'm not anymore!

Q: *Are you related to [author] Dea Trier Mørch?*
A: Maybe distantly so. Ohh, that was even worse!

Q: *Is there anything from your background that you have benefitted from in your work as a filmmaker?*
A: Yes, I think the analytical side has been of use. Logical thinking . . .

Q: *. . . that you use to create some highly irrational things?*
A: Fair enough. There are certain numbers, for example, and some are good and some are evil. We've worked a lot with that, like "after that scene, there will be four scenes, and then three scenes" and so forth. Mystical numerology. Again, that creates a frame for the process, just like with the visual ideas.

Q: *Peter Greenaway works a little like that as well. He's in love with statistics.*
A: Yes, I can sympathize with that technique. You need some kind of technique to be able to work—you can never free yourself from that. And if you wish to achieve something different from what you have done before, then

you have to change your techniques. Maybe use them for the "wrong" purpose, and then get something new out of it.

Q: *Were you good at mathematics at school?*
A: Yes, very. I had top grades.

Q: *Philosophy?*
A: Not really. But I loved mathematics.

Q: *Are there any filmmakers that you respect, especially active ones? Are there any out there doing something new and interesting?*
A: That's hard. I've seen Jarmusch, and he's quite splendid, but I don't feel religious—like I've felt with Bergman. I don't today—it's almost the opposite—but there was a time . . . and, of course, Dreyer. With him, I have an almost holy relationship. Tarkovsky—*The Mirror* was a revelation!

Q: *Did you like* The Sacrifice?
A: No, that was a big mistake. Really, as long as he was in the Soviet Union, things were great, but when he went west, it all went away. And Bergman— his greatest international breakthrough came with *Cries and Whispers*, right? And after that I don't think he's made any good films. My favorite is the trilogy around *Persona*, with *The Silence* and *Persona* and *Winter Light*. [*Persona* is not a part of this trilogy; *Through a Glass Darkly* is.] Extremely important films. *Persona* is very interesting, and I also like his older films, but I can't stand *Fanny and Alexander.*

Q: *What about Wenders?*
A: *Alice in the Cities* is wonderful. *Paris, Texas* is OK, I guess. It's all about being able to make a living from making films, but I hope I won't ruin something by having to compromise.

Q: *Many Europeans go to America nowadays. Do you have any plans on becoming an international director, too, one day?*
A: Most of all, I'd like to make films in Denmark. In English, but in Denmark. The only Danish films in Danish that I like are Dreyer's, and you can't get Danish actors to talk like that today. OK, *Epidemic* is partly in Danish, but that was Niels and me. We talked just like we always talk.

Q : *I read somewhere that* The Element of Crime *was a tribute to Orson Welles.*
A : I never said that. But *Touch of Evil* is a fantastic film. And there was something he made in Spain on TV recently . . . what was the title?

Q : Mr. Arkadin?
A : Yes. And it wasn't bad at all. Very interesting.

Q : *In* Epidemic, *you and Niels go to Germany. Why?*
A : That's Niels—a lot of *Epidemic* is from Niels's universe of ideas. We met when I did *Images of a Relief*, where I had a scene where a German officer reels off the names of some German cities. And we take a trip through those cities in *Epidemic*. It was actually that scene in *Images of a Relief* that made collaborators out of me and Niels. He was an extra in the film and we discussed that scene and here we are. Niels is very interested in Germany, especially the industrial side of it. For example, he maintains that "aspirin," as a phenomenon, has been more important to European culture than the collected works of Goethe, and I find that somewhat intriguing.

Q : *You also get to visit Udo Kier, who seems to be an old friend.*
A : I know him quite well. I met him at a festival. He has a good cultural résumé to his credit. He was in Warhol's *Dracula* and *Frankenstein* and he lived with Fassbinder for three years. It's a nice feeling to work with people with connections like that, just like Henning Bendtsen, Dreyer's cinematographer, who shot the fiction parts in *Epidemic*. You might find me romantic, but things like that are important to me. They allow me to pay my respects to Fassbinder and Dreyer.

Q : *Is that scene with Udo improvised? Is his story real?*
A : Only partly.

Q : *He talks about water and later on we see people standing in water. The elements figure largely in your films, but it's water more than anything else.*
A : Yes, Tarkovsky had a wonderful way of working with water, although everything got a little watered down toward the end. Kurosawa had marvelous fights in the rain. Water enhances things in cinema.

Q : *Does water symbolize anything in your films?*
A : I don't know.

Q: *Let's get back to the hypnosis scene at the end of* Epidemic. *The girl really becomes hysterical. Is she really hypnotized?*

A: You bet. We called in a real hypnotist, a notorious hypnotist at that, because he had spent three years in prison—he had had sex with a few women who were under his spell, about eighteen to twenty of them. So he was very skilled, and that's why we got him. He's very strange. He goes around and performs shows at schools and stuff. He got three girls and they all read a text we gave them, Daniel Defoe's accounts of the plague in London in 1348. They would then be put into a trance and asked some questions about the text. The girl we eventually chose went into a trance immediately—it took four minutes. Niels and I thought she faked it, but she was deeply hypnotized. She cried and screamed and hyperventilated. This was a very shy girl. First, we wanted her to act out a couple of things while she was awake, but she was too shy in front of the camera. She did all the scenes, except one short one, under hypnosis. Then she woke up and jumped up on the table. And there was blood and everything. I was in total shock!

Q: *But you have also used hypnosis yourself?*

A: I did it with the Negro in *Epidemic*. He was standing in very cold water and didn't remember his lines. And it's easier in English—especially if you use a foreign accent. Dreyer did it in *Gertrud*. He used some very strange words.

Q: *Dreyer seems to be your absolute favorite. Can you sum up your fascination with him?*

A: I'm going to use an old, worn-out word: honesty. I find an honesty in his films that I haven't seen in any other films.

Q: *I just saw a little film called* They Caught the Ferry *on French television.*

A: Oh, that's just like when I have to make commercials. He had to do stuff like that now and then, because they wouldn't give him any money.

Q: *Did you see his films at the university?*

A: I had seen them on TV long before. And when I was a little boy I was given a little projection machine and some snippets of film that I ran over and over for myself. And I remember I got a little bit of *Jeanne d'Arc* and also some footage with worms. I was fascinated by *Jeanne d'Arc*. That was my first Dreyer experience. I liked the worms, too.

Q: *Dreyer seems to have been more appreciated in France than in Denmark. How are you perceived in Denmark?*
A: Well, they hate *Epidemic*.

Q: *Will you have any problems to get backing for your next film?*
A: Perhaps. But the Danish system is very good. I probably would not have been able to make a film like *Epidemic* anywhere else. I had control over every single comma in the film. In any case, I can always go back to making more commercials.

A Conversation with Lars von Trier

MICHEL CIMENT AND PHILIPPE
ROUYER / 1 9 8 8

POSITIF: Epidemic *is presented as the second part of a trilogy that started with*
The Element of Crime.

von TRIER: Yes, I found some things in *The Element of Crime* that made me
want to go deeper into the subject. Granted, *Epidemic* doesn't share the same
approach, but to me it feels important that the films in a trilogy don't resemble each other. If the connection between the films is too evident, then it
quickly gets too banal. My screenwriter Niels Vørsel and I very quickly came
up with a story for the third part, which will be called *Europa*.

POSITIF: *Why "Europa"?*

von TRIER: "Europa" is truly a very beautiful word. I also think that, in
one way or another, all of my films are very European. In this third film, I
will tell the story of an American who goes to Europe. There was already an
American in mind in *The Element of Crime*, but he was going to Africa and to
Egypt. In *Europa*, the American disembarks to save Europe. The story takes
place in 1945, just after the end of World War II, and he arrives as a simple
soldier. But now I won't say any more about the story.

POSITIF: *You have, however, already thought up the subheadings to each film*
*in the trilogy (*The Element of Crime*—Substance: non-organic;* Epidemic*—*
Substance: organic; and Europa*—substance: conceptual).*

From *Positif, #334*, December 1988. Reprinted by permission of Michel Ciment.

von TRIER: The subheadings aren't there to explain the trilogy. While they remain logical, they're also independent of the films they characterize.

POSITIF: *Of course, but they're abstract concepts rather than impressions. You should therefore explain them—that's why we're discussing them right now.*
von TRIER: Please observe that you read them in the press material and not in the film credits. But if you insist, let's try to justify them. "Organic" obviously refers to *Epidemic*, because of the microbes and the bacteria.

POSITIF: *But* The Element of Crime *evokes the water and the sewers. These elements, too, are organic. . . .*
von TRIER: Certainly, but in *The Element of Crime* . . . the plot revolves around the notion of crime. And crime isn't organic. I'm not yet able to explain the "conceptual" of *Europa*. But you should know that this term refers to the very special rapport that this film will establish with its audience. Together with Niels Vørsel I will try to do something very original. I will not say more than that it has to do with the language of film, the contact between the story and the audience. This time I will do a very commercial film, that I promise you. But to return to the subheadings of the trilogy, let's say that that was all a joke, if you prefer that.

POSITIF: *Do you, just like the heroes of* Epidemic, *write your scripts in five days?*
von TRIER: Yes and no. *Epidemic* is the story of how Niels and I wrote *The Element of Crime*. We didn't really write it in five days, but we went through five different phases of writing.

POSITIF: *How do you work together?*
von TRIER: Exactly the same way as it's portrayed in *Epidemic*. We laugh a lot and we work on the dramatic progression along the way. You could say that *Epidemic* is a very private film. I like to see private films at the cinema—I think that things can get very interesting when they're private.

POSITIF: *What do you mean by "private"?*
von TRIER: What I mean is that, in *Epidemic*, the way we work is very thoroughly shown. There are things shown in the film that shouldn't primarily

interest the audience. But the important thing isn't to know how we work, but to show these details in a vivid way.

POSITIF: *Given the circumstances, why did you and Niels Vørsel choose to play the filmmaker and the scriptwriter in* Epidemic?

von TRIER: For obvious financial reasons. Thus we avoided having to pay for the services of two actors. We also had the liberty of shooting whenever and whatever we liked. If we didn't feel like shooting one day, then we didn't have to. We shot whenever we felt like it and this is totally impossible with a traditional film crew.

POSITIF: *How many people worked with you during the 16-mm sequences?*

von TRIER: Most of the time I was alone with Niels. This caused some problems with the camera movements, by the way. When we wanted to have a panning camera movement we used some external help. We also ran into some sound problems. We set the microphone in place ourselves and sometimes the sound came out inaudible.

POSITIF: *Is it because of the lack of money that the 16-mm sequences outnumber the 35-mm ones?*

von TRIER: Absolutely right. In the beginning we were gong to make another film with more money. But things dragged out to a point where I lost interest. When you've done a film ten times over in your head, the film no longer has any shape and it's very hard to materialize it on the big screen.

For *Epidemic*, we had a budget of a million crowns, which is a little less than a million francs. This tiny budget was part of the challenge. We wrote the script in two hours.

POSITIF: *Did you work with a storyboard for the fictional sequences?*

von TRIER: We intentionally used a very simple storyboard. I didn't want to remake *The Element of Crime*, which was full of refinement regarding lighting and camera movements. I didn't want to pursue this line of development any further—I wanted a break. This is why the image is grainy and not necessarily beautiful in *Epidemic*. These are images in a raw state. The style of the film is very bare-bones.

POSITIF: *Why did you use Wagner in the fiction sequences?*
von TRIER: Because it's very bombastic music. To me it perfectly corresponds to film music.

POSITIF: *Regarding those sequences, how did you work with your director of photography, Henning Bendtsen?*
von TRIER: I explained my perception of the film to him: that it was a return to simplicity through black-and-white pictures. Henning Bendtsen is simultaneously very technical and very open-minded. He's seventy years old, but when I explained my technical ideas to him he got very excited—he wanted to try out all the things I suggested. In contrast, every time I've worked with a young cinematographer, I've found them to be thoroughly conservative.

POSITIF: *Did Bendtsen work a lot with the lighting?*
von TRIER: Yes, especially when it came to the scene with all the doctors. He has done a remarkable job on the film.

POSITIF: *Did you talk about Dreyer on the set?*
von TRIER: Constantly. I found it very pleasant to have him on the team because he provided a bit of Dreyer's world. By the way, Bendtsen used the same camera and lighting equipment that he used when they made *Gertrud*. This may seem stupid and sentimental to you, but to me this meant a lot. And even more so, since I don't hide the fact that I let myself become inspired by Dreyer's simplicity and sobriety when making *Epidemic*.

POSITIF: *The last meal with the people around the table who are obsessed by an evil power also echoes the* Mabuse *films.*
von TRIER: Probably, but I'm not sure. With Lang I especially like the early films. But the Dreyer reference, on the other hand, is obvious. I've seen all his films at least twenty times, something I wouldn't say of all filmmakers.

POSITIF: *With this story within a film, you're making meta-film. Do you think it's impossible to make cinema without discussing cinema?*
von TRIER: I don't know anything about that. To tell you the truth, I never discuss this kind of problem with Niels. I look for images within my head in

order to transform them to the big screen. The main thing after that is to know which technique to use to achieve the desired result.

POSITIF: *Do you think that the choice of technique will determine how the forthcoming film will look?*
von TRIER: Of course. In order to realize a script, you have to find the appropriate technique, just like here, with the changes from 16-mm to 35-mm. It's all very obvious to me now, although I didn't think of using this process at all in the beginning.

POSITIF: *Was* Epidemic *produced by the Danish Film Institute?*
von TRIER: No, they support, but don't produce. They provided us with 80 percent of the backing, which wasn't a lot, since we worked with a small budget.

POSITIF: *What do you think of what is known as "the rebirth of Danish cinema"?*
von TRIER: Who said anything about any rebirth?

POSITIF: *Do you see a new generation of filmmakers coming out of Denmark? Is it a coincidence that this country won the Palme d'Or at Cannes and an Oscar in Hollywood?*
von TRIER: You know, Gabriel Axel is already old. Before *Babette's Feast* he had some fifty films to his name, among them some soft porn films. Regarding Bille August, I think he does far too commercial films. True, he's talented, but he never shoots anything exceptional. The Palme d'Or award is a political gesture. And at the moment people are looking towards Denmark—they're interested in this country. What can be said with certainty, though, is that the technical conditions have improved in Denmark. The films are more beautiful, more refined, even though there are only ten made per year. In order to have a true rebirth you would need a generation of young people who move in the same direction. And I see nothing like this. With few exceptions, like Jørgen Leth [*A Sunday in Hell*, 1976], those who seek to renew fail.

A Conversation with Lars von Trier, Henning Bendtsen, and Ernst-Hugo Järegård

EVA AF GEIJERSTAM  1990

EVA AF GEIJERSTAM: *"Europa"—when you hear this beautiful name, how do you react? Is the film a reflection on the modern Europe of today?*
LARS von TRIER: The name of the film is *Europa* and it takes place in 1945. Of course it's always interesting to view it in the light of current events. Yes, I would say that it's an interesting film to watch in relation to the modern Europe.

EaG: *The reason I ask is that the film states that we'll never succeed in putting that period behind us. Do you really think we'll never free ourselves from it?*
LvT: Yes, I do. We'll have to live with it—for better or for worse. So you can already grasp that, just from reading the script? You seem to have seen the whole film! And it's not even finished yet. Have you read the whole thing?

EaG: *I read it yesterday—I was so curious. There are a lot of technical instructions.*
LvT: Yes, more than in an "ordinary" script—it's full of technical descriptions. But when I wrote it, I wanted it to be more focused on the story than on the technical details—in hindsight that wasn't really the case.
HENNING BENDTSEN: No, definitely not. I never had that impression.
LvT: In my earlier films I worked much more with atmospheres that worked around the story, or sometimes in opposition to it, rather than just telling

Transcriptions of parts of these taped conversations appeared in *Dagens Nyheter*, 31 July 1990. Reprinted by permission of Eva af Geijerstam.

the story. This time around the story is the most important thing, even though there are other levels as well. But the story is the main thing. This film is much more commercial than my earlier ones. We have a bigger budget and we of course expect a larger audience. That's simple mathematics. But it's nothing like a restriction to me, mind you. Like everything else, that's something you can work with. And I would like to stay in this business, you know. And if I want to make films on a lower commercial level, well then I'll have to work with lower budgets, right? The film has to make money. But I haven't had any pressure from any producers—not the French ones, not the Danes. I have total freedom both as writer and director. Over the final cut and everything else.

E a G : *But it's quite fantastic that you could go ahead and make this film, that the Danes allowed you to do it so soon after* Epidemic, *whose box-office numbers weren't all that great.*
L v T : But it's important for me to make an *Epidemic* now and then. And *Epidemic* has influenced this film more than you might think at first glance. If you watch *The Element of Crime*, *Epidemic*, and this film together and compare them, then you'll see the influence of *Epidemic* on *Europa*.

E a G : *Together, they form a trilogy, right?*
L v T : They do, yes.

E a G : *I also think that* Europa *reminds me of* Images of a Relief *more than anything else that you've done, especially judging by the theme.*
L v T : Right, as far as the theme. But the story is much closer to *The Element of Crime* and *Epidemic*—it's more or less the same story. It's about time we stopped telling it, by the way. There won't be anything more of it after this. We've told this story now.

E a G : *I think it's very interesting and very nice that you work together with Henning here. How did you meet?*
H B : I met Lars while giving a lecture at the film school and he later asked me if I wanted to work with him on *Epidemic*. Although I was thinking a little bit about retiring at the time, I thought, this could be interesting, and said yes. I've never regretted it.

EaG: *Henning, of course, worked as cinematographer on* Ordet/The Word *and* Gertrud *by Dreyer. And you, of course, are a great admirer of Dreyer.*

LvT: Yes, very great. And I'd like to add that Henning really works *against* my ideas. It's the same with some of the actors: I like to have them work against my films, because that's where some interesting things start to happen. For example, visually, this film has a very cartoon-like aesthetic—it's much more clearly outlined in its clichés than how Henning usually has worked with images. His style isn't 100 percent compatible with my images. If you were to work in the true spirit of this film it would be much more expressive than, for example, what comes through via Henning's lighting methods. And I find it very interesting not to do it like that. It's the same with the actors—they should move against the grain of their parts a little bit, because it introduces some interesting qualities into the film and keeps it from becoming too unambiguous.

EaG: *From looking at the script, I get a truly expressionistic image in my head.*

LvT: You certainly do. And you could easily have done it like that all the way, and if I had asked Henning to do it that way he would have. But I know about Henning's style and past and for example *Gertrud* wasn't an expressionistic film at all—if I were to call it anything it would be impressionistic. I like to put things together like that—I would even say it's a prerequisite for this film: employing the talent to do their parts, not in harmony with, but rather in *disharmony* with the style of the film.

EaG: *But isn't there a limit somewhere to this reasoning, where there gets to be too much of all these "interesting" things?*

LvT: Well, yes—and it's up to me to see to it that that doesn't happen. It's all about spicing things up to get the perfect mix. You can't use an ingredient that doesn't belong in the dish, right? But you can spice it up to get a little exotic flavor—otherwise it gets boring.

EaG: *And this is what you thought about when you cast the film, then?*

LvT: Yes, I wanted people who played against their types. For example, the part of Colonel Harris was originally going to be played by a young dynamic American guy. But we gave the part to Eddie Constantine who is in his '70s and happens to have a very timid face. Despite all the pockmarks, he has this mild, timid expression and I think we've captured it for the film. And he has never been allowed to play anything related to that side of him before. He has always been tough and socked people on the chin and been very strong and brash all the time.

H B : Yes, he's very subdued in this one. He told me that he was a little unused to speaking with a soft voice because he always yelled and shouted his way through all those Lemmy Caution movies. But in this one he comes off much stronger thanks to the mild thoughtfulness of his personality. It's an added dimension.

E a G : *There's an interesting constellation of actors in the film.*

L v T : It's like a happening to me. Again, it's about getting good ingredients. I've got Henning, Eddie Constantine, Ernst-Hugo Järegård, Barbara Sukowa, Udo Kier, and so forth. That mix isn't very predictable, is it? It's quite unlikely that anyone else would use that mix. Then you can discuss the qualities of what you get out of it, but just to mix it like this, that's very exciting for me.

E a G : *The opposite of type casting? Or maybe not?*

L v T : No, I don't think it's the opposite. But it works on several levels. I find it very satisfying to keep some kind of cultural-historical flame alive. With Henning's background I feel the presence of Dreyer's spirit, *apart* from Henning's obvious qualities as a cinematographer. Udo gives me a little Fassbinder. And I feel that the past and the image of an actor mean a great deal. It's definitely something to take into account when you cast. If an actor has a back catalogue of work and even a private life that stands for something, then of course he brings it into the film. And you can just as well work with these things, take advantage of them.

E a G : *What did you find worth taking advantage of with Ernst-Hugo?*

L v T : Well, Ernst-Hugo represents part of the madness in the film. I'm mainly familiar with his television work in Sweden, like the series *Skånska mord* [*Scanian murderers*, 1986]. He's such a strong personality and I've worked with the fact that he represents a part of Swedish culture that I find exciting. At the same time his personal presence is very important, on top of his acting. Some actors have lives that always dominate their stage parts, and this is very true of Ernst-Hugo. It has influenced the film in a positive way, and this pleases me very much. Very exciting.

E a G : *And perhaps you can bring out the best in someone like that much easier on film than on stage?*

L v T : If you tried to do that with someone like Ernst-Hugo on stage? You wouldn't stand a chance! But here we approached it from the right direction, so to speak. He has been allowed to become the comical element of the film, or at least one of them. It's a good part for him. We haven't really cast it against his type, but we've added some new dimensions, I think. From my point of view, he really works well. But we have had to force him to downplay it a bit, compared to what he does on stage. I think that he'll be very pleased with his performance. I'm pleased, at least.

(Ernst-Hugo Järegård enters the room to general amusement.)

E a G : *How do you cope with his meticulous working methods?*

ERNST-HUGO JÄREGÅRD: At first, he reminds you of the early Picasso, or Johan Borgen's character Lillelord: polite, friendly. But when he starts shooting, then Mr. Hyde appears. He's exceptionally at ease also with us older thespians: "Take it easy, I know exactly how it's going to work out."

E a G : *How do you feel about this film? Are you having fun?*

E H J : It's incredibly stimulating. It's such an interesting group of Europeans.

E a G : *Have you had the opportunity to meet them?*

E H J : Yes, in my own way. You say a couple of phrases, you really don't find out that much about people. Generally, actors don't have the urge to articulate themselves verbally. In front of the camera, yes, but not when it's turned off. When we don't shoot, we talk about cigars or last night's menu. You never talk about your part, the why's, the how's or anything else—you just don't do it. And it was really funny with this Constantine character, he's a reasonably plain actor but he lived with *Piaf!* And you think to yourself, "Damn! His body must have had an experience that mine certainly hasn't had!" But when you ask him about it—nothing. Just a couple of inflated phrases. He doesn't remember a thing. And then he talked about Gabin, who told him, "Don't read verbatim. Always add something of your own in every line." That's so typical of an actor to remember something like that. He was impressed by the breaking of the rules. It's not as simple as that. Lars uses his face. He looks like hell, he looked like hell already back in the old days. He has this really huge stomach as well, he looks grotesque. And Lars likes that, more than working with top professionals. He's great with faces. And I think he's very amused by the fact that I've worked as hard with his script as I have.

(Ernst-Hugo Järegård leaves the room to general amusement.)

E a G : *Have you watched everything that you've shot at this point?*
L v T : Yes, of course.

E a G : *But you haven't started to edit yet?*
L v T : No, the continuity is finished. It won't be that hard, we'll just follow the numbers on the clapper board.

E a G : *How much work is left for you to do?*
L v T : About four to five weeks.
H B : We have some important studio sets, some front and back projections, some color and some black-and-white footage that we have to set right. And the underwater footage.
L v T : I think we have a week to work on the last four minutes. That should be enough.

E a G : *And then, come springtime, it's Cannes—*
L v T : Oh, let's see about that. I really want to go to Cannes with it and they have been incredibly sweet to us thus far. You never know, but Cannes would be very suitable—the film has a French co- producer, even. And they've shown my previous films. I'd like that a lot. Berlin would be suitable, too, this being a German story and all. We'll see. I'm not the producer, but it would give me great pleasure to go to Cannes.

E a G : *Would you have done this film as you've done it if you hadn't done* The Element of Crime *and* Epidemic *before it?*
L v T : Certainly not, and this is a big project for me. I learn all the time. I'm a schoolboy—from a very progressive school—but still a schoolboy.

E a G : *What have you learnt from your previous films?*
L v T : Simple—what works and what doesn't work. It's no more complicated than that. That a part of the audience might not agree with that might be the case—I can only follow my own instinct: what works for me?

EaG: *The next film, are you already planning that?*

LvT: Well, there isn't much space for that in my head. We're working quite hard at the moment and I'm a little tired. How are you doing, Henning?

HB: Well, it's catching up with me. You give a lot of yourself. A little fatigued, yes.

LvT: But Henning has become quite radiant during this project. And, if I may say so, he seems to very happy with this film.

HB: It's nice, yes.

EaG: *How old are you, Henning?*

HB: I'm sixty-five. Just like Dreyer was when we made *Gertrud*. I was a little over thirty then, but now the tables are turned—the director is a little rascal.

LvT: Well, then it's a little easier for Henning to take me down a peg or two when it's needed. But Henning has been so nice to me. He gave me a tuxedo.

HB: Yes, Dreyer had this thing about gifts. We got to be great friends even outside of work and we got together for birthdays and such, already back when we were making *Ordet*. And then he wanted me to have a gift. He had bought a pair of shoes at Illum, some really nice ones for a thousand crowns or something. But they wouldn't quite fit him and he was too embarrassed to go back and exchange them. So he told me that he had these really nice shoes that were a little too tight-fitting and a little too painful to wear, and if they fit me I would be welcome to have them. And they fit me perfectly.

But then, when we had made *Gertrud*, he had grown out of his tuxedo. He had put on a little bit of middle-age paunch at that point. So he asked me if I wanted it—he would even pay for the alterations. I didn't own a tuxedo at that point, so I said, "Yes, thank you very much," and had it altered. It's so great—inside, on the label, it has the name of a Danish tailor who had his business in Paris when Dreyer was at his peak. It has stripes and everything.

LvT: Very refined. It was made in 1926, so he was wearing it in Venice when he received the Golden Lion for *Ordet* in 1955.

HB: I recently went to Sitges and found out that I couldn't wear it anymore. But I had already promised it to Lars when we made *Epidemic*. With his fondness for Dreyer I felt that it should remain in the film industry rather than enter the civilian ranks. My own son isn't really the tuxedo type anyway.

LvT: And it fit me like a glove! It's the first time ever that an article of clothing has fit me so perfectly. That in itself was very moving.

A Romance in Decomposition

MICHAEL TAPPER/1990

I HAVE AN APPOINTMENT with Lars von Trier and his co-screen-writer, author Niels Vørsel. We are at the studios of Nordisk Films in Valby on the outskirts of central Copenhagen, where post-production on *Europa* has everyone hard at work—everything has to be completed for the grand opening at Cannes in May. Expectations are high, but Lars and Niels radiate calm self-assuredness when I show up at mid-workday to discuss careers, the fascination for technology, Nazism and the decline of European culture, plus a couple of other topics of interest to a young director who likes to be known as the bad boy of Danish cinema.

Who, then, is Lars von Trier? And why have there been so many more interesting things written about him in French film magazines such as *Positif* and *La Revue du Cinéma* than in the Danish and Swedish press?

Let's start from the beginning.

Lars Trier was born in 1956 and, just like Erich Stroheim, he later added a self-styled, aristocratic "von" to his directing name. He had already at an early stage decided to become a film director, so he didn't hesitate when he was offered the male lead in the Danish children's television series *Hemmelig sommer* [*Secret Summer*] in 1969.

"I was fourteen years old. I was working with 8-mm film, and I had a very strong fascination for film technology. The whole year after the shooting of the series, I used to skip school and run down to the studios and pester the

---

From *Chaplin* #2, 1991. Reprinted by permission of the author.

crews with questions and comments about the cameras and the lighting until I was thrown out."

Between 1979 and 1982, Lars attended the National Film School of Denmark in Copenhagen where he made, among other things, *Nocturne* in 1980 and *Den sidste detalje* [*The Last Detail*] in 1981.

"*Nocturne* was the more important of the two and it also won a prize at the film festival in Munich. I got the inspiration for it while watching the Swedish film review program by chance. There they showed a long clip from *The Mirror* by Andrei Tarkovsky. What I saw was a long take without cuts, a camera tracking along a road. It was simply unbelievable—like a revelation to me! At the time I had of course seen a lot of films with different aesthetics and I was always interested in the divergent—in unusual things—but the images from this Tarkovsky film seemed to me to have come from another planet."

Lars von Trier's graduation film *Images of a Relief* also seems to have come from another planet. This dreamlike, almost hallucinatory, mood piece tells the story of a German soldier and his experiences the day the Allies liberate Denmark. His spirit defeated and his will broken, the officer walks among the ruins of the illusions of the Third Reich, while his Danish girlfriend betrays him in opportunistic desperation, by helping some Danish resistance men set a trap for him.

As the story unfolds, von Trier inserts rarely shown documentary footage of "tyskepiger"—Danish girls with German boyfriends—getting their hair cut off by force, and of administrators who had collaborated with the Germans forced to run the gauntlet down the streets of Copenhagen. At the same time von Trier's film makes it very clear that it wasn't uncommon for the Danish resistance, just like the French, to collaborate with the forces of the German occupation. The compassionate portrayal of the German officer and the expressive reexamination of this publicly known secret from Danish history quickly made *Images of a Relief* a controversial film. Lars von Trier even got a reputation for romanticizing Nazism in the debate that followed. Despite these controversies the film was shown on Danish television shortly thereafter.

"They had bought the film before it was finished and there was no problem showing it since it was an 'art film.' When a film is provocative in its form the content is secondary—even if that also is provocative. An aesthetically provocative film gets away with telling any kind of story or delivering

In 1930's, mag qr(azis = Cartoon crooks

any kind of message. It still won't sink in. . . . Nazism is, of course, the great European trauma. . . . Well, what can I say about the charges? My mother was in the Danish resistance. . . . We'll have to see what will happen now, when *Europa*, which has many similarities to *Images of a Relief*, is released. Personally I see both Nazism and World War II as parts of our culture and as a logical development of forces within that culture. Already in the thirties many people made the mistake of dismissing the Nazis as some kind of cartoon crooks, but we've become wiser since."

The most striking thing about von Trier's graduation film is the elaborate expressions of form and his infallible stylization technique. The sets consist of grandiosely dilapidated backdrops, caressed by sensuously sweeping camera movements—both Vincente Minnelli and Max Ophüls come to mind. The acting is performed with strained theatricality and as a further expressionistic accentuation, von Trier soaks his scenery, using sodium lamps, in a pervasive yellow hue. *Images of a Relief* is in many respects a pilot study for *The Element of Crime*, von Trier's commercial feature film debut.

"I knew it would be hard to find backers for my first commercial feature. I don't think anyone wanted to see another *Images of a Relief*. Circumstances paved the way quite unexpectedly, though, and I got lucky. They had just hired an extremely unpopular film commissioner at the Danish Film Institute. Normally the film consultant gets hundreds of scripts sent to him, but when I arrived with my project he hadn't been sent a single one, so on the basis of my synopsis he gave me the go-ahead immediately. I then managed to get hold of Per Holst, the producer, who invested the rest of the money. The film looks like a big-budget production, but it was in fact the second-cheapest production in Denmark in 1984."

The Element of Crime is a rare bird indeed, being a Danish science fiction thriller. It takes place in a post-apocalyptic future where both culture and climate are in a state of collapse. Europe is now constantly swept in rain and has turned into a large, inundated swamp. Africa is slowly perishing under enormous sandstorms. Somewhere in Cairo we find Detective Fisher who is at the moment undergoing hypnotherapy in order to try to remember an investigation of the so-called Lotto killings, a series of sex-related murders of young lottery-ticket-selling girls, probably perpetrated by the elusive and enigmatic Harry Grey. In his pursuit of Grey, Fisher uses a criminological model, which is described by his former mentor Osborne in the book *The Element of Crime*. The model requires the detective to identify with the killer, which will enable him to predict the killer's plans. During the pursuit a pattern of clues emerges, all pointing towards Osborne. But when Osborne takes his own life the clues begin to point in another direction—towards Fisher himself.

Both *The Element of Crime* and *Images of a Relief* are romances in decomposition and set in a landscape saturated in yellow sodium color. *The Element of Crime* is a typical postmodern 1980s product with its mix of genres and its countless references to other directors, films, and clichés. One could, in brief, describe it as black-and-yellow film noir, modernized into a low-budget exploitation film à la Roger Corman and directed by Andrei Tarkovsky. The post-apocalyptic scenery has a lot in common with a number of films made during the same period: the *Mad Max* trilogy, *Escape from New York*, *The Final Combat*. . . .

"—and don't forget *Stalker* and *Blade Runner*," adds von Trier. "The film is definitely part of a fashion trend. I don't analyze the origins of my images. It's simply not up to me. The pursuit of not being influenced by others is something I think has defined much of the Nordic cinema. Paradoxically this has made it totally conform, a little like the new car models where all the different brands all look alike. Of course I hope that my stolen material has been processed into something new. I don't strive to reproduce my sources of inspiration mechanically. It seems like the fear of letting yourself be inspired by others has loosened its grip during the '80s and I find that good, but I don't feel related to the other directors at all. Except, maybe, in that we make films at the same time and maybe share some of the same sources of inspiration. Apart from any intellectual explanations—and I'm sure that you could provide some of those—about me choosing an apocalyptic landscape, the most important factor for me was to make a clean break from polished Danish filmmaking. I wanted a rough, patinated landscape, so we created one."

The Element of Crime was the first film on which Lars von Trier collaborated with Niels Vørsel (born 1953), an author, relatively unknown even in Denmark, of a couple of radio plays and three novels that have been released by small publishing companies (nothing from his production has been translated). Vørsel himself regards his books as "conceptual meta-literature" written with cold distance.

"I met Lars while I was working as an extra in *Images of a Relief*," Vørsel explains. "I hadn't seen any of Lars's films and he hadn't read any of my books, but we started to talk about an idea for a crime story that Lars had. The only thing we knew from the start was that we wanted to make it into a film noir. Lars had three images he had to include in the film and I suggested that he read Hammett and get some inspiration from that. Hammett is unsurpassable within the detective genre. Chandler was a great author, too, but his crime plots were simply a pretext for showing off his writing. Hammett, though—perhaps because he was a Pinkerton detective himself—is the real thing."

In connection with the opening of *The Element of Crime*, Lars von Trier published a manifesto, in which he attacks the old institutionalized directors—the ones he regards as the "old sexual masters," who today have become "impotent" in their opportunistic showmanship, churning out "well-meaning films with humanistic messages." Their former "passionate love affairs" with cinema have now turned into "marriages of convenience." Dreyer and Tarkovsky seem to be exempted from this condemnation. But with Ingmar Bergman, we suddenly get to the core of what von Trier is attacking—a phenomenon he calls "aesthetic rigor mortis."

"I have an intense love-hate relationship to Bergman," explains von Trier. "I've seen every single one of his films. In his youth and until the late '60s he made many masterpieces. *Through a Glass Darkly*, *The Silence*, and *Persona* have all been of tremendous importance to me. My mother died not long ago and I visited her at the hospital as she was on a ventilator. Suddenly she asked what time it was, and everyone there thought it was a miracle that she could speak although she was dying. That's how I think Bergman is perceived today, which is bad. Many of his earlier films are among the best in the world. Today he sits there as a big obstacle to Swedish cinema. And it's only now, when he's lost his significance as a filmmaker and has stopped making films that matter, that he is given that kind of power. Sadly, I see the same pattern everywhere."

The Element of Crime became a success for von Trier and Vørsel. The film was sold to thirty-two countries, won the Best Technique award at the film festival at Cannes, where it opened, and received several awards at other festivals. Then came the ensuing dilemma—finding the next project. *Le Grand Mal*, a screenplay that was completed in 1985, remained unrealized.

In the meantime and in between trying out new ideas, Lars did an assortment of commissioned projects in order to pay the bills. He has made around forty industrial films, commercials, and music videos. His most widely shown work from this period is without doubt the heavily rotated MTV hit video *Bakerman*. Here we see Danish rock group Laid Back skydiving from a plane a couple of thousand meters up in the air.

But it was on account of a commercial for a Danish evening paper that he was to gain even more attention. It was made in 1986 and called "Gå i bad med *Ekstra Bladet*" ["Take a Bath with *Ekstra Bladet*."] It can be described as a paraphrase on the voyeuristic Hitchcockian pastiches of Brian De Palma: a young man enters the gentlemen's section of a sauna and seats himself a little off to the side on the top bench. There he discovers a vent in the wall, and when he cautiously opens it slightly, his gaze comes to rest upon the ladies' section, where young female bodies reveal themselves in dreamlike slow-motion choreography. Suddenly he sees a stocky middle-aged female bath attendant staring directly towards his peephole. Cut. A line-up of shamefaced men stand at attention for inspection by the despotic bath attendant, and when she reaches the main character she looks down with a stern expression. An issue of *Ekstra Bladet* hangs, folded in the middle, over his erection, lustfully bobbing up and down. The caption reads [loosely translated]: "*Ekstra Bladet*—It's good to have around!"

"A lot of the attention was due to the fact that it wasn't allowed to be shown on the new Danish television network TV2," explains von Trier. "And when it got banned everyone wanted to see it, of course. The ban got a lot of coverage in the media—the Danish film magazine *Kosmorama* published pictures from it, and it was shown in the Danish television news. . . . Scandinavia is fantastic! A thing like this really couldn't have happened anywhere else."

Three years went by before the next von Trier/Vørsel project saw the light of day. This time it was an extremely low-budget black-and-white film about two young men, a director called Lars and a writer called Niels, who have been given money by the Danish Film Institute to write a screenplay. But the problems just pile up until, one week before the planned presentation of the finished product, they find out that the computer has crashed and that the only thing they have left of the script is the title—"The Inspector and the Whore"—and half of the first sentence.

Desperately they try to do a fast rewrite, but they remember nothing of the story, something they both take as a sign of the total worthlessness of the script—so "good riddance!" they say. They then decide to take a trip through Europe in the hope of conceiving and composing a new script. Lars dreams of a heroic medieval epic where he, as the doctor, tries to save a plague-ridden city, while Niels starts to tell absurd stories from his own life.

Epidemic is the first—and so far the only—film that has been produced by von Trier's and Vørsel's own production company, Elementfilm, founded in 1986. Vørsel and von Trier themselves play Niels and Lars in what seems to be a documentary about their real lives.

"_Epidemic_ is my own favorite among the films I've made," says von Trier, "because it's about what we ourselves have been fighting for—the conditions of film production. We were our own producers, secretaries, editors, cinematographers, lighting supervisors, and so forth. With the exception of my medieval episode where Henning Bendtsen used a 35-mm camera, the film was made with a 16-mm camera that mostly stood unmanned since we ourselves stood in front of it. The film looks like a documentary but is really fiction based on real events, chiefly inspired by things that happened during the preparations for _The Element of Crime_. It was fun to shoot and the budget of one million Danish crowns lasted for a long time, but it was a lot of work being in charge of all the different filmmaking tasks at the same time, so it's going to be a while before another Elementfilm film comes along."

Epidemic is a complete departure from anything that von Trier and Vørsel had ever done before. Here, we find an anarchic playfulness, with the film swinging wildly between bombastic Wagnerian tragedy and low-key everyday farce. The comical highlight of the film is a staged account from Niels Vørsel's life: at the age of thirty he starts a pen-pal relationship with an American teenager under the pretense that he is a Danish youngster of the same age. After squeezing everything out of her status-conscious soul by urging her again and again to write in detail about the composition, price, and design of every single artifact in the interior in her parents' home, Niels believes himself to have bored her into ending the relationship. Suddenly, she calls him from a hotel in the center of Copenhagen where she and her parents have checked in. He can't talk his way out of it so he is forced to put on a disguise (his wig looks like something inspired by Lemmy of Motörhead) to try to look like a teenager when he meets her.

In the spring of 1988, Lars von Trier made what thus far has been his only film for television, a film version of Euripides' drama _Medea_. Just as in the beginning of _Europa_, Lars von Trier's name appears dogmatically written above the title, despite the fact that the screenplay of von Trier and Preben

Thomsen is based on Dreyer's plan, left unrealized at his death, to film *Medea* in a Viking setting.

"*Medea* is based on one of the many unrealized scripts that were found in Dreyer's estate. I was fascinated by his very special ideas on color film—ideas he never got a chance to put into practice—since he never made any color films. *Medea* was shot on video, then transferred to film and then back again to video. In the editing we created the special color qualities using among other things chroma key to get the effects I wanted. Otherwise I tried to give the film an almost archaic character, like an old silent film."

Together with *The Element of Crime*, *Medea* is von Trier's most successful film. It has been sold to many countries, and in France—where von Trier seems to have most of his supporters—*Medea* was awarded the Jeanne d'Arc Prize, which probably helped pave the way towards the international financing of *Europa*.

When the time comes for us to discuss *Europa*, they tell me that there is a rough version of a trailer available, and we sit down and watch it. A droning voice phases in, then counts down in the manner of a hypnotist in order to lead the viewer back to postwar Germany, a claustrophobic landscape of labyrinths for the viewer, as well as for the main character, to get lost in.

The story starts at the railway station in Frankfurt just after the end of the war in 1945. American Leopold Kessler (Jean-Marc Barr) arrives from the United States to help in the rebuilding of the former homeland of his parents. Through his uncle (Ernst-Hugo Järegård), he gets a job as a conductor with the Zentropa Railway Company. His gullible idealism and naïve visions make him the perfect target for the manipulations of everyone involved in the power struggle after the fall of the Third Reich. The Alfred Hitchcock connection is emphasized on several occasions by moments of suspense, so-called red herrings, and, of course, by the use of Bernard Herrmann's music from *Vertigo*. Herrmann's score is also interesting in relation to von Trier's recurrent fascination for the music of Richard Wagner, since it is a paraphrase of none other than Wagner, in this case the opera *Tristan und Isolde*. And what could be more suitable for this tale of *Liebestot*? Leopold's passion for Germany and Europe blends with his love for the seemingly innocent but for him so fatal woman Katharina Adler, the daughter of Zentropa's president. As in all of Wagner's operas, the drama ends in a deeply tragic and yet aesthetically beautiful death.

There are close similarities to *The Element of Crime*—the suspenseful plot,

Europe in ruins—but the story of *Europa* is told without the digressions and self-irony of its predecessor. In other words, it is more conventional.

"*Europa* is probably the most commercial film I've made," observes von Trier. "And I don't mind that. On the contrary, I've had enormous freedom to develop my ideas, despite the budget of 26 million Danish crowns, which is five times more than on *The Element of Crime*, my previously most expensive production."

For the English-language production of *Europa*, von Trier has gathered an international ensemble from France, Germany, the United States, Sweden, Switzerland, and Denmark. The film is internationally financed, with contributions coming from the Swedish and Danish Film Institutes and, fittingly enough, from the European Union's Eurimages Fund.

Given his love for expressionistically styled landscapes, visual trickery, and often puppeteer-like direction, von Trier's aesthetics appear to be the total opposite of those of the *nouvelle vague* of the '60s. Is any improvisation at all possible given these aesthetics?

"Yes, if it works, then it's good, but all the images, lines, and details in, for example, *Europa* were planned beforehand in a 600-page scenario with a storyboard consisting of 800 pictures. We impose a structure as early as the scriptwriting stage, when Niels here decides how many pages will be written every day."

As already mentioned, von Trier has attacked older colleagues for being creatively impotent. But then, how about von Trier's own creative potency?

"My solution is fascination, and I've tried to cultivate my fascination for film by developing and renewing my technique for each new film I make. As you yourself have seen, there aren't two of my films that resemble one another. In *Europa*, for example, I use a lot of front and back projections, double exposure, and clearly choreographed camera movements to break down the realistic frame. Of course I borrow, for a moment, Hitchcock's camera and then place it in a landscape by Tarkovsky, but something happens in that process."

When *Epidemic* was released, von Trier published another manifesto, in which he sketches a film trilogy about Europe, which culminates with the film *Europa* and each part of which is given a subheading: *The Element of Crime*, "substance, non-organic"; *Epidemic*, "substance, organic"; and *Europa*, "substance, conceptual." Despite persistent efforts it has been impossible to get von Trier to explain the meaning of these subheadings.

"We wanted the three films in the trilogy to be entirely different from an aesthetic point of view. The subheadings most clearly represent some kind of working hypothesis, or a navigation point for the working process. Both the ideas as well as we ourselves have changed during the working process, so today I don't know if these terms are relevant anymore."

"As I see it," Niels Vørsel interjects, "the trilogy with the three totally different films about Europe produces a kind of relief effect, where the three films reflect and comment on each other."

Concludes von Trier: "So then, all three parts are about exactly the same thing—that logic and common sense are one thing and knowledge and insight something else. When the audience goes to the cinema to watch *Europa* they don't have to know anything about the two other parts. On the contrary, they'll have to leave all their knowledge at the counter when they buy their ticket."

Maniacal Iconoclast of Film Convention

NIGEL ANDREWS / 1991

SAY ''DANISH CINEMA'' to most cinephiles and their eyes glaze over. They think of farming families pounding butter in Nordic Technicolor or grim, impenetrable tales of seventeenth-century religious persecution in black and white.

Yet Lars von Trier had a different, *de*-glazing effect on last year's Cannes prize-night audience. He won two awards for his spectacular film *Europa* and even these, it was clear, were not enough for Denmark's new *Wunderkind*. The first prize for Superior Technique he disdainfully handed to a colleague saying, "He has worked on all my films and is very technical." For the second, grander Prix du Jury he thanked "the midget," by which we all realized with a shock that he was referring to jury president Roman Polanski.

But what would you expect from a man whose movies—from the Borgesian thriller *The Element of Crime* to the Nazi-era film noir *Europa* opening in Britain this week—place a bomb under film convention? Not since *Citizen Kane* has more maniacal fun been had with cinema's visual possibilities. Multiple exposure, color mixed with monochrome, 3D deep-focus effects, cameras passing through solid objects, back-projected dream images. . . .

"I don't like *Citizen Kane*," insists von Trier in a sunny Cannes garden. "I like Welles very much, but *Citizen Kane* is too obvious. I prefer *The Lady from Shanghai* and *Touch of Evil*."

But he clearly shares Welles's "best ever train set" view of cinema. Indeed von Trier has a different analogy.

From the *Financial Times*, 19 April 1992. Reprinted by permission of the author.

"I am a simple masturbator of the cinema," he told one French reporter. Meaning? "The only thing I have in mind when I make a film is my own enjoyment."

He also enjoys kidding people along: not just interviewers but audiences. *Europa* winds us up with its violations of stylistic orthodoxy and also with its plot about an idealistic American (Jean-Marc Barr) arriving in Germany after the war and falling in love with a beautiful Nazi sympathizer.

The terrorist group called the "Werewolves," who carry the Third Reich flame into acts of postwar sabotage, is depicted with alarming sympathy. At Cannes a well-known left-wing daily viciously attacked the film.

"*Libération*, which supported me before, was quite negative about *Europa*. This was an expensive multi-country co-production, so they don't like the commercial aspect. But also they think I'm siding with the Nazis, which I'm not. The film is seen through Leo's (the hero's) eyes: the Germans are victims at the beginning, but by the end that has changed. We had a joke, though, that I would win the Iron Cross for the film!"

People have been shot for jokes like that. Still, *Europa's* provocateur political postures are half the fun. The other half is its delirious mise-en-scène.

"The camera moves were so elaborate that we had to plan and storyboard almost the whole film. The shooting script was a thousand pages long. The whole film was made in the studio, except for some Polish location scenes we used for backgrounds.

"Some of the shots that look impossible, like the camera going down through two floors to the bathroom where a man cuts his wrists, were quite easy. We used dissolves that the audience can't see. But some difficult shots were done for real. When the camera passes out from the attic room through the roof of the house and then into a train passing by, that we actually did.

"Also we used a lot of back-projection, because I love how Hitchcock used it in films like *Vertigo*. Back-projection creates a dreamlike effect because it's so unreal. It divides the image into different layers, which in *Europa* we exaggerated by using color and black-and-white.

"When we wrote the script we spelled it out in terms of 'close-ups,' 'long shots,' and so on. And whenever we used color we called it 'super close-up.'"

The film has conjuring tricks aplenty, but also real magic. Most of all in its weirdly satisfying potpourri of influences, from British TV (von Trier stole the post-WW II "innocent abroad" idea from *A Family at War*) to Franz

Kafka. *Europa*'s humor, especially the scenes in which two eccentric railway examiners put the train-guard hero through his paces, is pure Kafka.

"I love Kafka. He was a great influence and I chose the title 'Europa' as an echo of *Amerika*. It's really the same story told in reverse. This time the innocent American comes to Europe. He enters a chaos of different lives, different traditions, loyalties, and opinions, which I think is the charm of Europe."

Seeing *Europa*, with its marriage between (almost) traditional plot and go-for-broke stylistic experiment, one realizes how visually tame most feature films are. "Cinema is so expensive, that's why it's so conservative," says von Trier. "At the beginning of the pop promo era, I was very hopeful. I thought film was becoming more experimental and that this would feed through into mainstream cinema. That hasn't happened. Today you still sell a feature film on its story, whereas a rock video can be sold on its images."

Trier is about to take another bash at the frontiers of convention. His next project is an epic thriller that will be shot over twenty-two years. "I wanted to do a 'monument.' We can't afford *Lawrence of Arabia*, so it's crime story that will end in 2024! I can tell you what the first scene is, because we're shooting it today. It's Eddie Constantine helicoptering over Cannes and delivering a parcel to Udo Kier, who's waiting in a Mercedes. We haven't decided what's in the parcel, so we're shooting with five different parcels. Oh, here they come now!" (Enter man bearing parcels.)

"We don't know the ending yet, but I can tell you the first line. Eddie Constantine says, 'This will be my last delivery.' That's all I can tell you. Now I must go."

Euro Paean

ANYONE WHO MAKES A FILM with a presumptuously compre-
hensive title like *Europa* must surely be a megalomaniac of the old school.
Especially if their name includes the ominous "von," usually a reliable indi-
cator of the whip-wielding martinet-with-a-megaphone. "The *von* is purely
fictional," confesses Danish director Lars von Trier, "like von Stroheim or
von Sternberg— it goes with a director, like riding boots."

Lars von Trier's cameo in *Europa* adds to the intense persona he's projected
in the past. As a Jewish survivor of World War II Germany, he's all cropped
hair, furrowed brow, and Walter Benjamin specs. Over the phone, though,
he seems in a constant state of mirth, as though he can scarcely believe that
anyone would take him too seriously. His 1984 film, *The Element of Crime*, was
generally received here as an overblown essay in *Sturm und Drang*. *Europa* is
bound to cause more dropped jaws. Set during Germany's postwar "recon-
struction"— or dismantling— it is only incidentally a state-of-Europe film,
since it mostly takes place in cramped railway carriages. "Europa" is what
you don't see.

Clearly there are problems in dealing with such a historically ambivalent
moment as Germany's "zero period." "If you're showing Germany in ruins,
there's always the danger that somebody will call you a Nazi, because people
who live in ruins will be victims and starve, whether they're the good guys
or the bad guys. That's one reason why there aren't many films set in that
period."

From *Time Out* #1130, 15 April 1992. Reprinted by permission of *Time Out* and the author.

It's clear that von Trier's first duty in *Europa* is not to historical realism but to the sheer drunken hit of being a movie brat on set. Dark as it is, *Europa* is essentially hedonistic, its panoply of trick shots and baroque trackings the work of a director so addicted to effect that he's almost masochistic in its pursuit.

"I want to do things the hard way, that's for sure. The reason they did all that back projection years ago was because it was the easiest way. Now the easiest way would have been to take the actors to Poland, but no, no, no. The thing about the train is more that I like the idea of being in a tight place and being taken through a lot of locations that you don't have to see."

The tableaux in *Europa* mobilize crowds with the parade-ground grandeur of a *Metropolis*, but von Trier denies that he's a power junkie. "But I like electrical trains, that's true. Bergman, I'm sure, loved power—I'm much saner than him. What's interesting is to create your own world. It's close to the idea of the electrical train—you build your own mountains, here should be a little street—that is thrilling. Many directors are quite sensitive people, afraid of the world and life—so when they control them, they build enormous things with horses, police, earthquakes."

Lars von Trier has waxed lyrical about the cheapness of his cinematic tricks. The power of his peculiarly grandiose tackiness is that the tawdrier the effect, the more transparent, and so the less manipulative the film. In this sense, *Europa* lays its cards on the table from the start, as mesmerist Max von Sydow hammily exhorts you to "Relaaaaax . . . , as you go deeeeper into Europa: . . ." The effect, paradoxically, is to put you on your nerve ends. "I'm extremely afraid to get into a cinema," von Trier confesses. "I don't want to be seduced. It's like that with hypnosis, asking you to relax—then when it has you in its grip, when you don't have any resistance, it can open up things in you."

Europa, it's true, aims straight for the unconscious, with its night-bound textures inkier than a squid's Rorschach test. "The best images are the ones created within the brain. But I don't want to do that again. Now I want to do an erotic film, in daytime and in color."

More immediately, he is making a film called *Dimension*. But not *that* immediately—it won't be completed until 2024, with two minutes to be shot every year. "We're writing narration for the whole film, trying to take into account what will be happening in Europe over the next thirty years. It's very seldom you can do flashbacks in real time. We're doing some with Jean-Marc Barr—we hope he'll be alive a long time, otherwise we'll have to throw them away."

Lars von Trier, Director

TOBY ROSE/1992

LARS VON TRIER, director of *Europa*, the most expensive and award-strewn movie in Danish history, is in something of a quandary as he sits at a table in the pine dining room of this clinically clean and typically Scandinavian hotel in the center of Copenhagen. "Oh, come on," he finally blurts. "Let's have some *Danish* beer."

Chuckling as he gets probably the world's finest lager after a hard day's filming here in the Danish capital, von Trier is, however, deadly serious about the importance of his homeland in the great European scheme of things, hoping that *Europa*—not to be confused with the German/Polish production *Europa, Europa*, to be released in the UK *next* month—will help movies replace this very lager, bacon rashers, and Lurpak as his country's most famous export. It has, however, been something of an uphill struggle for von Trier to maneuver himself into the position of directing a £7 million production.

"First I could fool a few people to give me some money," he laughs, "then I could fool a few more people to give me some money and now I've fooled a *lot* of people to give me a *lot* of money."

The third and final part of a trilogy which opened with the critically acclaimed *The Element of Crime* in 1984—starring Michael Elphick—and continued with 1987's *Epidemic, Europa*, set in the aftermath of World War II, caused a huge stir at Cannes last year (where it won the Special Jury Prize and Best Technique gong), not so much for its subject matter but for its

From *Empire* #35, May 1992. Reprinted by permission of *Empire*.

extraordinary visual wizardry, involving the overlaying of colored and black-and-white images and various other sorts of jiggery-pokery.

"Each of my films contains a technical innovation," says von Trier. "In *Europa*, we were working on image superimposition. Sometimes we had up to seven layers of images, in black and white and color. The main thing, though, is that we can combine two images filmed with different lenses. With a background shot on a wide-angle, we create an unsettling effect that isn't immediately noticeable, but which affects the audience."

The postwar period clearly holds a particular fascination for the thirty-five-year-old von Trier, who co-scripted this tale of a German-American returning to Berlin in 1945 and attempting to come to terms with what happened during the Nazi regime.

"Denmark has always been very influenced by Germany," says von Trier. "The war was a big humiliation because there was no resistance whatsoever in the beginning, it came late on. It was quite traumatic for many Danes. Norway was completely different, they fought quite a lot. And what really irritates the shit out of me today is to hear some German guy talk about the Danish-German border, and that it should be further north. I don't believe there *will* be another war with Germany, but if you go there, you realize that it is an enormous country. East Germany has a lot of resources, and West Germany is such an economic center that given those resources, it will be very, *very* powerful."

Slight, sandy-haired, and with the hallmark frown of a thinker, Lars von Trier gives this opinion, like all his others, in a clipped, deliberate manner, qualities that also come across in his movies, films which tend to be top-heavy on ideas and images, sparse on narrative. *Europa*, however, is a slight progression from the previous what-the-hell-is-going-on school of von Trier filmmaking, a policy, insists the director, that he decided upon quite deliberately.

"I'm not stupid," he says. "I'm not going to spend this budget knowing that ten people are going to show up at the cinema. It's part of my job to have as many people see this film as possible. If I'm Daneocentric, I'm also egocentric, and I want people to *see* my movies. Who doesn't?"

A Stone-Turner from Lyngby

LARS K. ANDERSEN/1994

RECENTLY TURNED thirty-eight-year-old film director Lars von Trier is the kind of artist who makes some people positively see red. Twelve years have passed since his watershed debut, the award-winning graduation film *Images of a Relief*, but he shows no signs whatsoever of having become less controversial with time.

The media turmoil of Cannes '91, with von Trier declaring his disappointment when his latest film *Europa* [U.S. title *Zentropa*] didn't win the Palme d'Or, still lingers in the air somewhere. At least to the extent that the image of the confrontational, self-promoting, arrogant, testy, stubbly scalped man is still what people see when they think about the gaunt little fellow with the fox-like face.

But does that image really hold up? Could it really be true of the almost forty-year-old co-founder of an unusually successful production company—Zentropa—that he still has a penchant for the media-manipulating statements he persisted in making throughout the dark '80s?

Even in recent interviews—for example, those from this fall—Lars von Trier comes off as the angry young artist. Something rings off-key here. And it becomes even clearer as I enter his messy little study at the recently renovated house in Lyngby, where he resides with his wife and children.

Granted, he can't help seeming somewhat affected, but he's also a friendly spirit, ironic at his own expense, playful, and childishly enthusiastic—like when he shows off his new CD-ROM driver, which stands beneath a crucifix.

From *Levende Billeder*, November 1994. Reprinted by permission of the author.

And more than anything else he is a man who—just like the rest of us who belong to the bourgeois middle class—has to deal with the little trivial things of everyday life. During the interview he has to put some time aside for a long phone conversation with the bricklayer since the archway in the backyard is too low: "Yes, it's a beautiful piece of work, it's not that. And I'm a pretty short guy myself, but I had a visit from a man who was 182 centimeters [six feet] tall the other day, and he bumped his head on it, and that's not very good, now is it?"

And he is a man who by his own admission has developed into "a ruthless opportunist," with more than fifty commercials and music videos to his credit, and he was glad to do what he earlier would have shunned: an entertaining TV series for DRTV [the Danish Broadcasting Corporation]. Moreover, he's also a man who has a hard time recognizing the picture the media have painted of film director Lars von Trier—but who at least confesses his complicity in creating that image and acknowledges the fact that rumors of its death have been greatly exaggerated:

"I've always thought that I've fought for a good cause. And that could easily be seen as reasonably brainless in a world where there are better things to fight for than the look of a film. But this is how I've always been: I should be allowed to do the things I do and all that jazz. Very moralizing, even though it could be seen as the exact opposite."

ANDERSEN: *The media, especially the tabloid press, welcomed your outbursts with open arms. You got mad at Cannes and all of a sudden it was all over the Danish front pages.*

von TRIER: It was out of proportion—the way it's always been. Documentation is just as fictitious as film. In a review of [TV show] *Lærerværelset* [*The Teacher's Room*] in *Berlingske Tidene* I was almost described as diabolical: "Trier the Mad Prince." There's not a damn grain of devilry in me. It's only an image they've constructed. The media were the first to believe in it.

ANDERSEN: *But weren't you also a part of creating that version of Lars von Trier?*

von TRIER: Well, yes. I'd like to put it like this: I was crazy about Bowie and people like that, people who created an image. And I'll accept that side of showbiz in the same way that a pop musician will—the way in which people promote themselves has always been important to me. From my point of view, John McEnroe was a good tennis player while Björn Borg was really boring. Granted, McEnroe couldn't control his temper, but it was also an image he himself created and which the media subsequently built upon.

ANDERSEN: *So, you went for star quality in a way?*
von TRIER: I don't know if I was that conscious of it, but I've always respected that side of the business. At the same time I was thoroughly able to stand up for the things I did. I had the feeling that there was a correspondence between my films and the things I communicated with my person. But as time goes by, the media become more and more difficult to control. Because if there's one thing the media won't accept, it's change. I'm still remembered as having a shaved head, so that hairstyle doesn't interest me anymore.

Most of the works of Lars von Trier—including his debut *The Element of Crime*, the made-for-television *Medea* (based on idol Carl Th. Dreyer's posthumous script) and *Europa*—have gained attention through their sophisticated visual ideas, but they've also certainly had their limitations. In hindsight it's not unfair to maintain that these are the gifted, stylistic exercises of a fledgling director.

Epidemic, a startling commercial fiasco made in 1987, is the odd film out. Just like with the others, this is not an actor's film—the director himself and his regular script collaborator Niels Vørsel are the main characters—but it is a film that, with its grainy images and handheld camera, anticipates the television series *The Kingdom*, which looks like it's going to be Lars von Trier's first major success with a mainstream audience. At least by judging the reception the four episodes recently received at the Venice Film Festival.

"A major event," "better than *Twin Peaks*," "a gem of ambiguity from Denmark"—these are just some of the kudos from an enthusiastic Italian press on the subject of this bizarrely humorous, gory, ghastly ghost comedy that takes place at the Copenhagen University Hospital, Rigshospitalet. An endless stream of actors is featured. In the leading roles we see Kirsten Rolffes, Holger Juul Hansen, Søren Pilmark, Jens Okking, Ghita Nørby, German Udo Kier and Swede Ernst-Hugo Järegård. And surprisingly—because, remember, we're talking about von Trier—there is some phenomenal acting to be found.

von TRIER: I haven't always been able to strike a balance between the style and the plot in my previous films, but this time around I certainly have.

I had a discussion about it with my editor Tómas Gislason before we started working on *The Kingdom*, and we started to move in the direction of using handheld camera. It's one of the big waves in American cinema at the moment. Woody Allen has used the technique, but it was around before that. For example, John Schlesinger and Ken Russell did it, and it was there in the British cinema of the '60s, when the editing was also much freer. Take *Help!* with The Beatles, for example—that film certainly contained a lot of mischief and fooling around. But with the exception of *Epidemic*, where I worked a little with handheld camera myself, I've always been very concerned, ultimately, with aesthetics: panning, dolly shots—with parallel movements especially. However, what really opened things up for me was an American television series called *Homicide: Life on the Street* by Barry Levinson, a show they stuck in the middle of the entertainment package on Saturday nights on TV2. Its generous view on the 180-degree rules of filmmaking—something they spent two months banging into our heads at film school—was very interesting. The 180-degree rules are the ABC's of the whole film industry. It's basically about always having cameras on both sides if you crosscut between two characters. But Barry Levinson started to crosscut without any concern for which side of the axis the actors were standing on. Barry Levinson is a really good guy and *Homicide: Life on the Street* is an excellent series. We've used the things that Levinson did there, and pushed them even further.

ANDERSEN: *It's particularly visible in the scenes between Ernst-Hugo Järegård and Ghita Nørby, but to how large an extent have you made general use of these violations?*
von TRIER: You can see it in those scenes, yes, but we do it all the time. We've thrown out all those 180-degree rules, and it's really so cool. I'm crazy about it.

ANDERSEN: *It really affects the way the viewer perceives* The Kingdom. *It produces an almost physical effect. . . .*
von TRIER: Absolutely. But it's not just the 180-degree rules that are absent. We've also brought another great animal to slaughter: the continuity. When

you do the scene, you normally have one set idea about how the actors will play the scene—they'll all stand at the same time on the same side of the room, holding the glass in the same way, et cetera. We asked them to play the same scene five times in five different ways—cheerfully, gloomily, et cetera—and at different places in the room every time. We then intercut these different takes, and then when you watch it, you'll perceive it as a perfectly normal take. You create the missing links in your brain. But performance-wise, you really get into some territory that makes for more interesting characters.

Lars von Trier describes the absence of continuity of the separate scenes as the actual basis for "the ultimate love-cutting.": "Just edit like the Americans do. Cut when the actor's good. In an average American film you might be able to use 50 percent of the takes, for the simple reason that you have to respect the 180-degree rules and the continuity. In my older films we could perhaps use 10 percent, just because there were so many things to take into consideration. But with this new way of dispensing with all 180-degree rules and continuity, we can use 98 per cent. It's the ultimately actor-friendly technique, because it animates the players. They never know where the camera is placed and they're forced to play to each other—as opposed to playing to the camera as it used to be under the old-fashioned conditions."

ANDERSEN: *While visiting Venice, a Swedish critic wrote that Ernst-Hugo Järegård had never been better on film. This is news in connection with your films. The word is usually that you're not very interested in actors.*
von TRIER: I've been bad at giving directions, my excuse for this being that I'm not very interested in it—and this is true enough in a way. But with *The Kingdom*, I've tried to look at it from the actors' points of view. It's much easier, of course. It's one thing to be a little testy man who insists on having the actors standing in a corner, talking to the wall. That's hard work. The easiest thing in the world is to approach them and ask them if they have any ideas. Just rub them the right way. I used to argue with the actors, but today I have a wonderful relationship with them. I've become very popular. But the fact that I brought Morten Arnfred along as my assistant has also meant a lot. He's very experienced with actors. This was already decided in advance of course, because this time it was clear that the style demanded some serious acting. I've tried everything in my day, hypnotized the actors and whatnot.

But it goes without saying—if you want that strong, personal, psychologically well-founded expression, then there's nothing better than actually working with the actors. I just never had any use for it before. But I have to say that I had some brilliant actors on the set. They actually play reasonably well. I've had good actors before, too. But they were never allowed to play at that point.

ANDERSEN: *Are you also more flexible, now that you're older?*
von TRIER: Possibly.

ANDERSEN: *But there have to have been some other considerations, apart from the actor-related ones, that made you reject the ABC's.*
von TRIER: Of course. In many ways, *The Kingdom* is an absurd story and when something is absurd, then you need some kind of realistic foundation. The fact that the story takes place in a hospital where they perform real operations and everything was as important as any. And as you can see, the operations look really good with this handheld style. It's the added dimension of the documentary style. In documentaries you never had to abide by the 180-degree rule: if a man gets shot you can't just say, "Let's do another take." And that's accepted in documentary films. So now we're only waiting for the makers of fictional films to follow suit—and it's coming! Our generation, as well as the younger ones, has had phenomenal training in the reading of images. The 180-degree rule was invented in the days when people saw one film per year and were in danger of getting confused. Today we see films around the clock. If you showed a modern television report to somebody from those days, they would be totally unable to comprehend what they saw.

ANDERSEN: *So you're not afraid of alienating the older audiences?*
von TRIER: I don't think it will happen. I've shown it to some elderly people, who didn't have any problems keeping pace. They understood who was speaking to whom. And that was just it—*that* was the whole justification for the 180-degree rule. I now believe that we've suffered under certain film dogmas that have no significance whatsoever. Five years from now, the 180-degree rule will remain in a few cinematic works, but it'll be gone from mainstream films.

ANDERSEN: *In other words, the handheld camera is your new standpoint?*

von TRIER: For the moment I'm crazy about it, but I also enjoy being a little at the forefront of things. When everyone else is doing it, then I'll probably do things differently. There's a difference between finding the source of the Nile and going on a guided tour, right?

ANDERSEN: *How did the idea of* The Kingdom *arise?*

von TRIER: DRTV [the Danish Broadcasting Corporation] asked me if I wanted to do a little thing for them. I wasn't interested in that, but I suggested a series. I had three suggestions, of which I only remember *The Kingdom*. And they jumped at the offer.

ANDERSEN: *Were you inspired by the old song that can be heard in the film—"I en seng på hospitalet" ["In a Bed at the Hospital"]?*

von TRIER: No, I was inspired by *Twin Peaks*. I really enjoyed the early episodes, despite the fact that I've never been a very big fan of David Lynch. At the time, I thought that *Eraserhead* was a terrible piece of Kafkaesque crap. But I was really crazy about *Twin Peaks* and I realized that it was so good, so different, because it was a piece of left-handed work: God knows Lynch didn't really care to make a TV series, he just needed to pay the rent. All right, so let's do it—*Twin Peaks* is quite obviously the work of a director without the fear of having to live up to any expectations of a great feature film. In other words, I had the desire to do something just as pleasurable. And it worked. On the other scripts, it's taken a year and a half for Niels Vørsel and me to get the job done. *Breaking the Waves*, the one I'm starting to shoot this summer, took me three years to write. But we did *The Kingdom* in a month and a half, by just letting things roll. Automatism and full freedom. That was great fun.

ANDERSEN: *And you never lost track?*

von TRIER: Well, yes, I admit that we lost track now and then, but the work is so pleasurable and that makes *The Kingdom* more entertaining than anything else I've ever put my name on. It's very much of a comedy with a layer of realism and a layer of horror, just to give an edge to the comedy.

ANDERSEN: *Did the recent medical controversies, malpractice and such, inspire you?*

von TRIER: No, not at all, but then I've never been interested in the authority of the medical practice. I don't care for authorities, and when you're sick and have to go and see the doctor there's no doubt about the power balance.

And any quack that tells you that he can help will get the upper hand on you. And then I liked Rigshospitalet as a location. The clash between death, evil, and the otherworldly. A modern building with an old ghost.

ANDERSEN: *Do you have a spiritualistic interest? It is a very crucial element in* The Kingdom.
von TRIER: I regard myself a religious person. But spiritualistic? No—I'd rather say that I find the supernatural quite titillating.

ANDERSEN: *In other words, the mission has been to tell a good story.*
von TRIER: Yes, I'm afraid that I happen to have told good story. I've always said that I'd be through the day I told a good story. But what the hell, it can happen to anyone.

ANDERSEN: *How do you regard your production thus far?*
von TRIER: I haven't seen my films in many years and I'm not on good terms with them, really. The one I like the best is *Epidemic*, and that's the closest to what I'm doing now. There are scenes I like in my films—as well as some perceptions in and around them—but there are many things I'd do differently today, many things I feel are really embarrassing. Well, it's like when children reach puberty. They're awful, pimply and cross-eyed, but they're still family, so you're forced to care for them.

ANDERSEN: *You just tried your hand at the handheld camera. What would you say to the possibility of computer animation? Are you going to get into that as well?*
von TRIER: I probably will, I've gradually lost all my principles. So why shouldn't I sell out on the principle that says that we should be able to determine the origin of an image?

ANDERSEN: *You sell out, and you do things that you never imagined you'd do. . . .*
von TRIER: It's called opportunism. . . .

ANDERSEN: *Could you also imagine breaking with the traditional dramaturgy of cinema?*

von TRIER: I greatly admire directors who have done that, but these are very esoteric films. *The Mirror* by Tarkovsky is unintelligible, to put it mildly. Then I think there's more to be extracted from the break with the 180-degree rule and the continuity rule and what that can lead to. It could very well be that there's even more to be done than crosscutting between characters across a given space. You could imagine some even wilder things, like moving an actor around, having him stand at 117 different places around the world, saying the same lines—and then cutting it all together. The very different locations would add color, but the only thing you'd primarily concentrate upon would be the story. Maybe it would make for good cinema, but it's an interesting train of thought. With *The Kingdom*, we see to it that at least you will find the story comprehensible enough and the plots interesting enough, so that we then can allow ourselves all the liberties imaginable with the camera work.

ANDERSEN: *Would that allow you to target the subconscious more precisely?*

von TRIER: It would at least provide you with some very good tools for doing so.

ANDERSEN: *What about working on commercials and music videos?*

von TRIER: I've recently made some French commercials that were incredibly well-paying. I never knew you could make so much money, but they only pay you to put your name on it and then shoot what they've decided upon. There's a saying that you're allowed to experiment when you make commercials, but I've never experienced that. Well, yes—it was fun to do the music video where Laid Back jumps out with parachutes. I don't fly myself, so I stood down on the ground and ordered them up again once they'd come down. They were horrified.

ANDERSEN: Lærerværelset *[The Teachers' Room], which you made for TV2, has been met with a very mixed reception.*

von TRIER: I myself had fun with *Lærerværelset*. I love television where the actors all speak at the same time. I'm crazy about chaos. Television needs more chaos, because normally it's purged of every form of it. And in journalistic broadcasts there's always someone telling you how you should interpret what you're seeing: before you've had time to form an opinion of your own, you've been made to understand that these people are behaving badly towards these other people and blah, blah, blah. There always has to be a meaning, a point. But *Lærerværelset* really has no point. At least it's very shallow to say that the point would be to regard the culprits as idiots. The idea behind *Lærerværelset* came about when *Ekstra Bladet* was hounding Ritt Bjerregaard [Minister of Education at the time] when she got herself that flat on Vesterbrogade. The thought was to create a television show where Ritt could make a rebuttal and gain some sympathy in the eyes of the public. If you see people there on the screen just telling her off, you also see the absurdity in telling someone off at all—the absurdity of having anything to do with it at all. More than anything else, *Lærerværelset* is a depiction of staff-room philosophy. The thing about a smug group of people who sit around and bully others by virtue of being a flock and being in power.

ANDERSEN: *First and foremost,* Lærerværelset *has confused people.*
von TRIER: Confused them enormously. But I don't think that the ordinary viewers are so confused, they just watch it. The intellectual viewers, on the other hand, have been greatly confused and insanely angered by the show—for what's the point of all this? It's just one great question mark. It's apparently the most terrible act you can commit. I've always believed that it was thoroughly honorable to produce something that doesn't have a coherent message. It was the same thing with *Medea*, and I got criticized for that, too. I'm not that crazy about *Medea*, but I do think it has some really stylish images, and most important, it was an attempt to make alternative television. But I've never received any credit for that, anywhere. There has never been a reviewer anywhere who has approached me and said, "I think what you do is crap, but it's really great that you do it, because it's interesting that someone turns the camera upside-down." I just can't understand that these people don't exist. People who say "keep it up" to people who move against the stream. Not that it was any stroke of genius, the way the person moved against the stream, or that there was any point to it, but simply because he bothered to do it. I really wonder about this, since there are papers and magazines who pat themselves on the back because of their foresight and their intellectual and cultural insight, but the very simple thing of detecting that someone somewhere is turning over a stone, well, no one sees that. It bothers me in that things tend to stiffen up under such circumstances—I'm really

delivering a whole election speech. And what the hell is this? Everyone has surely thought that "This Trier guy has been running around at our expense and had himself a one hell of a time." And in a way I have, but apart from that I've also been on a crusade that should interest everyone. Take, for example, *The Element of Crime*: Stephen Spielberg was interested in seeing it. He knew, of course, that what we did when we went out and fooled around with the camera might contain something that he could use ten years later in some commercial film. Maybe one or two camera angles. He was smart enough to see that.

ANDERSEN: *But it's not exactly new thinking that characterizes Danish cinema.*

von TRIER: No, you can't say that, but it's also being criticized—and for all the right reasons, I'd like to add. But I don't demand that. For me the main thing is that something is *well made*—and then it can be as traditional as anything. Reproduction annoys me, however. At least if it's bad reproduction and that's when you find out. No, I do not demand new thinking, but new thinking should be respected. It's like that in science. It should be like that in culture and all other aspects of society. I will stand by this until the day I die. Because this is what mankind is capable of, dammit. It's also taken us to the edge of the abyss—that everyone's been going around turning over stones—but it's a basic need. Otherwise we'd never know what the Indians of America were up to. Maybe that would've been for best for all parties concerned, but that's the way it is when you turn over a stone. Now and then there's a really horrible bug underneath it. I'm almost excited. Can you hear that? I don't know what the hell has happened. Maybe it's all just a cover-up for the popularity swamp I'm in at the moment. . . .

ANDERSEN: *You seem to have made yourself very comfortable there.*
von TRIER: Yes, it's been fun to do *The Kingdom*, that's true. I feel very relaxed about it. Probably age has something to do with it.

ANDERSEN: *Are you pleased with the results of The Kingdom?*
von TRIER: For the moment I'm reasonably pleased with it. There are some isolated scenes here and there that I find really funny.

ANDERSEN: *But you expect to be displeased with it two or three years from now?*

von TRIER: That may very well be, but there's a clearly visible brand of humor in it, the same humor that Niels Vørsel and I have always made use of, also in *The Element of Crime* and *Epidemic*, especially in the latter. We screened *The Kingdom* in Venice and they were really laughing there. I have this theory about making things as specialized as possible, as opposed to making them generally accessible. A clash between a Swedish senior physician and a Danish hospital is very specialized in relation to an international audience, but they had a blast in Venice.

ANDERSEN: *All countries have their little feuds.*

von TRIER: Of course. But that's the interesting thing about it: watching a symbolic representation of our situation from an exotic point of view. I just never thought about it like that. At one point there's a line where the Danish chief surgeon says of the Swede, "He comes from a totally different cultural background." They screamed with laughter—ovations from an international crowd—it was really wild. And you'd think it was a very domestic, Nordic concern.

The Kingdom is not yet completed. In fact one leaves the first part of the series in a most disturbed state of *interruptus*. The continuation, currently being written by von Trier and Vørsel, is planned for next winter. Lars von Trier plans a total of thirteen episodes of *The Kingdom*.

His exiting line to *Levende Billeder* is that he hopes for a good reception: "At least *The Kingdom* is made in good spirit—so why not, this time around? But then again, I've had the same thought before every premiere."

I Am Curious, Film: Lars von Trier

STIG BJÖRKMAN AND
LENA NYMAN/1995

Q: *Lars, there's a problem. I've heard that you're such a devil with the actors.*
LARS VON TRIER: Oh, in what way?

Q: *Well, I don't really know, now that I've met you. And I can't imagine that a man who is as sweet, as nice, as good-looking as yourself, could be a devil. Well, what's the deal?*
LvT: Well, no, I'm not a devil. But it's like this, you know, that, earlier in my work, I was very interested in technical aspects and such. Which made the actors think that I wasn't interested in them. And actors, as you know—especially female ones—want to be loved, and I do love them, of course, but only part-time. And that's not good enough for actors, I eventually found out. So, therefore, I've changed my character so that I now love them full-time.

Q: *All right. I'm thinking about the film* Europa *and whether you neglected the actors or whether the technique took over. I mean, for the actors it seems to have been a hard film to shoot.*
LvT: Yes, I might have been too hard on the actors, I admit that now, but I think I'm better today. Don't you think I'm better today?

Q: *I think you're wonderful, but you're not directing me right now.*
LvT: No, no, no, I'm no longer hard on them. Never. Not anymore.

From the film *I Am Curious, Film*, 1995, by Stig Björkman. Questions written by Björkman and presented by Lena Nyman. Reprinted by permission of Stig Björkman.

Q: *I'd like you to tell me about Dreyer. How he has inspired, or influenced, you. You said that* Medea *was made with an old technique.*

LvT: I would say that Dreyer's own technique was very simple. He had a couple of guiding theories, but there was no sensational technique. But what I've done with *Medea*, for example. . . .

Q: *Yes, why did you choose to do* Medea?

LvT: Well, it was nothing less than a case of blackmail. I accepted the project because someone else would have taken it if I hadn't. And it would have been horrible for me if someone else had taken it—to have to see someone else doing it. So I did it. But I would say that I'm not really directly inspired by Dreyer so much as I'm inspired by his way of directing. For I think that he's a very honest director. He never made anything in a calculated fashion. Or, in other words, he always, so to speak, went against what was in vogue.

When he made his first sound film, for example . . . he had already done some silent films, so when he made his first sound film, he had almost no sound in it. It was interesting, because all the other directors, the Americans and what have you, made use of music and effects. But Dreyer said no, this is the way we should do it—just a little bit of sound. There are only three lines, maybe—it's *Vampyr* I'm thinking of—and just a little bit of music.

Q: *I know that there are those who call him a gloomy old amateur. . . .*

LvT: But you can say that they're right in a way—when they say that Dreyer was boring. As a person, I believe, he was unbelievably boring. He was an office clerk. But I would say that, as opposed to Bergman, who has always, so to speak, opened himself up and talked about himself and maybe dared to make the most of that openness, that Dreyer is more of a mystic.

Take for example the last film he ever made [*Gertrud*]. He made it in Denmark, by the way. No one liked it, absolutely no one. It was a tremendous setback for him. The film was totally panned in Denmark. In that last film he didn't direct his actors, he hypnotized them. But he didn't hypnotize them in Danish, he hypnotized them in some sort of quasi-Hebrew that he would read aloud, because he thought that it formed a magical link between the actors and the director.

Q: *Cinema celebrates its 100th birthday this year. What do you think that the next hundred years of cinema will bring?*

LvT: I don't know about the next hundred years, but I do know about the future. If we compare cinema to the art of painting, then painting started with someone drawing in some cave in France or wherever they did it. And they did it like that for a hundred years, I think. Anyway, it started with something like that and then gradually it became more complicated, something like an ox or whatever it was. So if we compare it with that, then we have to say that where painting is today, many centuries later, those cave-painters could never have foreseen. They could have never guessed what painting would look like today. And I think it's the same with cinema. We've reached the end of the first hundred years, we've just managed to make it look like an ox. So I look towards the future in a most optimistic way. But, of course, we'd better think it through carefully. . . . Yes. I have nothing more to say.

Edge of Darkness

WALLY HAMMOND / 1995

IT'S JUST WHAT YOU NEED for the New Year—a spine-chilling ghost story. The darkness, the diabolism, the fear in Danish director Lars von Trier's remarkable new film, may come as no shock to those familiar with *The Element of Crime* and *Europa*, his brooding earlier features. What does come as a surprise is the delirious humor and the escalating farce in his highly eccentric, iconoclastic four-hour hospital-soap-opera-cum-occult-social-satire, *The Kingdom*.

Funny as they are, the characters in von Trier's latest release would frighten the denizens of Dante's *Inferno*. The patients are bad enough: Mrs. Drusse, a malingerer from hell, turns out to be a psychic investigating the murder in 1919 of a child whose spirit still haunts the building. As for the staff: the houseman extracts cocaine from drugs in his basement lair; the Dane-hating Swedish consultant, under investigation for being an impostor, is seeking refuge in the Santería cult; the incompetent administrators have formed a self-protective lodge the Masons would be proud of; and the chorus-like kitchen staff have Down Syndrome. As the cauldron begins to boil, heads are cut off and a surgeon decides to transplant a necrotic organ into himself for research. Where will it end?

Talking in an exclusive Knightsbridge hotel, the fortysomething von Trier casts a less daunting figure than expected. His casual clothes, stubbly face, and flop of hair make him seem quite avuncular—less the piercing, prickly intellectual than a discreet retired security agent. There's a feeling of a mas-

From *Time Out* #1324, 3 January 1996. Reprinted by permission of *Time Out*.

sive ego present, but under wraps. He adopts an air of cautious friendliness, a prudent response, no doubt, to his previous penchant for indiscretion, whether his infamous diatribe against Roman Polanski at Cannes or his hurt reactions to charges of racism over *Europa*. When I query a quote of his about how people should approach his films as if they were dreams, so as to use the subconscious as well the conscious, he answers smilingly: "Well, that's my problem. I've said so many things!"

The ambitious *Europa*—a bad dream of a movie about a German returning to the Heimat and its post-WW II ghosts—divided the critics and his previous fans alike, and was a box-office underachiever. This disappointment may explain his tetchiness. There have been long gaps between his features (three films in ten years), though these have been plugged with regular TV work, which has been of such an innovative nature as to make him a considerable force and celebrity in his own country.

Lars von Trier accounts for the newfound humor in *The Kingdom* in terms of the need for speed and responsiveness when working for television. He scripted the 35-mm miniseries quickly with collaborator Niels Vørsel, "and we certainly had a lot of fun, and almost no time to think things over too much. But the inspiration is serious enough because it's based on the fear we have of science, of A&E departments, of hospitals, of the power people might have over you there. But it's shown in a humoristic way, although we allow ourselves to be more than humoristic sometimes. What I think is disturbing about the film is that we sometimes allow it to break its borders. Like at the end of episode one, with the girl with brain damage, suddenly it becomes much more serious than you ever thought. It sometimes makes these little jumps. I like films where you're not really sure what's going to happen; it makes you a little bit more—how shall I say—alert."

That edge-of-the-seat quality also derives from his continued surreal, disquieting cinematic style: *The Kingdom* has the same powerful hallmark images—the jaundiced colors, off-kilter camera angles and disturbing overlay of sound—as his earlier work. The use of surreal atmosphere, the subversion of soap opera clichés, the modernist palette, the horror beneath the overturned stone bring to mind another director of the unsettling and the bizarre—"Don't mention Lynch!" von Trier exclaims, with a laugh stiffened by severe intent. And indeed, while *The Kingdom* has much in common with, say, *Twin Peaks*, the informing mind comes from an altogether different direction. Perhaps it's a matter of the Old World and the New World, Europe and America. Von Trier's work is haunted by an often-unwanted penetration by a specific European past into the present, not least the legacy of Nazism and the Holocaust. For me, his nearest European counterpart is Umberto Eco; certainly *The Kingdom* is as great (and entertaining) a compendium of conspiracy and paranoia as Eco's *Foucault's Pendulum*. But cinema is a very different medium from that of writing.

"The subject of everything I have been doing has actually been the clash between nature and the mind, if you will. In *The Element of Crime* it was nature taking over again, and in *Europa* the same thing. So it's more or less the same story I'm telling here. Of course I'm a sceptic [he takes an age st-r-i-n-g-i-n-g out the word], well, not a sceptic in the sense that I'm frightened of science. I'm not so frightened of science, I'm fascinated by science, but the problem is maybe, more inside myself. . . ."

On a personal note, he describes the softening effect of having children, embracing the Catholic Church, and recent revelations about his ancestry. Nevertheless his new project, *Breaking the Waves* (shot recently in Scotland and Denmark with newcomer Emily Watson and *Naked*'s Katrin Cartlidge), about a couple coping with a near-fatal accident and recently described to me as a "*Götterdämmerung* romance," suggests that the forces of darkness still occupy his mind.

Control and Chaos

CHRISTIAN BRAAD THOMSEN/1996

IN 1981, WHILE GIVING a guest lecture at the National Film School of Denmark, I noticed that one of the directing students was listening with a strangely ecstatic smile on his face. At first glance one might have found it flattering, but I soon discovered that he was sitting there with his Sony Walkman on, listening to something other than the possible words of wisdom coming from the lecturer's mouth. What an arrogant bastard, I thought—he'll never amount to anything in the film industry.

I later found out the name of that student—it was Lars von Trier. Fifteen years later no other Danish film—ever—has had the impact on me that *Breaking the Waves* has had. And hardly any other contemporary film director is a more permanent feature of the international media scene than Lars von Trier is today. He is often described as coming off arrogant, but you wouldn't have to know him for very long in order to decipher this arrogance as an at times slightly awkward protectiveness, on account of an underlying vulnerability, which with *Breaking the Waves* is given full expression.

CHRISTIAN BRAAD THOMSEN: *Lars von Trier, what has happened to you—what made you abandon the cold formalism of* The Element of Crime *and* Europa *and suddenly make a film that goes straight to everyone's heart?*
LARS von TRIER: Actually, my family doesn't care for *Breaking the Waves*

From *Politiken* (Denmark), 5 July 1996. Also published in *Sydsvenska Dagbladet* (Sweden), 23 August 1996, and in *Positif* (France) #428, October 1996. Reprinted by permission of the author.

that much. My brother, for example, called me up yesterday to tell me that he found it even more repulsive on the second viewing. But I think that this film is precisely my reaction to the tastes that ruled my childhood, where sentimentality was totally forbidden.

The first film I wept while watching was the one about a little boy who gets a little wild pony and at the end he has to say goodbye to it—and when the horse is walking off toward the horizon, it turns around and gives him a last goodbye look before it moves on. That was really powerful. I don't remember the name of the story, but I guess it has several variations. It works every time, because it's also a story about having to say goodbye to your own childhood and venture into the unknown.

The values I present in *Breaking the Waves* are in total conflict with the conditioned responses of my childhood. Morten Korch[1] used to be a four-letter word, and in my family we were atheistic with almost religious conviction, so everything in cinema with religion and cheap sentimental effects was something that I was taught to avoid. I was taught, rather, to shoot for something more complicated—something that might not work as well. But that doesn't matter, there's no reason to exhibit things as shamelessly as I do in the film. Here you have the sappiest of lines, over and over—

CBT: *Well, I wouldn't agree with that.*

LvT: But it's true. On her deathbed, Bess says: "I'm sorry that I could not be good, Mother." That's nothing less than crying to heaven!

CBT: *But that's what you would say in a situation like that. When else would you say it?*

LvT: And she says, "Forgive me," just before she dies. No, kiss my ass, it couldn't be any worse.

---

1. Danish novelist (1876–1954) whose popular novels about rural life and conflicts between peasants and landed gentry became the basis for numerous widely seen adaptations during the '50s and '60s. At their worst, these films might be comparable to *Little House on the Prairie* directed by Ed Wood with music rejected by Lawrence Welk. *De røde heste* [*The Red Horses*], the first of these adaptations, was directed by Alice O'Fredericks and Jon Iversen and produced by ASA. In the mid '90s Zentropa/Lars von Trier purchased the rights to Korch's work, and to date this has led to two productions: *Stillebækken* [*Still Brook*], a popular TV series, was shown on Danish TV in 1999; the first Zentropa-produced, Korch-based feature, *Fruen fra Hamre* [*The Lady of Hamre*], directed by Katrine Wiedemann, was released during the spring of 2000.

CBT: *The same is heard from Fassbinder's* Effi Briest *on her deathbed.*

LvT: Yeah, and that's pretty bad, too.

CBT: *Was it Douglas Sirk who got you thinking along these lines?*

LvT: My interest in Douglas Sirk is really quite shallow. He has this really big cult name, but his films never really got to me on any emotional level, although it's interesting how he takes feelings seriously and works with them so uninhibitedly. It's also interesting how Fassbinder took off from him and then, evidently, reached emotional deliverance via Sirk.

CBT: *But what has led you into the themes of more direct emotional conflict that you are now working with?*

LvT: It's from religion. I was baptized a couple of years ago together with my daughter—which didn't turn me into a good Catholic, you definitely couldn't call me that. I mean, I just got divorced. But religion and the miracle have to a certain extent been present in my films from the start. At the end of *Images of a Relief,* the protagonist is raised over the treetops, and all of the films end with either some kind of deliverance or from God's point of view. This goes for *Europa* as well, where the protagonist drifts down the river and out to sea. When you drown, you tend to float in an upright position, because you still have a little air left in your lungs. Our original idea was, as he arrived out in the ocean, to let him unite with all of the other thousands of dead people, but that couldn't be done for practical economic reasons.

CBT: *It's interesting that your three cinema releases thus far—*The Element of Crime, Epidemic *and* Europa—*all attempt to depict a hypnotic state, although the films themselves have no hypnotic effect on me, while* Breaking the Waves *is a totally hypnotizing experience without using any means of hypnosis.*

LvT: We're definitely talking about a shift in style and I maintain that it's about what I was taught at home, which is: Show the method! If you have a table, for instance, you should show its rough surface and not try to polish it. I've always worked like that. Whenever I've used an effect, I've always shown it in the same frame, using back projection and whatnot. In *Breaking the Waves,* however, I venture further in my aim to deceive. We try to make it look like reality with the semi-documentary style, which means that it *is* hypnosis, while the other films are *about* hypnosis. Maybe it's all about going back to the hypnotizing look of the horse in the film from my childhood.

CBT: *Are you saying that you became a Catholic as a reaction to your childhood?*
LvT: Yeah, I think so. Religion was totally forbidden, and it has always interested me. At the same time I'm a neurotic person and my biggest problem in life is control or the lack of control. I can get insanely frightened of not being in control when I need to be. The greatest form of happiness for me, as I see it, would be to be able to accept the lack of control,—but that's an almost masochistic thought for me. For me, all the situations that cause anxiety are about the lack of control, especially bodily control, which is so maddeningly frightening to me.

As a child, you create all kinds of rituals to maintain control. I was very scared of the atom bomb, so every night when I went to bed I had to perform all these rituals to save the world. And from a psychological point of view, religion is a continuation of these childhood rituals, which are there to prevent everything from reverting back to chaos. But of course you can't consciously approach religion in that way, because then it's something other than a religion to you. I regard religion as I do miracles in that I don't believe in them but I hope for them to occur. Right now I guess I'm standing at a crossroads where the child who creates rituals in order to control the world meets the adult who creates a faith, in order to wholeheartedly embrace a religion. I'm in great need of a faith, dammit!

CBT: *What would you say if I said that I perceive* Breaking the Waves *as a blasphemous rather than religious film?*
LvT: That's very probable. Basically, I acquired my religion, so my situation is fundamentally different from the people who have grown up with it as a part of their culture. So it's probably blasphemous, but it also reflects a wish to encounter the naïve, because religion also contains a lot of naivete.

CBT: *But it's quite possible to be naïve without being religious—or religious without being naïve.*
LvT: Definitely. But for me religion is also a quest for a childhood I never had. And the fundament is this book from my childhood, called *Golden Heart*, a picture book about a little girl who goes out in the woods with some bread crumbs in her apron and on her way she gives away both her food and her clothes. And when the rabbit or the squirrel tells her that now she doesn't have a skirt on, her answer is the same every time: "I'll be all right." And my father always mocked those words. For him, they embodied the

spirit of Morten Korch. She was some kind of martyr, which was the most ludicrous thing to be in my childhood home. In *Breaking the Waves*, I've taken as seriously as possible all the things that were never taken seriously in my family—and that's why my family now reacts the way it does towards the film.

On the other hand, the film is inspired not only by the children's story, but also by De Sade's *Justine*, which I for years have had plans to adapt for film. It's a quite short story about a girl who is the victim to a series of evil acts, who's repeatedly exploited, raped, or whipped by everyone she meets. But at the same time, Justine possesses some kind of self-righteousness that my protagonist does not possess. In the end Justine thanks God for his goodness in letting her survive all the calamities—after which she is struck by lightning and burns to death.

I set out to make a melodrama with a female protagonist, like Dreyer, who always uses female protagonists. And I wanted it to include a real miracle, and it had to be credible. Not like in *Miracle in Milan*—

CBT: *And probably not like the miracle in Dreyer's Ordet [The Word]. That couldn't be called credible either?*
LvT: I don't think I agree with you on that.

CBT: *Well, at least not after Dreyer deleted Kaj Munk's line about those coroners not doing a thorough enough job!*
LvT: But it's credible enough. It's about taking the miracle seriously. Dreyer's film about Jesus was supposed to end with the crucifixion, but he stressed that he wouldn't mind having it ending with the resurrection, that is, the miracle. It was just more practical to end with the crucifixion. As a general rule, Dreyer goes for the miracle.

CBT: *But here it's possible to experience the film without ever experiencing the miracle.*
LvT: Yes, but my starting point would be that I'm trying to depict a miracle. I would believe in it myself.

CBT: *But is it still a miracle if we other ungodly souls don't experience it as a miracle?*
LvT: You would accept it in the context of the film. It would seem credible

in the film, but it can of course only be credible in relation to the film. If I could depict a miracle that was credible in relation to reality, then I would say that I've reached a higher level that I'm at today. But on the other hand, a miracle shouldn't have to be credible in relation to reality, for then it's not a miracle.

C B T : *But to me everything that happens in the film is believable, in relation to reality as well. It could just as well have happened in real life, and then we wouldn't have called it a miracle.*

L v T : Well, except for those bells—

C B T : *Now, don't be so hard on the bells. As I wrote to you in my thank-you card from Cannes, I have now, after having seen the bells, retracted my warning to you against using them at all. They work in the film, but as a concluding comment on the part of the director and of course not as a realistic feature.*

L v T : The thing that makes the bells a little bit unfortunate is this recurring thing we have with the chapter headings, which is some sort of abstraction. And of course it can be fun to have the layers melting together in the end, but there's still something unfortunate about the fact that the bells will be regarded in the same way as the chapter headings, and that wasn't what I intended.

C B T : *My personal opinion is that it was Dreyer's tragedy that the talking picture was invented. But wherein lies your fascination with Dreyer?*

L v T : Primarily in his pure, absolute style, which I find very beautiful. There's a little of Hammershöi [Danish turn-of-the-century painter] in it, and not only visually—the themes and dialogue are also very minimized. And then I respect him for always going against the flow of the age. I have a tremendous respect for the rebels, and I definitely think that he was one of them, Or—if you will—a martyr. He suffered at any rate as the result of con- demnation.

C B T : *To how large an extent did you base* Medea *on Dreyer's original script?*

L v T : It is Dreyer's script that is the foundation of *Medea.*

C B T : *And your Morten Korch trip, that has to be a part of your childhood rebel- lion, right?*

LvT: Yes, in a way. I asked his son Morten A. Korch which of the films his father valued the most, and it was the two earliest, *De røde heste* [*The Red Horses*, 1950] and *Mosekongen* [*King of the Moor*, 1950], both by Alice O'Fredericks—he thought all the rest were terrible. And you have to say that he's right about *De røde heste*—it's actually a good film—but I don't think that *Mosekongen* is very good. The crucial thing about *De røde heste* is that the film is very close to the book.

CBT: *Are you going to direct some Morten Korch yourself?*
LvT: It's not my plan for the moment but you never know. For the time being I will act as some sort of creative producer and be a part of the design of the projects. There's no doubt that we will try to be true to the original form, and that we'll try to film the novels as literature, completely without irony but still with the cheerful tone of the books. In *De røde heste* there are for example no songs, but on the other hand it has a rather complex story line. But then already in the next film they get scared of the story line and start to simplify it. In *De røde heste* they get married without being in love and that happens in a lot of the other books as well. And either love comes strolling down the path or it doesn't come at all.

The later Morten Korch films are pure muck, awfully shallow, and they get gaudier and gaudier and there are more and more insipid songs and show numbers in them. They've done their share to ruin our image of Morten Korch. But all those conceptions that we have of Morten Korch clichés, they don't hold up. It's not all cotton candy at all. Of course there's always a happy ending but the road that leads to it is much more nuanced than we think. He often tells some really good stories and they could definitely be the basis of a serious film. So my idea is to perceive these books as literature—because there's also a bit of *Ditte, Child of Man* [*Ditte menneskebarn*, 1946; an award-winning film and one of the true classics of Danish cinema] in them—and then treat them cinematically with the appropriate seriousness. I think the time is ripe for that instead of those superficial [popular heist comedies] Olsen Gang-like Morten Korch films, that we're accustomed to seeing.

Lars von Trier does not care to lift the veil on the four new episodes of the television series *The Kingdom*, which he is currently shooting. When they are completed, an additional five episodes will be made. The only thing he (somewhat triumphantly) wants to say about it is that—unlike David Lynch with *Twin Peaks*—he knows full well how it all is going to end. Which Lynch didn't.

CBT: *With all the research that you've done at Rigshospitalet, have you got any opinions on the unrest they've had during these last couple of months?*

LvT: Of course I'm opposed to cutbacks in health care. They can save money in so many other places. I'm glad my old father isn't around to see all this happening under a Social Democrat majority. My father was a Social Democrat of the old school and had a strong social conscience.

Already beforehand I felt a great deal of anxiety about everything connected with hospitals, and now there's no doubt that the level of service will go down. Both my kids were born at Rigshospitalet and the level of service wasn't that high, even then. I don't understand how they could lower it even further.

CBT: *When I saw* Epidemic *again some time ago, it amazed me that you with your phobias dared to attend an autopsy at all. But perhaps it's all fake?*

LvT: Of course it's fake. We did something very smart: we covered the face of the man that they were going to examine, and that was a stroke of genius because then the audience would think that it's a real autopsy since they wouldn't see the identity of the person getting cut into. The cutters were indeed real pathologists, but everything took place on Niels Vørsel's dining-room table and they took tissue samples from the organs of a pig.

I really have a warm relationship with that film. Of my earlier films it's the one that I like the most. But, incidentally, something very interesting about that film was precisely the reaction to our mix of realism and fiction. I showed it to five members of the Danish Broadcasting Corporation, DRTV, who wanted to buy it unseen on the grounds that they had been so pleased with *The Element of Crime*. But I still thought that they should have a look at it first, and afterwards they said that never before had they been so in agreement as they were now: this was the worst film they'd ever seen. So they didn't buy it.

And Morten Piil from *Information* was furious. We had already started to play around with the documentary look back then, particularly in a scene we were roundly criticized for by Morten Piil. It was the one where Udo Kier tells the story about his mother's death in a bombing raid during the war. Morten Piil's opinion is that we're exploiting Kier's private grief and ridiculing it in the way that Niels Vørsel and myself are shown listening to it. But first of all, we filmed the shots of us listening at a different time. It does not reflect our real reaction to the story—it's pure fiction. And second, Udo Kier's story is also fiction. It's a text that I wrote for him, based on some things he told me. Third, we were never in his apartment in Cologne—we couldn't afford to go there—so that scene was shot in my home, and the park where the bombs supposedly rained down is shot in Copenhagen. It's all fiction, but this supposedly reflected our arrogance towards Udo Kier's tragedy.

In connection to *Breaking the Waves*, Lars von Trier has not shied away from admitting that he suffers from serious phobias. For instance, during the shooting of the film, he would under no circumstances allow himself to be flown by helicopter to the oilrig where some of the crucial scenes took place. So he sent his director's assistant Morten Arnfred instead, together with the crew, while Lars remained ashore, where he then via closed-circuit television could follow the happenings on the set and give his instructions accordingly.

Two months before Cannes, Lars called me up and asked if I knew of a psychiatrist who might be able to help him out with his phobias, since he very much would like to go to Cannes with his film and since the condition he was in at the moment made it unthinkable for him to go.

I attempted what would later turn out to be a rather bad joke about the fact that one should cultivate one's phobias in our business for they can indeed be a source of inspiration. To which Lars quietly replied that he had all the inspiration he needed and would like to have a little less of it.

In contrast, von Trier's producer Peter Aalbæk Jensen has taken those phobias in stride. He is quite certain that it will never be possible for Hollywood to get its hands on von Trier, as he simply won't dare to travel there.

CBT: *Lars, what happened, really, when you failed in your attempt to attend your world premiere at Cannes?*

LvT: If I'm going to do something I'm afraid of, I usually start to worry months in advance, picturing in my head all the things that can go wrong. It was unthinkable for me to fly to Cannes. I was going to go by train because that's where I feel the safest. But when Bente and I arrived at the Copenhagen Central, it turned out that it wasn't a German Intercity train we were going with, something I'd been counting on the whole time. It was a Danish IC-3, which would have meant a very claustrophobic experience for me. It's an awful development, I think, that you can no longer open a window—

instead they have electronic air conditioning and automatic locks. You're totally locked in, in contrast to the German trains, where you can still open the windows and get some fresh air. They're wonderful, those German trains.

So Bente and I sat for a quarter of an hour and waited inside the train and considered the situation. And just before the doors shut, I had a panic attack and rushed out. So then and there the Cannes trip was cut short, because the mental preparations had collapsed. We did, however, rent a car and we got all the way to Puttgarden, but that night I realized that it was no use. I have no anxiety when I'm driving on a freeway, as long as things are moving, but I imagined all the traffic jams we were going to get in on the way down and even that made me claustrophobic. When things stand still I become afraid of the fear.

I think phobias in themselves are to a large extent a form of self-punishment. If you've worked for five years on a project that you have a good feeling about and that you expect will be well received, then you're punishing yourself when you won't allow yourself to enjoy the good reception. The same thing, kind of, happened at the grand opening here in Copenhagen last week—it's an event you look forward to from the first day of shooting, but I had to decline again. I had the dinner jacket on and off several times, but had to give it up in the end, because I had the feeling that I'd be trapped in the middle of all these people. Adversity and setbacks are easier to handle than prosperity and good fortune, which are very difficult to handle—and anxiety-provoking! I work much better with my back to the wall. Once there, I'll fight to the last drop of blood.

My own thoughts on these phobias are that I have been living too long with the philosophy that I have to go through a lot of evil before things will turn good. This reasoning has permeated my whole existence. It's very hard to make a film, but when it's finally completed and I can enjoy myself, I won't permit myself that period of enjoyment, I won't allow myself the satisfaction. It's like a birth trauma, some kind of repression I have to get through before I can enjoy it. And my whole life turns into this great act of repression that I'm stuck in. It also has something to do with control: what counts in this life is the ability to enjoy the ride out of the maternal womb because after that there's nothing more to it. If I can reach that point, it would be a great step.

CBT: *It's like the old saying "The journey is the goal and the answer is the question."*

LvT: Yes, there's no doubt about that. And I realize this intellectually, but I can't yet feel it emotionally. Because I think that these ideas about control and chaos stem from my upbringing, which was unbelievably lax. There were no rules whatsoever, which creates a lot of problems, like deciding when you should go to the dentist, because everything's up to you yourself. And in that case, you end up not getting things done and that creates a lot of anxiety. I also had to force myself to do my homework, because no one told me when I had to do it. When there's nobody to enforce discipline upon you, then you have to enforce it from within. That, in return, has made me incredibly disciplined at my work today—I work all the time. But at the same time it's a tremendous source of anxiety that everything is *your* decision. Of course this has given me great faith in my own creativity—almost like a christening gift.

I'll soon turn forty, I have a wonderful girlfriend, I feel content with my work, and I can finally start enjoying life instead of anointing it with rules and rituals in order to survive. Now I would like to relax and enjoy life, and I have tried—which has resulted in this bubble of anxiety.

Both *Breaking the Waves* and *The Kingdom* have been an outlet for these things. It's been a great pleasure to do these films. They are freer, looser in their language, while my earlier films were characterized by discipline, and that's why you call them cold and that's what they are. They were difficult to make—there was hard and unpleasant work connected with them, whereas the collaboration with the actors on *Breaking the Waves* was a great, great pleasure. And *The Kingdom* was fun to make. Together, those two films express the fact that I'm now enjoying the journey, and not only the final destination. But then there's also the backlash: the phobias that have always been there and which I've until now been able to keep in check, they're blooming like mad these days. But my hope is of course that during this flowering season I'll be able to root them out, once and for all.

The Man Who Would Give Up Control

PETER ØVIG KNUDSEN/1998

PETER ØVIG KNUDSEN: *Is the purpose of both Dogme95 and* The Idiots *to give up control?*

LARS von TRIER: Yes, you couldn't put it more precisely. Now you've pigeonholed them. So we don't need to talk any more. .

The film director Lars von Trier is not inclined to describe his artistic achievements in words; he would rather show clips and out-takes from his new Dogme film, *The Idiots*, about a group of young adults who move into a large empty house in a leafy suburb to "spazz about"—i.e., act like spastics or idiots. Lars von Trier has donned the big clogs and placed this journalist in a pair of muddy rubber boots with the mission of forging out into the similarly muddy yard behind the von Trier family house on the outskirts of Lyngby—the same backyard where he shot his first 8-mm films as a boy. At the edge of the yard, he has erected "Puttely," an oblong wooden building, where he, with a view of Ravneholm Forest and Søllerød, has just finished the editing of his new film, using the latest version of the Avid computer editing equipment.

PØK: *You are very pleased with the film?*

LvT: I am very pleased with the film. I tried to imbue it with life and light-ness, and I've succeeded. Some people say it's all very silly, and yes, that is

From *Weekendavisen*, 11 May 1998. This article, in abridged form, also appears in the press kit for *The Idiots*. Reprinted by permission of the author.

exactly what it is. In some places, disastrously silly: malicious, foolish, and meaningless silliness. But the film contains other facets.

If you examine the history of the cinema the way I'm constantly doing, I've tried to seek some of the lightness and enjoyment possessed by the films I refer to with *The Idiots*: the French New Wave, and what I call the Swinging London period—including the Beatles films where they ran through London carrying a giant iron bedstead. The New Wave was a breath of fresh air, and in the same way Dogme95 has been designed to provide a breath of fresh air, to regain lost innocence.

P Ø K: With *Breaking the Waves you wanted to make women cry, and you succeeded. What kind of reactions are you hoping for this time?*

L v T: *The Idiots* is a more complex, far weirder film, a film you ought to be amused and moved by, but also a bit disturbed by. The film is dangerous because it plays with the concept of normalcy—with the way we ought to and ought not to behave. And if one devalues rationality, the world tends to fall apart.

P Ø K: *Some people will be indignant about some scenes, but hardly about the film as a whole. For one of its features is that it keeps giving off contradictory signals.*

L v T: In old-fashioned terms, you might say it's a more political film than the ones I've made before. On the surface it's about our attitudes to the mentally handicapped and how much we appreciate them. At a deeper level it must appear to be in defense of abnormality.

The idea for *The Idiots* arose at the same time as the Dogme project. At one level the Dogme rules emerged from a desire to submit to the authority and the rules I was never given during my humanistic, cultural-leftist upbringing. At another level they express the desire to make something quite simple. In a normal film production you are hampered by having to make decisions about and control an infinite number of things such as filters and colors. The Dogme95 rules basically say that you mustn't do any of that.

P Ø K: *You're responsible for the script, which states that it was "written May 16—19, 1997." Surely you didn't complete it in four days?*

L v T: Yes, I did. Actually it's a phrase I got from good ol' Marquis de Sade, who wrote *Justine* in the Bastille in a fortnight, I believe it was. Of course I'd toyed with a couple of ideas beforehand, but I hadn't written a single cue, and it was a wonderful feeling to just write away. I haven't even reread it, as you can see in one place where a character has been given the wrong name for an entire scene."

In the past I spent years writing each script, but it was more Dogme-like to give up control. The whole idea is to shake the dust off yourself. Or maybe "dust yourself off" sounds too easy—"cast off the burdens" is more like it. If you go on correcting a script you may lose your enthusiasm. It almost happened in this process, too, when we spent ages changing scenes and moving back and forth. But in the end we returned to the original, and the final version of the film is very close to the script. So unless *The Idiots* exudes enjoyment or at least the joy of filmmaking, the project will have failed completely.

P Ø K : *In your introduction to the script you write about "avoiding dramaturgy"?*
L v T : Yes, but then, it would be difficult to avoid breathing while you're still alive. It's a contradiction in terms, because no matter what choice you make, it's dramaturgy. Dogme95 contains a few impossible, paradoxical rules, but the same goes for religious dogmas, too.

The essence of my dramaturgical considerations is that I want to chuck out the most superfluous, habitual constraints and escape from rigidity, but at the same time film is a means of communication. Joyce also wanted to escape from rigidity, but it gradually grows difficult to communicate with others apart from yourself. I liked *Ulysses* very, very much, but *Finnegan's Wake* is not easy reading—you have to have a command of at least four or five languages and have considerable knowledge of the customs of different culture groups.

P Ø K : *Compared to the script, some of the scenes must have been improvised?*
L v T : Yes. I encouraged the cast to make up their own lines. Altogether, my initial approach was pretty nursery-school-like: "Come along, let's see what you can do and what you feel like." And of course everything ground to a halt, as many people have been forced to realize before me. Actors need bricks to play with, and in fact we rejected all the improvised fragments we had made without a plan. Improvisation without a plan is like tennis without tennis balls.

The do-as-you-feel approach also resulted in people taking a very relaxed view about turning up at work on time. The same applied to the idea that the crew would do its own cooking and housekeeping, which resulted in the worst manifestations of house-sharing: everything was a mess and got incredibly foul. So in the end I had to make the great "freedom with responsibility" speech.

P Ø K : *Did the spazzing spread to when you weren't shooting?*
L v T : In the weeks preceding the shooting we worked a great deal on the spazzing, and the cast became very fond of spazzing. But gradually they simply got bored if they didn't have to spazz. And as an outsider, as time goes by you become quite unaffected by spazzing, whereas at first it was pretty distracting to have someone drooling down your trousers.

The spazzing bit finally functioned quite naturally, as did the nude scenes, which we had loads of. One morning I greeted the cast naked on the front drive and insisted that today was to be a nude day. No, we didn't have any nudity problems.

In many ways the six weeks of shooting was the most intense film experience I've ever had. Also because I operated one of the cameras myself, and my own footage actually comprises 80 or 90 percent of the finished film, I was frantically geared up the whole time and practically didn't sleep at night.

Lars von Trier clicks on the editing computer until he gets to footage of the two female leads, on whom he spends hours using therapeutic techniques in order to invoke authentic feelings of grief—filming nonstop all the while.

P Ø K : *You once said you preferred having as little to do with actors as possible because otherwise they insist on your playing the therapist. And what are you doing now . . . ?*
L v T : Only a fool doesn't fear actors, but you can't beat them, and if you can't beat them, join them, as they say. As I've gotten older I've become very interested in that part of the work.

Trier clicks forward to a "forest scene" to illustrate the consequences of the Dogme rules:

L v T : During shooting it turned out that the Dogme rule that sound and picture must not be produced separately was a very interesting rule. In fact it was in this way that the very first sound movies were made, but since then it has become more and more of a virtue to produce the two facets separately. The rule means—as I interpret it—that you're not allowed to do anything with the sound or the picture after shooting: sound and picture hang together, and neither may be changed or moved afterwards. This means that we often edited according to the sound instead of the picture, because if you require a particular sound or cue, you have to use the picture that accompanies it, which has meant weirder pictures and peculiar differences between the sound and the picture, compared to the intended result.

In the forest scene we had put a mike up a tree to capture the ambient sound. . . . It's like reinventing movie-making, don't you see? Bringing the ambience forward instead of the sound of the scene itself is a common, simple effect, but now it suddenly became difficult to achieve because the decisions had to be made on the spot. A load of cinematic effects that otherwise seem easy or cheap to me suddenly become difficult again. . . . Can't you hear that this is the only way of doing it? I was thrilled to bits after that day in the woods. It was like returning to the poetry that I encountered when I began making films as a child.

PØK: *There is also music in the scene—isn't that cheating?*

LvT: No. We used a harmonica, the kind you could buy through *Mickey Mouse Magazine* in the old days, and simply brought in the harmonica player when we had scenes with music. In the forest scene he stood in the forest with a microphone as we shot the scene, and the sound engineer mixed the music and speech as we shot. When we do the closing credits tomorrow, he'll play in the same way while we're filming them.

He clicks forward to the "skiing scene":

LvT: Another Dogme rule is that you mustn't bring in props, but in the house we found some old skis, and we took them with us to the ski jump in Holte and shot a ski scene in midsummer—that's Dogme in a nutshell. And the dogs you hear in the background now I would normally have avoided, but all of a sudden they fit! But of course it's possible that I'm the only person who can take pleasure in things like that.

Also, we weren't allowed to use artificial tears or artificial blood. When it came to the tears, the actors had to cry for real, and the same went for the blood. Nikolai Lie Kaas got a real nosebleed, and Bodil Jørgensen cracked an eyebrow and was already on her way to the emergency room when I managed to stop her and get my shots in the can.

PØK: *The film also features countless visible mike and boom drops and even a couple of cameramen. . . .*

LvT: Yes, after a while you get really tired of counting all the mistakes! The agreement with the audience is the most important thing, and it's perfectly all right to include both mikes and booms in the picture. If you're present at a fire, you won't notice the photographers—you'll watch the fire.

PØK: *But have you even downright aspired to include as many boom mikes as possible in the film?*

LvT: No, when you shoot, you of course try to avoid the boom mikes, but at the same time I haven't been that afraid to include them. If I'm shooting something really interesting, then I couldn't care less about boom mikes— and I expect the audience to feel the same.

In many of the scenes, the actors change clothes from one shot to another. According to the rules, the actors were supposed to wear their own clothes and if they changed, it sometimes meant that we in the finished film cut back and forth to a person who alternately would have his shirt on and off. The interesting thing is that people hardly notice.

PØK: *When you made* Europa, *a technically advanced film, you told me that it was such a joy to carry out these "hitherto unseen technical achievements." Is it, this time around, a joy to do the opposite of that, maybe a little revolt . . . ?*

LvT: That's probably a part of my nature, yes. But it's also a question of liberating oneself from the inconsequential, in order to be able to focus on the essential. In order to find our way into reality, we don't give a hoot about boom mikes and other conventions. And if we do find a second of truth, well, then screw the rest!

PØK: *And what is truth, then?*

LvT: To hang a mike up in a tree, to use a couple of toothpicks instead of a gigantic technical apparatus, this provides one form of cinematic truth. Or at least it gets more real. Truth is about searching an area in order to find something, but if you already beforehand know what you're looking for, then it's manipulation. Maybe truth is finding something you're not looking for. . . . Wasn't that very poetically put?

P Ø K : *Is the next step to do a pure documentary?*
L v T : It's very easy for us to get into a lengthy discussion on whether documentary is reality or not. Fiction is still important to me, however. I have always enjoyed English parks, where the landscape is imitated with a little cave and a slightly neglected area overgrown with ferns—it's all calculated coincidences. But the next step could be a semi-documentary form where you put some fictional elements in, to provoke psychical reactions. You could perfectly well take *The Idiots* idea one step further, towards the psychodrama.

P Ø K : *This movement exists in order to approach emotions more than they were approached before, right?*
L v T : Yes. The emotions have always been the inspiration. Before they were a little stiffer, whereas they now express themselves to a fuller extent. Vibeke Windeløv, my producer, asked me if *The Idiots* was number two in my "Golden Heart" trilogy after *Breaking the Waves*, and I can only confirm that she is right about that.

P Ø K : *Do you also have a need to spazz out in the cream cake in the middle of afternoon tea in the closing scene?*
L v T : Oh, I think I've always had that need. Tom Elling, my old cameraman, always talked about "the dirty trading stamps." There are two kinds of stamps—the dirty ones and the decent ones—but the dirty ones are just as good. I mean the ones you get for negative coverage or behavior.

P Ø K : *But the "idiot" and "spazzing" themes go well with the desire to lose control?*
L v T : Yes, that was my intention, but the film contradicts itself in a way, because the group does not succeed. Maybe it only works out for the lead, Karen, and that might be the moral of the film. My films have become highly moral recently.

P Ø K : *And the moral is . . . ?*
L v T : The moral is that you can practice the technique—the Dogme tech-

nique or the idiot technique—from now until kingdom come without anything coming of it unless you have a profound, passionate desire and the need to do so. Karen discovers that she needs the technique, and therefore it changes her life. Idiocy is like hypnosis or ejaculation: if you want it, you can't have it—and if you don't want it, you can.

PØK: *Have you become more of an idiot through making this film?*
LvT: I don't think that's possible. . . . No, it's probably kind of like my own therapy: I sit there pouring out my woes year after year, coming up with one enormity after another about my mother and the way she let me down, but it doesn't make me any less fearful.

PØK: *Your films and your success have no therapeutic effect on you?*
LvT: I don't feel they do, no. The last year has been more full of fear than ever before. . . . But on the personal level, each of my films is a little monument . . . and this film has been a very cheap, though very tiring, monument. The genesis of these monuments becomes what life is all about, and so it's hard to quit. . . . It becomes an addiction of sorts.

He is silent for a while.

LvT: My biggest problem, down deep, is that I can't allow myself to be happy.

He grabs his bangs and smiles.

LvT: Have you seen this—I've cut my bangs. They were hanging down in my eyes and Bente was very displeased. So I picked up a pair of scissors from the kitchen. That's how vain a person I am. . . .

Tracing the Inner Idiot

EBBE IVERSEN / 1998

A FRIENDLY LARS VON TRIER greets us in the charming wooden building that functions as his study high up in the hilly garden behind his big white house north of Copenhagen. The idyllic spot has a view of green nature, and it's absolutely clear that this internationally admired filmmaker feels very comfortable here, far from the turmoil of the outside world.

And far from the media—for Lars von Trier does not give interviews. But he once promised that if he one day did in fact give one, it would be for *Berlingske Tidene*. And being a man of honor he now keeps his promise, and—seemingly—without for one moment regarding it as a tedious duty, at that.

On the contrary, for he makes us tea and asks us where we would like to sit. But before this he has asked us to remove our shoes and offers us a pair of soft slippers, ready at hand for the purpose. Lars von Trier explains that this rule is not his own, but his cleaning lady's: otherwise the beautiful floor gets so dirty that she won't clean it. "And one better listen to one's cleaning lady," he explains with a smile.

The topic of our conversation is of course the fact that Lars von Trier's new film *The Idiots* has been chosen for competition for the Golden Palm at the Cannes festival—which will commence tomorrow—where the forty-two-year-old director already has reaped honors for both *The Element of Crime*, *Europa*, and *Breaking the Waves*. But let's start with the question about Lars von Trier's reasons for choosing to avoid the media.

From *Berlingske Tidene*, 12 May 1998. Reprinted by permission of the author.

LARS VON TRIER: When you become a person of public interest—and this continues to amaze me—you will be asked questions on everything between heaven and earth, as if you had a well-thought-out opinion on everything, and of course you don't. For me personally, I've reached the point of nausea, and I feel very comfortable no longer talking to anyone.

EBBE IVERSEN: *Two years ago, when* Breaking the Waves *competed at Cannes and was the favorite of many, you did not attend the festival. Do you plan to attend this year?*

LvT: Yes, I will try to go to Cannes this year, but I still haven't made any promises. Whether the director is present or not should not affect the evaluation of his film. I was, however, very sorry not to have been there at that point. Of course you want to be present at the opening of your film, and two years ago I did in fact manage to get into Germany on the way to Cannes, but that was it. And having to spend the night in Puttgarden couldn't be anyone's idea of a dream come true.

The reason for Lars von Trier's abortive attempt to reach the festival was his problematic relation to traveling and has nothing to do with arrogance. And this day in May, in the well-cleaned study of Lars von Trier, there are certainly no signs of arrogance, awkwardness, or the other troublesome character traits attributed to this director, who could not be more accommodating, cheerful, and relaxed. He is a likeable man, who tells us that he really hopes to get to Cannes this year, because he feels he is in much better shape at this point.

Just like Thomas Vinterberg's *Festen* [U.S. title *The Celebration*], which also has been chosen for competition at Cannes, *The Idiots* is a so-called Dogme film, based on a "vow of chastity," whose ten commandments among other things dictate that the film be made on location and take place here and now, and forbid all superficial action (murder, weapons, etc.). Lars von Trier explains the Dogme principles:

LvT: In 1995, I called Thomas Vinterberg up and asked him if he wanted to come along and create a new wave. He said he'd be delighted. The Dogme rules are—just like in a religion—impossible to abide by, but they provide some guidelines, and I needed some of that at the time. I needed to lose control, and in that way I was very egotistical in inventing these Dogme rules. Yes it's true, they're pretty tough to abide by, but that makes it a scream to make the film, and I think that Thomas would agree with that, in spite of the big differences between the two films we've made based on this concept. His is a modern one while mine goes back to the roots of the—nowadays ancient—French New Wave. But in those days things really happened with cinema, also in Sweden and in Great Britain.

My film is about a group of young people who try to live like idiots. It's inspired by the French film *Blow-Out* and the Danish film *Weekend,* which is a great movie, and *The Idiots* could very well be said to be the modern version of *Weekend*—a kind of group portrait or an ensemble comedy. The film was made in five weeks and I've shot about 90 percent of it myself, with a small handheld camcorder for amateurs. This gives a great difference in that if the camera is curious, it's really you yourself who are curious. And all this talk about the handheld camera—we started to use it in *The Kingdom*, inspired by the American television series *Homicide: Life on the Street*, and there's even more of the handheld camera in *The Idiots*. The advantage of shooting with video is that you can record very long scenes—we created scenes that were up to an hour long and then we cut them down later on.

E I :   *Sexually—at least according to rumors—your film is supposed to be very candid.*

L v T :   I don't agree at all. Well, maybe a little, but only in a small section of the film. I'd rather not go into it any more at this juncture, but I can promise male frontal nudity, and that will probably not be approved in America. Of course you could place a black rectangle in front of the guy, but then the question is whether it should go horizontally or vertically. But *The Idiots* is not an erotic film at all. I have always wanted to make a porno movie, but unfortunately this one hasn't become one of those. In fact, I feel that this one is rather quaint.

E I :   *You have included the frequently nude model Trine Michelsen in the cast, however. . . .*

L v T :   Yes, she was brilliant and very sweet. It was somewhat of a psycho-drama, the birth of this film, and I'm a little proud of the fact that I wrote it in just four days. And, no, not because there was a great creative out-burst—we just had to have the script ready in time. It will, by the way, be available in printed form from Gyldendal Publishing and my detailed diary from the making of the film will be included.

At this point, a very interested Lars von Trier asks me how Bille August's *Les Miserables* is doing in America at the moment. And when I tell him that it's doing great and that it was the fourth biggest motion picture at the box office after its opening weekend, he looks pleased—no jealousy to be found here. Lars von Trier tells us that *The Idiots* will open in Denmark in early July, while the French will schedule their premiere to coincide with the Cannes Film Festival in May, in no fewer than seventy prints. And with a contented smile he adds:

LvT: We've also made a recording with the film. I only sing on one side, though—the other side is pure idiot stuff—but I've taken singing lessons from [Blue Note recording artist] Cæcilie Nørby, and it will be a tasty morsel for any discophile! And then we have the Morten Korch television series where I've been involved at the script-writing stage, and we're also preparing a Morten Korch feature, which I will not direct. And then I hope that after Cannes I can move on to my planned musical, with the working title *Dancer in the Dark*. Originally it was going to be called "Taps," but that title was already "occupied" and we have to be careful, otherwise we might be stampeded by a whole herd of brief-toting lawyers.

EI: *So, your forthcoming film won't be pure Dogme, then?*
LvT: No, but it would be fun to make a couple more of those. I'd really like that, it's so much like going on vacation. It's like being a nudist and not having to worry about what you aren't wearing—there is, by the way, a little bit of nudism in *The Idiots*, which is one of those ingredients that makes the film a little old-fashioned. I had an uncle who was a nudist and used to open the front door of his home dressed in nothing but his cigar.

With this we remove the soft slippers, and it's on with the shoes and out in the green surroundings, so that the photographer can get a couple of good pictures of Lars von Trier. He himself suggests that he stand on the nearby railway track—then the photographer can get a really good shot when the train comes. And just before we say our good-byes, he tells us that he has written a letter to the Japanese master director Akira Kurosawa and suggested that he make a Dogme film. Since the project would be so straightforward, Kurosawa could do it without worrying about the fact that he's reached a rather high age, no? We then set course for Copenhagen again, with that nice feeling that comes from spending an hour's time, not only with one of Denmark's most original and visionary filmmakers, but also in utterly pleasant company. One crosses one's fingers and hopes that he will reach Cannes this year.

Dogme Is Dead! Long Live Song and Dance!

JØRN ROSSING JENSEN/1998

DANISH DIRECTOR LARS VON TRIER and his three co-signatories of the Dogme95 manifesto—Thomas Vinterberg, Søren Kragh-Jacobsen, and Kristian Levring—have decided that they will no longer authorize new Dogme films. In the future any film may achieve a Dogme certificate, if the director claims in a sworn statement that it was produced from the Danish 1995 vow of chastity.

"Of course they can cheat, but they are essentially cheating themselves. Dogme was never intended as a shield you could hide behind. The more fashionable it has become, the more boring," said von Trier, as he called off the condition of approval by the four directors. "At some stage I had to get out of it anyway [well, "I've got to get out of this shit" is how he actually puts it]. I was never born to participate in collective resolutions."

Von Trier, Vinterberg, Kragh-Jacobsen, and Levring will all leave their—somewhat different—interpretations of Dogme95 on the Internet (www .dogme95.dk). If a filmmaker feels that his or her work applies to one of them, they are free to demand their certificate from a Dogme secretariat shortly to be established in Copenhagen. The licence will arrive by mail.

"The manifesto was in itself without any value, but it states a couple of limitations which can be useful to work from. I have always thought that the most important rule was that picture and sound should be recorded simultaneously. It excludes manipulation—you cannot cheat afterwards in the editing room. I am still using it as a principle when shooting.

From *The Independent*, 5 November 1998. Reprinted by permission of the author.

"When we originally discussed the vow of chastity, we had no ambitions to change the world, such as—for instance—the French *nouvelle vague*. But if in twenty-five years some film students accidentally excavate the manifesto and find the ten rules interesting, we will obviously be happy, but it was never our initial purpose," added von Trier.

Meanwhile, von Trier is halfway through editing his $15 million musical, *Dancer in the Dark*, starring the singer Björk and Catherine Deneuve ("She sent me a letter saying that she would like a part, and that has never happened to me before"). After having seen the first forty-five completed minutes of the film, Zentropa Entertainment's chief executive, Peter Aalbæk Jensen, decided not to make any presales at MIFED, but to wait for its presentation at Cannes 2000 as The Millennium Movie and demand a higher price.

"I have never before refused that much money," said sales director Thomas Mai, Thrust Film Sales, representing the film in Milan. Following von Trier's award-winning *Breaking the Waves*, *Dancer in the Dark* has so far sold the U.S., the U.K., Germany, and Scandinavia, besides going to France, Italy, and the Benelux through co-production agreements.

Originally signed solely to compose the score, former Sugarcube Björk (Guðmundsdóttir) makes her feature film debut[1] as Selma, a Czech immigrant and single mother working at a factory in rural America. Her salvation is a passion for music, especially classic Hollywood musicals. But she harbors a sad secret: she is losing her eyesight, and her ten-year-old son stands to suffer the same fate.

With a cast including Jean-Marc Barr, David Morse, Stellan Skarsgård, Peter Stormare, and Udo Kier, *Dancer in the Dark* is described by von Trier as a big film, a musical melodrama colliding with real life, "with dance sequences shot simultaneously by 100 fixed Sony DV-cam cameras." In the end Selma makes the ultimate sacrifice—giving her life—to save her son's eyes.

"When shooting I felt like Albert Speer, who was able to control everything. We filmed one special dance routine, moved the cameras once, and ended up with 120 hours of footage from the same scene. It's definitely the most difficult production I have ever undertaken," he said of the film, which concludes the trilogy of *Breaking the Waves* and *The Idiots*.

---

1. Contrary to general assumption—as well as Björk's own statement of *Dancer in the Dark* being her "first and last film"—her acting debut was in 1987, in the Icelandic-American film *Juniper Tree* (in a leading part). She also appeared in Robert Altman's *Prêt-à-Porter* in 1994.

"I have always loved film musicals, and looking for a new challenge, *Dancer in the Dark* came at the right moment. But I am sort of ignorant about music—I only listen to ABBA—I had never heard the music of Björk before we started looking for a composer. Now I have, and I am very fond of it."

Lars von Trier is also outlining the Dogme brothers' last stand—another world's first, to take place by the turn of the millennium. With Vinterberg, Kragh-Jacobsen, and Levring, he will stage a television project, which will for the first time unite Denmark's national broadcasters (DRTV, TV2/Danmark, TV3, and TvDanmark), while providing audiences with their own DIY film production kits.

On the first day of 2000, at 19:30—just after the State Minister's annual address to the nation—the films will be aired simultaneously by the four broadcasters. Supplementary channels will follow the events in the control room, regularly transmitting split-screen signals, so viewers can see what happens in all four films, creating their own personal version by zapping from one station to another.

In between, von Trier is preparing the grand finale of his DRTV soap *The Kingdom*, which critics described as *Dr. Kildare* meets *Twin Peaks*. Different from the previous installments, it will unspool as one long 110-minute episode. Some of the cast have passed away since the first series was produced in 1993, including Swedish actor Ernst-Hugo Järegård, but they have signed contracts that posthumously they are willing to appear as ghosts. Von Trier actually rang me to ask whether I thought he should show the latest installment at the Venice Film Festival, given that it was made for TV. Having reminded him that *Heimat* and Kieslowski's *Decalogue* series were shown at the festival, I told him yes.

"How stupid can you be?" he barked, and put down the phone. Oh Lars!

Lars von Trier: The Man Who Would Be Dogme

SHARI ROMAN/1999

JULY 9, 1998 — THE COPENHAGEN PREMIERE of *The Idiots*. The sitdown interview with von Trier was the next day at his home on July 10. I returned a little over a year later and interviewed him at the new offices/army barracks of Zentropa on August 31, 1999.

Lars von Trier, Denmark's foremost filmmaker, settles himself on the couch of his spacious production offices, located in his private bungalow residence. "I am completely relaxed," he says in his accented English. He stretches out, with a large satisfied exhale. "I am not afraid of you." He fidgets, acknowledges the tape recorder, sighs, then suddenly drops his head, cradling his face in his hands. "I am not afraid of you," he says again, softly. In the airy, largely windowed space, there are no apparent shrines to *The Idiots*, the work made in accordance with Dogme95, the no-frills film aesthetic von Trier created in 1995, after he filmed his Oscar-nominated *Breaking the Waves*. To his left stands a mint condition *Raiders of the Lost Ark* pinball machine, to his right scattered videotapes form a trail to the large, dark TV set. "I am not afraid of you," von Trier is repeating into his palms. "I am not afraid of you. I am completely relaxed. But," he adds, halting the incantation by throwing a mischievous sideways look. "I could be afraid of you later on. So, maybe you would like a whiskey, or something? For your nerves?"

Originally written for *The Face*. Re-written for and excerpted from *Digital Babylon: Hollywood, Indiewood and Dogme95*/IFILM Publishing/. Published October 2001. Reprinted by permission of the author.

He rises and selects a regal bottle from the side mantle. A sweet old tune tinkles as he lifts it from its cradle. It turns out it doubled as a prop in *Dancer in the Dark*, his $15 million upcoming musical feature starring Iceland's moody pop-chanteuse Björk (who also composed the film's music) and French icon Catherine Deneueve, about an Eastern European woman circa 1964 who imagines America as one big musical. "I'm sorry I can't talk to you about it," he says. "I promised Björk I wouldn't talk about working with her." Lars von Trier, who loves to sing, co-wrote the lyrics with Björk's partner, Sigurjon B. Sigurdsson. He points to one of the cassettes on the floor—cine-punkster Harmony Korine's *julien donkey-boy*, the first American film to be approved by Dogme95. "Harmony is a completely crazy guy," he says. "That's good. That's what we need. I'm for the craziness."

He presents me with a small paper cup brimming with dark liquor. "Here—Jack Daniels," he says with a smile. "From America. To which, as you know, I will never go. I would have to fly to go to America, and that I don't imagine I will ever do. But I have seen a lot of films about America. . . . You shouldn't underestimate that."

Nor should one underestimate von Trier. Regarded as one of Europe's most principled and iconoclastic auteurs (with all the "old school" honors that implies), he has had every one of his feature films appear in the official program at Cannes. From his debut, *The Element of Crime*, in 1984 through *Epidemic* in 1987 and *Europa* in 1991, to *Breaking the Waves*, which won the Grand Prix in 1996. As fascinated as he is by culture (and other people), he will not board an airplane. Not ever. When he does travel, it's rarely far from the modest suburban home where he was born and that he has lived in, on and off, his entire life. These days he shares it with his new spouse Bente, and their two-year-old twin sons. Three stories high, with a large grassy backyard, it includes a separate cottage that serves as his home office, a carefully cultivated organic vegetable garden, and a large playhouse, the province of his elder daughter from his first marriage. Hanging inside is a genial photo of another Danish icon, Hans Christian Andersen, whom von Trier detests, calling him a celibate wanker. There are also trees on the property, which (it has been rumored) he practices climbing down, via a long rope that he takes with him on his rare excursions, in case he should have to escape out a window in the event of a fire.

Having control, or being controlled, percolates throughout his work; von Trier says candidly, "All my anxieties you can find in my films," which are rife with black humor and populated with characters who find themselves mentally, emotionally, or physically impaired—their inner nature trapped in a war between their intellect, spirituality, and sexuality. In *Europa* the lead character literally drowns in his own emotions. Bess in *Breaking the Waves*, the "simple" girl in love (played by Emily Watson) who is dragged through heaven and hell by a wrathful God, von Trier says, would also be a case in point. And although his Bess howls at the sea, he himself is not adamantly against water per se (since he loves kayaking).

But when it came time to move shooting locations for *Dancer in the Dark*—it was filmed partly in Sweden, near the Trollhättan forest (where they make the SAAB cars)—von Trier balked at the endless, churning vista and initially refused to board ship. When he went to Cannes for *Breaking the Waves*, he made it halfway there, then turned around and went home. When traveling to Cannes last year for the premiere of *The Idiots* (the second of the films under the Dogme umbrella, which will have taken nearly two years to reach America when it is released in February 2000), he did so in an ancient camper van that broke down on the way, twice. But once there, he skewered his reputation as a dour perk-aesthete by lodging at the ultra-ritzy cash-only Hotel du Cap, showing he is capable of cool irony, especially about himself, when stepping into the public eye. Even when speaking of his most commercially successful film to date, *Breaking the Waves*, the transcendental Wagnerian wrencher about the nature of goodness, fierce religious faith, and the passion of true, ill-fated love, he has opined, "For more intellectual audiences, the style will excuse the tears. The intellectuals will be able to permit themselves to cry because the story is so refined."

Giving birth to the Dogme95 (excepting the religious connotations, there is no kinship with Kevin Smith's film *Dogma*) manifesto, says von Trier, has caused him great joy, as well as deep stress. Outlining a set of ten stringent rules heralded as a "vow of chastity" (which reads like a cross between Moses' Ten Commandments and a naughty anarchist pamphlet), it dictates the use of handheld cameras and location shooting, bans production design, soundtrack scores, optical work, and genre story lines, and eschews directorial credit. If one breaks the rules (although it's vehemently discouraged), redemption is allowed via a printed confession. But one shouldn't confuse the irony or the playfulness with a creative loophole. The manifesto's higher intention is to bring about a new attitude towards filmmaking. And if you don't approach it seriously, says von Trier dourly, "It defeats the purpose. Yes, I broke a couple of rules, but you know, it gave me no pleasure."

On this side of the Atlantic, the raspy-voiced Korine, twenty-five, who began his insurrectionist climb as the teenage screenwriter of *Kids*, has been spearheading his own loony brand of artsy filmmaking; *julien donkey-boy*, his largely improvised tale of a schizophrenic (played by *Trainspotting*'s Ewen Bremner), was grudgingly applauded by the critics as an improvement on *Gummo* (which was termed a "scuzzball atrocity" by the *New Yorker*). Jumping onto the Dogme bandwagon after a telephone conversation with von Trier, Korine declares he thoroughly enjoyed embracing the monastic, inspirational principles (although he did snap several of the rules in the process), referring affectionately to his eccentric guru as a madman. "I went to Copenhagen, and I got a call from Lars's assistant for me to come to see him, alone. No producers. He didn't really want to come to the screening, he didn't want to leave his production company, Zentropa, so I went to this place that looks like a big concentration camp and played pinball for few hours before we really talked about anything. I'm not very good at pinball. He beat me. A few times. He kept getting really upset that I wasn't a really serious pinball player. He's one really serious guy. The other side of him is really almost maniacal."

Notoriously moody, wary of outsiders, von Trier likes to make an appearance on his own terms in his own good time. I haven't seen him in over a year, since the Danish premiere of *The Idiots*, to which he arrived somewhat stiffly dressed in a tuxedo, one eye on the theater's exit signs. We are meeting today at Zentropa, which in the past eight years has emerged as one of the most successful film and television production companies in Scandinavia. Recently relocated to an isolated midpoint between Copenhagen airport and its former quarters in the center of town, the sprawling complex previously served as the site of an old military barracks. And despite the throngs of employees wandering the grounds, who look like stunningly healthy denizens of a J. Crew catalogue, architecturally, Korine is right on. It looks like a somewhat friendly concentration camp.

Lars von Trier is a quiet man of forty-three, of average height, with watchful, almond-shaped eyes and a newly nearly shaved head, head shaving being an old "renewal" ritual he sometimes performs at the end of a film shoot. Dressed casually in a loose anorak, comfortable pants,, and sandals with socks, he turns and motions for me to follow him to his small army-style jeep. Sitting down in the driver's seat, he flexes his arm up and down, and mentions he has just come from a successful two-hour tennis game, where he trounced his opponent. He smiles. "Maybe you'd like to play?"

It's slightly overcast, as is the norm, but as we do a mini-motor tour of the Zentropa grounds (a landscape dotted with faceless buildings, which house production offices, edit bays, soundstages, and all the typical, glittering swami tools of a Hollywood studio), von Trier remarks expansively on what an extraordinarily beautiful summer it's been. "Next week," he announces, "I am going to Jutland for four days. Fly-fishing. Me alone. No one else. Just me." Running into friends on the drive, he is laid back and chatty, whipping out a Palm Pilot to scribble down an appointment and cheerily waving goodbye. I had forgotten how charming he is when he isn't forcibly squeezed to spout film rhetoric.

Back at his home base, he is as candidly relaxed and "just folks" as a famous auteur can be when confronted with a shopping list of intrusive, poking inquiry. Feeling vulnerable, but not threatened, he playfully counters, and offers to hypnotize me, a control technique he said he used with some actors, early on.

"The American approach would be the power you have over another human being. But this is a normal technique, it's not a big deal, it's kind of European. And probably more effective," he smirks Svengali-like, "with an accent like mine." He names German filmmaker Werner Herzog (who also plays the father in Korine's *julien donkey-boy*) as a practitioner of the art, as well as director/countryman Bille August's father, who, he points out, was a hypnotist who traveled around with the circuses. And most significantly for von Trier, another fellow countryman, Carl Th. Dreyer, hypnotized the woman who played Joan in his famous silent film, *The Passion of Joan of Arc*, which he used as inspiration for his own *Breaking the Waves*. "Of course," he laughs, "to get that look, Dreyer also had her have sex before shooting the scenes. But I would say that hypnotism itself is not so strange. The difficult part is being the one who is being hypnotized."

"Control is a key thing in my production and in my life, that's for sure," he agrees. The idea for the Dogme film aesthetic, he says, emerges from a desire to submit to the authority and rules he did not have as a child. Von Trier's upbringing in a free-form, hippy-Marxist setting, which he describes tartly as "humanistic, cultural-leftist", left him feeling untethered and deeply fearful. "Being too free is a lot of responsibility for a child. It gives you a lot of anxiety." He shrugs, "I don't think that there are a lot of people who don't have phobias to some degree, but to talk about it, especially to the degree I talk about it, I don't think is common. It makes them sound like jokes." And despite the Woody Allen-ish parallels, he adds candidly, "I'm afraid it is not a joke. It's just a way of trying to get rid of it." In fact, his fears only increased, when seven years ago his mother shocked him, on her death-bed, by confessing, "My father was not my father, and I was not really a Jew. She told me she had done this, so that I could have more artistic genes. . . . It was a very 'Dallas' moment."

His mother, who had given him his first super-8 camera when he was ten years old, and the opportunity to pursue his passion, had lied to him. Lars von Trier shakes his head: "Not a Jew? Not a part of the great 'victims' of the world? I was devastated." His visually stunning *Europa*, which unfolds like a nightmarish *Shoah* death dream, von Trier wrote when he still believed he was Jewish. "But not when I directed it," he says. "I had found out by that time. I remember I used to go around to the cemetery and put rubble (small remembrance stones) on all the graves. I remember that when I told this reporter from an Israeli paper this, he cried, 'No! It's not true Lars. Say it's not true!' But, it was true. It was true."

After his mother's confession, von Trier decided to convert to Catholicism and thereafter filmed that fiercely religious impassionata, *Breaking the Waves* and created the canon for a religion he could use in his creative life, Dogme95. A cleansing ritual. Asked if he would call Dogme a kind of "cine-matic high colonic" von Trier fixes me with a hateful look and barks, "Why do you ask these questions? These stupid questions. Why are you laughing? Is it the whiskey or are you nervous?" He straps his sandals back on and shakes his head. "These stupid questions you ask."

Before Dogme, he was feeling strangled by options, by freedom. The color of a film always had to be just right. Scripts would take years to write. Actors were treated like props to be moved within the visual mythology. He longed for immediacy, the juicy, truthful moments that are born out of controlled chaos. But how could he give himself freedom, without falling into the abyss? He would take on the role of both "higher power" and disciple, and construct a new universe. . . .

Hammering out the rules in around an hour, over some wine with fellow Dane Thomas Vinterberg, whose incestuous family drama, *The Celebration* (a.k.a. *Festen*, officially *Dogme #1*) caused its own stir by winning at Cannes last year, von Trier emphasizes that the aim of all these mandates was to "escape from rigidity" and to "regain lost innocence" in the way films are made. "At another level they express the desire to make something quite simple."

Vinterberg, twenty-nine, a rangy charmer, who needlingly refers to Lars as his older, more clever brother "who did not win at Cannes" (at Zentropa, Vinterberg's bungalow is just a stone's throw away from von Trier's), says, "There's one problem. It seems that the ideas of Dogme scare people more than they entice them. Lars sent out invitations on Dogme's behalf, and he's not humble. He sent them to Kurosawa and Bergman, big guys like that. When I was at Cannes, I actually asked Scorsese. We spoke a lot about the Dogme concept, so I said, 'Join the club. Jump over the barricades.' He laughed, and was pulled away by his bodyguards. End of conversation."

Even so, it has had a positive, positively decorative effect on the two other Danish signatories who complete the four official corners of the Dogme brotherhood: Kristian Levring, a thirtysomething commercials director who is currently editing the *King Lear*-derived *Dogme #4—The King Is Alive* with Jennifer Jason Leigh; and Søren Kragh-Jacobsen, a thoroughly established and beloved fiftysomething filmmaker whose baroque love story *Dogme #3— Mifune* will be released in the States in February 2000 after winning top honors at last year's Berlin Film Festival. So far, besides Korine, there is only Jean-Marc Barr (who has appeared in *Europa*, *Breaking the Waves* and *Dancer in the Dark*) who has made the first French film to be certified: *Dogme # 5—Lovers*, with *gamine gaulloise* Elodie Bouchez [*Dream Life of Angels*], which will be released in Europe in December. Fittingly, Paul Morrissey, the iconic director of the Warhol-produced *Trash* and *Heat*, is said to be making a Dogme of his own.

Meanwhile, von Trier's stripped-down, posh-free call to arms, which some feel could "save the art of filmmaking" from being swallowed by technological sorcery, has received a simultaneous white-hot drubbing and loving embrace by the film community and the media at large. In a recent *Time* magazine article, even mainstream mega-weight Steven Spielberg stepped out of line to champion the ethic, enthusing about the possibility of making a Dogme film. Otherwise the Hollywood gatekeepers, in a familiar case of the pot calling the kettle black, satirize its austere tenets as publicity-seeking "emperor's-new-clothes" hucksterism, a Trojan Horse calculated for maximum effect.

Perhaps. Lars von Trier knows a thing or two about showmanship. Even when he was in his twenties, at the National Film School of Denmark, he antagonized his teachers by adopting a false "von" into his name to lampoon the equally feigned grandeur of fellow avatars "von" Stroheim and "von" Sternberg. But when it comes to Dogme, von Trier says, "I don't think there's any point in only provoking. But I would say that any kind of discussion, and any thinking about the media and how you're working with it, is a good thing and that is what can provoke. And it did at Cannes; everybody was talking about it. You can think that it's worthless, but you're still talking and here you are still arguing about why it's worthless."

Even so, Dogme for von Trier is less about picking a fight with Goliath over film etiquette than about a self-imposed self-referential vehicle for spurring his own development as an artist. Parenthetically, when he was a young man, clarifies von Trier, he became fascinated by David Bowie. *Station to Station* was his favorite album. He watched him at three concerts when he came to Denmark and listened to his albums over and over again, hypnotized by his fluid reinvention of his persona. "All artists have their time. When Bowie was at his peak, he was developing every album from the next. With filmmakers, like Dreyer for instance, there's a similar kind of developing, meaning that he could, over a long span of time, do very interesting films. You could say the same of Kubrick. On my scale, I'm trying to do the same, in that I'm never doing the same film again. It's a big problem, commercially, of course. After doing a film like *The Idiots*, which is for a much narrower audience, it's not as easy to finance a big film like *Dancer in the Dark*, because after *Breaking the Waves*, everybody wants to see "Breaking the Waves II" done as the next film. But I can't do that, and I don't want to do that. Because I want to move on. And that's why it's important for me to make a film like *The Idiots* now and then. And if people don't like it . . . I couldn't care less."

With *The Idiots*, von Trier is positively irrepressible. Written in four days, with 80 percent shot by von Trier himself on a hand-held Sony VX 1000, the project has been sanguinely declared by von Trier to be "a film by idiots about idiots for idiots," which points to a playfulness which is often overshadowed by the perceived stolid Dogmatism of Dogme. (Even Dogme95's logo is purposely cheeky. It is literally "in a pig's eye," as it features the rear end of a pig, with a huge unblinking eye placed directly in the anus.)

"People ask, 'Is Dogme tongue-in-cheek?'" continues von Trier. "Yeah, it is an experiment, but I do take it very seriously. To me it's like horseback

riding. Here in Denmark we have a discipline called 'school riding.' For people who are interested in horses this is very interesting. And I'm sure that
this experience from this strange way of riding can be used in other areas of
life. So, if you want to do it, you should follow the rules—otherwise it's nonsense. If you want to get carried away and ride over the prairie, be my guest.
I think there's a certain beauty to that, too."

Peter Aalbæk Jensen, a large, expansive man, who is von Trier's long-time
friend, Zentropa partner, and (along with Vibeke Windeløv) producer, says
that from his point of view, the ideals of Dogme are not really viable and are
maybe even a little silly. The downside being that many of the people who
are embracing it view it as merely another way to grind out cheap movies.
"But from a silly little country that makes silly little movies, to have this big
noise being spread around the world, that's a whole lot of fun. I can also say
that it has certainly helped Lars to become more flexible. On *Dancer in the
Dark* (which is not a Dogme film), Robby Müller, the cinematographer for
Breaking the Waves, was responsible for lighting camera, but Lars was the
operator," Jensen continues. "The handheld camera rule that came from
Dogme, made it all the more possible for him to have more contact with the
actors, instead of just looking at the monitor and screaming at them. Things
used to go from the storyboard directly to the camera, which was good to
look at, but boring. And the actors love it. With this, there is nothing else
but the actors and their talent, the director and the story. Nobody can hide
behind anything, and there are no excuses. Sure, it makes him more vulnerable, but it's also given him a lot of freedom to create."

Even so, *The Idiots* meanders, struggles at times. And it is not the most
visually attractive film in the world. Indeed, the roughness of style of both
The Idiots and *The Celebration* assaults the viewer with grainy images, visible
sound equipment, choppy camera movements, and unsettling jump-cuts
that remind one of a film-school student gone wild. Lars von Trier has said
that, by using this method, he was after some of the lightness and enjoyment
of the French New Wave and of the "Beatle-esque" Swinging London period.
In fact, he says Godard himself asked for and screened *The Idiots*. "I think
until *The Idiots* [Godard] thought it was rubbish what I was doing. Now,
maybe, I've kind of," he offers with a touch of shyness, "well, come home.
But the 'new wave' is a wave that's always coming. They didn't put anything
down on a piece of paper. I guess we're doing it a little bit more dogmatically,
in a sense." It was a bit of a throwback to the '60s, he says, with the free-

flowing use of improvisation. And in order to help the actors feel more comfortable with some of the more intense nude scenes, von Trier disrobed on the set one day and announced "naked day." He may travel with ropes, refuse to fly, obsess over diseases, but being bare-assed in front of friends and strangers is not one of his hang-ups.

"I had no problem being naked," he says. "They were so tired in the end of seeing me naked," he laughs. "'Put on some clothes Lars!' they said. I think it helped them anyway. Because some of the nude scenes are quite relaxed. It was good we were shooting in the summer—it was very hot. But I would've been naked anyway. The Nordic winter wouldn't have stopped me."

Among the film's taboo-busting scenes is a birthday party, where a request for a gang-bang transforms into a full-on orgy, featuring erect penises and a twenty-second sequence with actual penetration. It has already caused censorship problems in Europe (but not in Denmark, as the country abolished film censorship back in 1969). When it arrives in America, there has even been talk of using the old skin magazine technique of blacking out the offensive body parts in the hardcore scenes in order to gain an R rating. T & A aside, the film's subject matter, particularly to the extent that it reflects von Trier's attitudes toward the mentally handicapped, is potentially far more provocative and offensive. Not strongly narrative in nature, often caustically funny, the film explores concepts of normalcy and societal codes, by focusing on a commune of white middle-class adults who unlock their creative energy and emotional needs by pretending to be retarded. They evince their solidarity, releasing their "inner idiot," most often in public, by entering into a frenzied, near religious collapse they call "spazzing." Eventually the group fragments into madness and the challenges become more daring, leading to an emotional denouement of surprising power. Says von Trier, "And maybe it's a cliché, somewhat, maybe, in that scene, all that crying, yelling. There was a little Bergman, a little Dreyer. But somehow . . . it's still quite touching, I think."

After all the ruckus Dogme has caused, you'd think an anxious man like von Trier would be satisfied for a while. Not yet. Next autumn he has his sights set on the small screen, with the third part of his quirky supernatural soap opera The Kingdom (which has also achieved theatrical release). And on New Year's Eve 1999, he and his fellow Dogme95 brothers will regroup together in a Zentropa war room of sorts, to create D Day—four separate seventy-minute films shot in "real time," to be broadcast simultaneously on four different channels. Each of the four directors, from their position of safety in the film "bunker," will send a camera team along with each individual actor or actress into the Millennium fever, directing them by means of microphone. Viewers will do their own editing by zapping the remote.

He has no plans of doing another Dogme film (although he thinks it would be especially interesting to do a porno film, Dogme style). Once you've done one, he says, and learned from your experience, according to all the adherents, there is no need to do another. That possibility exists somewhere in the future, should your creativity once again require a stay at this Spartan cinematic spa.

He says, his face lighting up, that what he has "always dreamt of doing is a soap set in a concentration camp. The hierarchies between the inmates have always been very interesting to me. I've done a lot of research on this. The status they had before they took with them into the camp. If you had some money, you would have a tailor, and you couldn't really tell the difference, but it would be little trendy things in the clothing. These are the things that would become so important. In this milieu, you can't get out of it, but at least you could say, 'I'm the strongest of the mice.' It became more important than whether somebody died. Very cruel. It would also be good, because if the actors caused any trouble, it would be very easy to get rid of them." He mimes a deeply concerned look: "Oh you look so tired. So tired . . . and a little dirty," he laughs. "Maybe you'd like a nice, long shower?"

Lars von Trier carefully pulls his jeep up to a large building that contains the editing suite. "Would you like to see a little bit of *Dancer in the Dark*?" he asks sweetly, extracting a promise that I won't write about what I see. Yes, I say. He appraises my face, nods, then waves me inside. Of course, he says, his hope is that *Dancer in the Dark* will preserve his famous perfect score, by being presented at Cannes 2000. What he hadn't envisioned was the scrutiny and renown the seemingly "mad" tactics of Dogme has garnered him. More triumphantly, it has freed him, somewhat, to make movies that are satisfying to him. But idiocy, on one level, says von Trier, is like hypnosis and ejaculation: "If you want it, you can't have it—and if you don't want it, you can."

"The thing is," he says, as I follow him down the long, winding hallway, "for whatever else Dogme is, it was a wonderful experience. I found it was so much fun—it was like finding Paradise. Pacts with God? I haven't made any. But maybe you can say I have one with somebody like him. All the time."

Dance in the Dark

GAVIN SMITH/2000

LARS VON TRIER HAS ALWAYS made for good copy. A precocious *enfant terrible*, he quickly developed a cult following with *The Element of Crime* (1984) and *Europa* (1991), constructing a kind of pastiche authoritarian aesthetic out of his oppressive mastery of stylistic artifice and defiant art cinema rhetoric. When he hit a creative wall, he repudiated the idea of cinema-as-giant-train-set and embraced a more direct, personal form of expression with his half-parodic, half-serious Dogme95 manifesto. In 1996's *Breaking the Waves*, von Trier seemed to have discovered "real life," and re-directed his energy into an intensive collaboration with his actors. With *The Idiots* in 1998, he took another step towards self-liberation by trading in 35-mm for the chaotic immediacy of handheld video. Five years on, the one-time *enfant* is no longer quite so *terrible*: a figurehead of the impending "digital revolution," von Trier now has the demeanor of a humble, bemused visionary.

His new film, the already infamous *Dancer in the Dark*, is some kind of a first: a genuinely tragic musical. An unfashionably earnest celebration of spiritual fortitude, *Dancer* is rendered in a subdued, death-row-drab palette. Though it has a period setting (Washington state, ca. 1962), there are few period markers to speak of, and the digital video images add a certain tonal dissonance: the film is technically state of the art, yet opts for a sketch-like, almost primitive cinematic articulation, pushing the wavering handheld camera and jumpy, discontinuous cutting that von Trier began with *Breaking the Waves* to new extremes. Though epic in emotional terms, and initially

From *Film Comment*, September 2000. Reprinted by permission of the author.

promising grandeur with its lush musical overture, the action is so scaled-down in scope (the film basically consists of six locations) as to be miniatur-ist. There's a painstaking modesty and economy to *Dancer*'s dimensions and gestures: this is a profoundly interiorized reworking of the most exhibitionis-tic of movie genres.

And at the film's center, there's the enigma of Björk, the world-famous Icelandic rock star, in a triumphant performance whose greatness is equaled by its artlessness. An introverted, pixie-like, yet formidable and emotionally volcanic presence, she plays a Czech immigrant factory worker and single mother who's slowly going blind. In the course of just over two hours, she endures one emotionally agonizing ordeal after another, ending with an excruciating trip to the gallows. *Singin' in the Rain* it ain't.

It's all too easy to find yourself not getting along with von Trier's films, and *Dancer in the Dark* might seem like an especially tough pill to swallow. But if you're prepared to make a leap of faith and get past the story's willful naivete and the deliberately flat, neutral images, you might just have a tran-scendent experience.

Selma (Björk) toils in a rural wash-basin factory, saving every penny for an operation on her son's eyes to ensure that he doesn't inherit her failing sight. She rents a house from the local sheriff (David Morse) and his wife (Cara Seymour). Although Selma is a loner, sweetly rebuffing the romantic advances of Jeff (Peter Stormare), she finds release through musicals: she goes to see them at the movies with her friend Kathy (Catherine Deneuve) and takes the part of Maria in a local amateur production of *The Sound of Music*. When her hard-won savings are stolen, she is forced to commit a murder to recover them. After visiting a nearby eye clinic and paying in advance for her son's treatment, she is arrested and put on trial, after which her devotion to her son is put to the ultimate test.

As with *Breaking the Waves*, *Dancer*'s contrived, old-fashioned melodra-matic scenario packs quite an emotional punch. The new film takes its place alongside *Waves* and *The Idiots* in what von Trier has dubbed his "Golden Heart" trilogy, named after a children's story that made a strong impression on him as a boy: a little girl goes on a journey and gives away all her posses-sions to the needy people she encounters along the way until she's finally left destitute, yet she carries on undaunted. It makes sense—all three films are marked by emotional regression, fear of abandonment, and deliberately

Simplified personal and moral dilemmas. Each one features a pure, childlike, selflessly giving heroine who comes into conflict with the social order: her uncompromising emotional absolutism and freedom from self-consciousness are sufficiently disconcerting to raise questions about her mental state. And at the center of each film is the harrowing spectacle of this childwoman sacrificing herself body and soul for love, as represented respectively by a husband, an adoptive community, and a child. In the process she achieves a kind of sanctification and transcendence through martyrdom.

The primal terrain of family is at the emotional core of *Dancer in the Dark*, specifically a parent's unquestioning devotion to her child. Von Trier treats this devotion as a given and expends little effort to flesh it out: the mere invocation of the mother-son bond is sufficient to unleash powerful emotions. You could call this the filmmaker's "opportunistic" side: there's a sneaking suspicion that von Trier is capitalizing on a deep-seated cultural yearning for simple and palpably "moral" narratives. Moreover, it must be said that there's a troubling correspondence between von Trier's quest for a purer form of cinema and the emotional endurance tests to which he puts his actresses and the characters they play—it's hard not to see a measure of misogyny in the films' idealized yet masochistic conception of femininity.

Lars von Trier is nothing if not ambitious, and the scope of his ambitions is global. Like Luc Besson, who stood as president of the Cannes jury that gave *Dancer in the Dark* the Palme d'Or, this "Danish" director has wholeheartedly embraced the phenomenon of the English Language Foreign Film, of which his tragic musical is a surpassingly strange example. Lars von Trier presents us with an entirely simulated America, in which Washington state is patched together from Swedish locations and Danish sets. The cast is also a patchwork: of the thirteen leading actors, only five are American, and the rest are Icelandic, French, Swedish, English, French-Canadian, and German. This is less a question of melting-pot realism than pastiche, and the main ingredient in this pastiche is the musical genre itself. In terms of form and style, aside from the device of the roadshow overture, *Dancer in the Dark* seems to have little in common with Hollywood musicals—if anything, the movie's decidedly proletarian milieu is more suggestive of Eastern European Communist musicals from the '50s and '60s. But in another very important sense, *Dancer in the Dark* isolates and amplifies a central component of the Hollywood movie musical.

To be reductive, let's say the classic musical consists of song and dance numbers that expand on the emotional and expressive epiphanies of the characters, and that these numbers are typically linked together by expositional filler that makes up the action. *Dancer in the Dark* redistributes the balance of emotional emphasis—the privileged moments of expressive release aren't reserved for the musical numbers, but can also be found in the dramatic scenes. Because the numbers themselves convey something quite specific: Selma's intermittent mental dissociation in the face of crisis or malaise. Von Trier accentuates this sense of dissociation through both the texture of the image—the color suddenly changes to a more vibrant register—and the montage, in which the performances are dissected and fragmented by his one hundred stationary cameras into a hallucinatory swirl, an alternate happy reality in the process of being imagined. The songs and dances exist strictly in Selma's mind, and they're her way of coping with an unbearable reality, which she converts into an imaginatively empathetic form. In essence, the musical numbers are a form of refuge for Selma, and they allow her to carry on as a functional individual. Von Trier imbues the imagination itself with divine properties.

When it comes down to it, the director's ongoing project is a spiritual one: the reduction of human experience, and its representation through cinema, to its essence. And on the eve of the cinema's imminent digital transformation, von Trier has taken it upon himself to purge it of impurity. *Dancer's* premise and raison d'être is vision itself—a nearly blind mother's struggle to preserve her son's sight. The allegoric dimension is irresistible—as darkness descends on film's old magic of chemistry and optics, its offspring, video, is coming into the light. From a more circumspect angle, you might say that it's von Trier's good fortune to have his own creative evolution coincide with a pivotal moment of technological change. Come to think of it, that's a fairly serviceable definition of the visionary.

GAVIN SMITH: *What inspired* Dancer in the Dark?
LARS von TRIER: I set out to make a musical. This is more or less the same story as *Breaking the Waves*, only as a musical. At my age you try to go back and think, Where did it all start, what did the first film I saw look like, what was so fascinating about it? I always come back to some Christmas when they showed Gene Kelly musicals like *Singin' in the Rain*, and I thought I must cherish this. Then I thought, what would I like to do to a musical? I'm at a point in my life where I'm quite fond of melodrama, so I thought, why not

try to put this together and get something that is more like the emotion of an opera? That is, melodrama with music. The musical has a tendency to be something in between, where you can't really go all the way with the feelings. I'm not sure it is a musical, but it has musical elements in it.

G S : *How do you reconcile the search for realism that has become one of your goals with the artificiality and contrivance of the genre material in* Dancer in the Dark?

L v T : The task of this film was to make a connection between the dream or the musical and real life, and we do that through the main character. The story is extremely simple, about poor, simple people, and I like the collision between the monumental and the small and between the artificial and the real, or less artificial.

G S : *Why did you resurrect the device of the musical overture before the film begins?*

L v T : Well, I love it when *West Side Story* starts with the overture. The first moment when you sit down to see a film is very powerful, you kind of make a statement—with any film that always makes a statement. Other films I've done prepare the soil for the seed, so to speak. I like to prepare the audience.

Prologue

G S : *There's a sense of ritual about it, too, like the hypnotism that begins* Europa *and* Epidemic.

L v T : Music and suggestion are closely related, and I think the connection between the hypnotism of Max von Sydow's voice-over in *Europa*, and the overture here, are the same things as the chapter headings in *Breaking the Waves*, which represented an artificial or God's point of view.

G S : *It's interesting that you went back to your earliest cinematic experiences for inspiration. Your recent films concern childlike, fragile characters—are they vehicles for exploration of your own childlike aspect?*

L v T : I haven't thought about that. I think my wife would be very sorry if I became much more childlike. She thinks I'm enough of a child. Bess in *Breaking the Waves* and Selma in *Dancer in the Dark* are supposed to be strong, even though it's a fragility they themselves refuse to accept. The films that I have made have all had to do with a clash between an ideal and reality. Whenever there's been a man in the lead role, at a certain point this man finds out that the ideal doesn't hold. And whenever it was a woman, they take the ideal all the way.

G S : *So in a sense you see women as stronger.*

L v T : My mother was strong. I think maybe that's why. I can see that it's a pattern, and I'm sorry, but that's how it came out. Also, I think it would be more difficult for a man because he tries to find a logical solution to things. And if he sees that an ideal doesn't fit, then he has a tendency to do something to it so it works. I think that a woman, and this might be terrible to say, would tend to find an emotional solution. That's what they say, and that is what I think, to some degree. But let's not talk in terms of men and women. I feel kind of female, myself, to some degree.

G S : *What was your conception for the musical numbers in terms of what we experience?*

L v T : It would be too easy to say that it's escapism every time Selma goes into a musical number—it's actually just her seeing another side to the characters and reality around her. She can understand that the DA in the courtroom has to be tough on her because it's his job, so in the musical number he's still a DA, but he's not tough when he dances around. She just changes everything a little bit because there is always another side to things.

G S : *Why is it that the dramatic scenes are filmed with tremendous visual freedom, whereas the musical numbers are more mechanically and rigidly constructed?*

L v T : I wanted to mark the difference between these two levels of reality. When I thought about making a musical, when I was younger, I always thought that I should track and crane because that is what I'd done a lot of in my earlier films. But then I thought, No, it's too easy, and it takes too long. It would take me half a year to make the movie. The reason why I laid down the Dogme rules or put a camera on my shoulder was to get away from all this perfectionism and concentrate on something else.

After I made *Europa* I'd had it with craning-shots. It was so technical that I'd come to the end of my rope. If I went back to the earlier style, it would drain the life away. I was thinking, What kind of musical would Selma do in her head? And I thought it would not be this perfect kind. So we had a lot of theories and they don't hold water, but the idea was that we took the hundred non-professional video cameras that we could afford, and we placed them all around, and the idea was to cover the dance in one go, so that the singing could be live, and we would only do the whole thing once, accepting all the mistakes. The dancers could go almost anywhere; the dance didn't have a front to it, and we found out that this might be a good idea. You can see little pieces of it here and there. You can really feel the difference between a transition done by cutting between two cameras filming the same movement, from one to the other, and one where it's two different takes. That's a world of a difference. Especially in the intensity.

But a hundred cameras isn't nearly enough, we found out. The result unfortunately is something in between. Far too fast editing, because the images didn't last long enough. We should have had a couple of thousand cameras, but as the price is dropping that's also possible. But with all these good intentions, we didn't have the financing to do it. The good thing I can say about it is that for our budget we got quite a lot out of it. A dance like the one we had on the train would normally have taken two weeks to shoot. We did that in two days. First we had the hundred cameras on the train, then we moved them to the ground. But I still think there's a future to this way of thinking, that we want the live performance. I'm very sure.

G S : *Do you feel you've been trying to find a way to make films that are less authoritarian and cold in form?*

L v T : I have become more interested in other people. It's as simple as that. When we improvise, it's because I want to take some of the qualities that are there already and use them, instead of making an actor stand in a corner, count to four, take one step to the left, etc., which was the way I started. I think that when you mature as a person, you attempt to dare to let go of some of your technique—I'm talking about style and surface in a sense. You allow technique to stay in the background. I have to navigate on my curiosity. Whatever I'm fascinated by, whatever film is deep in my head, I follow it to the end. If I'm anything, then I'm very stubborn, and I don't stop until my vision of the film is reached.

G S : *Why at the same time have the stories become so simplified?*

L v T : It comes very much from the work of Carl Th. Dreyer, which I admire very much. He worked for years and years on his scripts and started with five hundred pages and ended up with twenty. So for me this search for the essence is found in working closely with the actors. When you improvise, you have to know exactly what you're doing—it can't be one way or the other, you have to be very clear where you're going, so you start with a very simple setup. That's the part of the process that I think is interesting. The story line is almost reduced to mathematics, and then my job is to pour my essence into it. *(not technique.)*

G S : *Your use of handheld camera suggests a kind of struggle to find the subject of the shot or the scene—as if you're constantly trying to capture the moment.*
L v T : On this film and the last one I operated the camera myself, and when you use a handheld camera, the search for the object becomes part of the story. I have tried to be very precise but I also like it to be a little bit sloppy. So when I hear someone say something, I pan to a reaction, or not, and this is part of storytelling with a handheld camera.

G S : *So in a sense you become a participant in the performance of the scene.*
L v T : Exactly. Before I'd be sitting by a monitor somewhere else. But the moment when the actors deliver is the moment you really want to be close to them. The perfect place is right next to the camera lens. My technique is to film every scene for a full hour, so if a scene is two minutes long we film over and over, and talk in between and let the camera roll and suggest different things and play around. We don't rehearse, we just start off with the actors standing where they want to stand, doing exactly what they think is right for the character, and then we shoot. From that first take I know where we should go with it or what the potential is and I usually talk about what different colors I need on the palette, so that I can paint the scene. After that I might make some suggestions about how to stage things or give a different weight to the scene, and then the emotional peak of the scene from my point of view usually comes after two or three takes. After that, we would talk, and then I'd go for different things that I need for the scene.
   I like it very much when the emotional development of a scene isn't completely logical and not one-to-one in real time. I like to make time cuts where we jump and cut out maybe a psychological transformation of some kind—we work a lot with time cuts. So when I'm shooting I'm planning all the time and taking risks, trying weird angles—you could say I'm sampling.

G S : *Is this why there's such a sense of suspended time in your films?*
L v T : I think it comes from my technique of getting the actors to act the

scenes much slower than they will be shown. A scene that should be ninety seconds in the film may take twelve minutes to act—don't ask me why, but I've often told the actors, Take your time, don't say the line until you're ready. When it's compressed and cut together, you have the scene.

G S :   *Will you continue to shoot on video or do you foresee shooting on film again?*
L v T :   I hope that I will change. I feel like a scientist searching for new things all the time, but I don't think I'll go back. Video is a revolution because everybody can make films for very little money and that means a lot of films can be made that we otherwise would not have seen. But I'll say one thing: everybody says, We'll use video when video looks like film. But this is not really logical, because the techniques of film were there before. I'm sure that we will see films that don't look like either film or video today, but something completely different, and I will try to go there if I live that long.

Lars von Trier Comes Out of the Dark

ANTHONY KAUFMAN / 2000 *age 44*

O PENING THE N EW Y ORK F ILM F ESTIVAL tonight, Lars von Trier's *Dancer in the Dark* will have its first true test with North American audiences. If its Cannes premiere was any indication, don't expect the reception to go down easy. Reviled as a failed experiment, hailed as a masterpiece, it's hard to believe that any one film could yield so many different and passionate responses. But this is Lars von Trier, after all, the director who began making visually stunning, highly stylized cinemascapes like *Element of Crime* and *Europa*, and then went 180 degrees with *Breaking the Waves* and Dogme95, tossing out breathtaking imagery on 35-mm in exchange for intimate turmoil on digital video.

Even though his latest DV opus went on to win the Palme d'Or and first-time actress Björk took home the Best Actress prize at Cannes, von Trier appeared to be a tormented figure in France, lamenting the struggles he endured while making his movie musical, *Dancer in the Dark*, the tragic story of Selma (Björk), a factory worker going blind in an unjust 1960s America. But months later, speaking from the comfort of his company just outside of Copenhagen, a very different figure emerges: relaxed, thoughtful, even laughing, von Trier is nothing like the tortured artist I was expecting after meeting him at Cannes. With directness and honesty, von Trier spoke to indieWIRE about working with actors, authenticity, technology, pushing the medium, and his new Alfa Romeo Spider.

ANTHONY KAUFMAN: *There was so much pain in your face at Cannes. Now that some time has passed, do you still feel so distressed about the whole experience of making this film?*

LARS von TRIER: No, now, I'm much calmer. We had a lot of time problems going to Cannes. The print was ready one day before it was shown. Now I feel very good, thank you very much.

AK: *But is the process of making films an emotionally difficult one?*

LvT: I don't find that. This has been special, in the sense that I had to fight so much for the film. It was not very pleasant, but it's rewarding in another way. But it has not been pleasant.

AK: *So* Dancer in the Dark *was an exception?*

LvT: This way of working with actors that I have found now is normally a great pleasure, because it means giving a lot of freedom to some people—and to see them enjoy that freedom and to give to the project is usually very nice. Maybe, I'm romanticizing it, but I remember that there were some films that were nice.

AK: *Can you talk about this process that you've worked out with actors?*

LvT: Since I'm holding the camera and operating it, we are in the same room, so we can actually—it's kind of a little game. We have a little text of two pages of the scene and then we start with that in one hand and then we start the camera and roll for one hour and then after one hour, we make different games with this text and then we end up with a lot of little cuts that I can use and put together for a film. It's a jigsaw puzzle, but it's very relaxed if you compare it to how I worked before. Before, I worked with a storyboard, and that meant that the image wasn't good. There were a lot of things that you had to live up to. Here, working in this other way, you actually start with nothing and whatever you get, it's good. If you start with a complete idea of what you want, then you can only go down—it can only be less good than what you thought. It's a very positive way of filming and freeing the actors, because whatever they come up with, it's where we start. So we start with their interpretations.

AK: *So do you think that gets at a more truthful representation? Do you believe in any truthful representation?*

LvT: No, I don't really believe in that. But, of course, that's one way of making sure there's good performance. It's authentic. Maybe not true, but more authentic.

AK: *At Cannes, you spoke about your using one hundred cameras to shoot the musical scenes and that was supposed to make them more authentic. You had also said that a hundred cameras were not enough, two thousand would be better. Can you explain why?*

LvT: If I made a musical in the beginning of my career, it would have been crane shots and tracking shots and people coming out of cakes and whatever, but these techniques are something that I've left behind me. The basic idea here was that we wanted a feeling for the event. That any song-and-dance number should be only done once. So that we really made a television transmission of it instead of film, so you have a feeling that this is really happening, and if people made a mistake or whatever little thing happened, it would be a gift, because it was how this live performance really worked. I still think it's a good idea, but it demands much more than a hundred cameras. And that's why—since we only had the hundred cameras—we had to go into different takes, which was against the original idea. The original idea was to make Björk sing live. But we couldn't handle it technically, unfortunately. But I'm still sure that is what the future will bring, more and more real events in the sense that it's not created afterwards. If we see someone singing, we want to know that it was done for real. I'm sure that this is where technology is bringing us.

AK: *You're a big fan of technology?*

LvT: I wouldn't say that. I think technology right now is great, because it makes filming so easy, you know. Early on, when I was young, everyone would say, No, you can't make films, it's too difficult to make films. Which was always a lie, it's always been a lie that it's difficult to make films. But now, nobody believes it anymore, because of the technology. That's the most important thing to teach a young person, that it's not difficult.

AK: *I wanted to ask you about the look and color of the film. You had said that it wasn't exactly what you wanted?*

LvT: We had to turn up the colors in the dance sequences to make people feel that there were different levels of the film. I was not so fond of that, because it made the dancing more glamorous in a superficial way than what I really wanted, but it was necessary for the understanding of the two levels.

A K : *Do you think that's like a standard Hollywood movie musical when things get all bright and shiny?*

L v T : That was what we didn't want. It should all come from the main character's idea that life is beautiful anywhere. It doesn't have to be lit with spotlights and blue lights and slow motion or whatever, life is great anyway.

A K : *Do you think the movie looks beautiful?*

L v T : I think some of the acting scenes with Björk look beautiful. Yes, to me, they are beautiful, but I am quite fond of Björk.

A K : *So how did Björk get involved?*

L v T : I had my first meeting with Björk two years ago. We sat down, the two of us, and said the challenge is, that we should work together. And that we should submit to each other. But the problem was that, first of all, I didn't know how she acted. I only saw her in a small music video. But she fascinated me and I still am fascinated, but the problem was that she was so goddamn talented. That's the only way I can put it. She has this little girl kind of way that she is, but she is extremely clever, I must say. I've never worked with anyone like her. And that is, of course, the good side of it. The bad side of it is all of this gave her this big pain. From feeling the whole thing.

A K : *Do you consider your films experiments in some way? With each film, are you trying to break ground?*

L v T : It's an experiment for me, because I always do something that I've never done before, but I wouldn't call them experiments. It's just how I see . . . I give myself a task. This time, the task was to do a musical. And this was what came out of it. Maybe, it doesn't look like a conventional musical, but it's a musical to me. So it's not like I'm trying to change anything. This is what came out of it.

A K : *But you do like to upset the system, don't you?*

L v T : If you like something, you want it to develop. And I'm very fond of films, and I think that all the films that I really like have pushed the medium a little bit. It's like if you love a woman or a man or whatever, you want this person to develop. You want to free this person a little bit. I would like to think I do this with film.

AK: *Did you have any inspirations for this film, in particular?*

LvT: I'm very inspired by a film called *In Cold Blood*. I started with *Breaking the Waves* and then I thought, we can make it better. We can change the man that she loves for a child that she loves! I made a cynical little synopsis. But this about the blindness came much later, after I wrote the first script. I was thinking in more opera terms. Opera is more like melodrama. And the good thing about opera is that if you can accept that people sing instead of talk, then you don't have to go in and out of it. And that means you can have your emotions with you. The problem about a musical is that it's a little hard to swallow that suddenly they're like dum-dee-dee-dum-dum—this is always a little difficult. Whereas in an opera, they play all the time. But a more honorable way to do it, the way I have done, is to use her imagination to go in and out of it.

AK: *What are some of those favorite films that pushed the medium? You're a fan of Carl Dreyer, yes?*

LvT: Dreyer, yes, he was a terrific filmmaker. I was just talking to another journalist and we talked about how the first film I remember seeing and that I liked very much was *Billy Liar*, a Schlesinger movie. That was a fantastic experience, this new London wave, it was fantastic.

But no, it's not a matter of reproducing. Reproduction is a little stupid. You have to put a little something in. It's like in the church you pay a little money to the collection plate. I think everybody has to put some money in—they can't just let it pass. I think a lot of directors just let it pass and kind of live on what all the other people have given. And I think it's important that we all try to give something to this medium, instead of just thinking about what is the most efficient way of telling a story or making an audience stay in a cinema.

AK: *At Cannes, you said you had no plans for any films—is that still the case?*

LvT: I'm having a vacation and it's so beautiful and maybe I'll never get another film idea in my life. I'm moving to a new house. I moved away from where I was born. I lived there for forty-four years, so I just moved. So I'm actually trying to grow up. And I got myself a sports car—that's fantastic—an Alfa Romeo Spider. It's a two-seater. I have four children. I feel like I'm eighteen years old.

A K : *But from what I've read in the press, when you're not working on films, you're suffering panic attacks?*
L v T : Yeah, but right now, I'm enjoying this open car. I don't know. My sweet wife says to me, "Try to enjoy things." So I bought a very immature car. I'm enjoying it much more than I ever thought I would, and my mother would have hated it, oh, she would have hated it. Maybe that's a good thing. Right now, I'm relaxing. I'm happy that I'm alive. I feel like someone coming back from Vietnam, you know. I'm sure that later on I'll start killing people in a square somewhere, but right now, I just feel happy to be alive.

There Will Be No Fun-Poking Today

JAN LUMHOLDT/2000

T HE FILM TOWN OF AVEDØRE is a quaint—very "Danishly"
so—and worn-down old garrison. Hardly the stuff that dreams are made of,
you might be tempted to think, and hardly where cinema history is being
made. The gates of Paramount Pictures, Cinecitta, Bollywood, Toho, Mosfilm
(and even the little Filmstaden in Råsunda outside of Stockholm, where Bergman made some serious magic in the '50s): those places certainly seem more
suited to moviedom magic. But this? If it resembles anything, it would be
the notorious "Christiania Free State" in Copenhagen, where Danish hippies
moved in the late '60s to be able to "turn on, tune in, and drop out" without
interference from the authorities of the establishment with their reactionary
views and their rules and regulations.

Coming to think of it—isn't that exactly what Mr. Lars "Rebel-with-a-
cause" von Trier and his boisterous partner Mr. Peter "No-holds-barred"
Aalbæk Jensen have set out to do, only more in the lines of "Lights! Camera!
Action!"? So, on second thought, this might be just the place for these head-
strong Danes who have set out to do their own thing without the interference from the authorities of the film establishment with their similarly
reactionary views, rules, and regulations (incidentally, Christiania is still
there, very much alive).

The last barrack at the end of the garrison yard. Young volunteer workers
run around in the building where von Trier soon will be receiving. A canteen
has some of its walls covered with enormous sheets of cardboard (probably

From *Filmhäftet* February 2000 (#111).

made by one of the volunteers or maybe even two, judging by their size) bearing Xerox enlargements of press clips featuring the ever-sniggering, ever-cigar-smoking Aalbæk, a.k.a. "Ålen" ("The Eel"), delivering yet another of those audacious statements that he seems to have a compulsive urge to deliver at least once a week. That man certainly has a reputation to live up to. How does he find the energy—and what's the deal with that ever-present cigar? Has he ever thought about taking it out of his mouth on occasion? But it's obviously a big image issue, and that takes its toll, of course—and at the end of the day "Ålen" comes off as much more fun than, say, Harvey Weinstein, as well as more interesting in his vision of cinema as a business. So puff away, just like they do in Christiania (but there all similarities end, for there they don't smoke cigars all that much).

But it's the other guy I'm meeting. Lars Attacks! Mr. Bad Boy of Danish Cinema. Mr. Making/Breaking/Shaking the Rules/Waves/Games (not necessarily in that order). Mr. Cannes 2000. Le Grand Danois. The First Danish Cinema Giant After Carl Th. Dreyer. And so forth—only James Brown has got as many *noms de guerre* to bask in. And just like Aalbæk Jensen, von Trier is an entertaining rogue. While giving interviews at Cannes, he comes off like a master of quirky one-liners (his accent helps, echoing that of the great Victor Borge), some of which are not very useful to those seriously interested in his cinematic visions. So instead of the Riviera, together with some 210 other journalists (60 in 1998 and 150 in 2000, reportedly), we prefer the old worn-down garrison, where he was found, lounging away like a little garden gnome in the comfy sofa of producer Vibeke Windeløv (who is out of the office for a while), and drinking Jolly Cola out of the bottle—handheld, of course.

JAN LUMHOLDT: *There's been quite a lot of pieces written about you through the years. Do you read them?*

LARS von TRIER: I've read the books by Peter Shepelern and Stig Björkman, at least I think I have. I feel a little like you do when you're a child and don't like to listen to your own voice on tape—and this applies to my statements in the printed interviews as well. It's something I don't regard myself as being very good at. I think I'm better at making the films than I am at talking about them.

JL: *And the questions you get? Do you feel they are relevant in relation to your ideas and visions or do you tend to get over-analyzed by some and merely regarded as an amusing* enfant terrible *by others?*

LvT: The French are generally the most serious. Very deep. Others ask away until they get what they came to hear—simple critical journalism—and then they throw away everything except what they wanted from the start. And then there are those who ask about all the usual stuff. Right now it's a lot about the rows between Björk and me.

JL: *"The usual stuff" also includes pornography. You were probably the most sought-after interview at the festival, and a comparatively small number of journalists actually got to meet you, even got into the press conference. And then we get to read far too much about your alleged plans to shoot porn. Don't you ever feel like changing the subject to more relevant topics?*

LvT: Of course I do. But it's tit for tat—what they ask for is what they get.

JL: *But it probably came from a joke you yourself once made—one that many chose to take seriously.*

LvT: I'm actually getting a little haunted by the fact that I've given so many interviews that I'm starting to forget what I've said. I frequently get to hear things like "in nineteen hundred something-or-another you said this about life after death." I never discuss life after death with my friends, but when a journalist comes along and asks the question, then I always have to have an opinion on everything between heaven and earth. And then it snowballs into something bigger than myself and becomes a vicious circle. Maybe I should get better at simply saying, "I can't answer that question."

JL: *You do seem to like to poke fun at journalists, right?*

LvT: When I'm in the right mood, yes, then I'm happy to do that. But right now I'm a little off so there will be no fun-poking today.

JL: *Is that fun-poking a part of "the little, little game that the little, little Lars has started," perhaps?*

LvT: Is that something I've said? You see, I don't remember anything.

JL: *You discuss it with Stig Björkman and he quotes it from your diary from the making of* The Idiots.

LvT: Ah, well. Fair enough. Of course it's a game. And it's very important to be a good game master, as they say in the role-playing world. I think I've got that talent, as well as the stamina and the art of persuasion. But it demands the participation of others, who also want to play "the little, little game that Lars started." That's a very important angle of my creativity.

JL: *A game that gradually has elevated you into a world elite of filmmakers.*
LvT: World elite? Well, I don't know about that.

JL: *At least* Dancer in the Dark *had a high budget. The film has a high-quality international cast. It's something as supposedly unfashionable and uncommercial as a musical, et cetera, et cetera. A lot of money involved, a lot of wills, a lot of risks. Is it still a game?*
LvT: Well, first of all a hundred million didn't make it less of a game. When we did *Epidemic*, we had one million and that was a lot back then. It should always be a game to make films. But it hasn't been with this latest film, I think. Not enough. I didn't enjoy making *Dancer in the Dark*. It was just too much hard work. For the record, we *had* prepared for a lot of fun and playfulness during the shoots, but it turned out to be an unenjoyable experience all the same.

JL: *Looking at the finished result, do you think that's visible?*
LvT: I don't think it's visible, no. Because the happiest moments during the working process were when the camera was rolling. Then we got along well, Björk and I. But only when the camera was rolling did we connect—and really well at that. Then we were suddenly free from all the reservations and misgivings. But as soon as the camera stopped rolling, it was really, really burdensome.

JL: *At the end of the day the film got both you and her the top prizes at Cannes. Wasn't that something that made the both of you feel that it was all worth it, maybe even inspiring you to reconcile your differences?*
LvT: Well, yes, but if you divide it all and consider the time when the camera was on, then those prizes only went to that part of the work. The rest has only been a lot of brawling and bickering between Björk and me—and that's a mess you can't just wash away, prize or no prize.

J L : *It is possible that the two of you can look back and laugh at all this in, say, five years?*

L v T : The strangest things happen in this world, but I do not think so, no,

J L : *Like most of your films,* Dancer in the Dark *is filled with references and quotes from well-known and lesser-known cinematic favorites and further evidence of your affection for cinema. . . .*

L v T : Yes, I had all that—until I made this one. No, seriously—I still have it. But I have the favorites I have. I haven't seen very many new films recently, to tell you the truth.

J L : *There seems to be a nice little tribute to Fred Astaire in the first scene. When Selma sings "My Favorite Things" at the amateur group's rehearsals of* The Sound of Music, *someone says, "She sings funny and her dancing isn't all that great either." I couldn't help thinking of the first screen-test evaluation of Astaire: "Can't sing. Can't dance. Can act a little."*

L v T : Really? I didn't know about that. So that's what they said about him? That's very funny! I have to say that I'm not in agreement at all, especially that third opinion—his acting ability has never struck me as very overwhelming. But of course I saw his films on television. We had a lot of Astaire and Gene Kelly—*Singin' in the Rain* is still very popular. Unfortunately very few Busby Berkeley films were shown in Denmark. Did you get him in Sweden?

J L : *We had some Eddie Cantor, but that was twenty years ago. Nowadays they don't show anything like that anymore. I'm a little puzzled by the comparisons between* Dancer in the Dark *and the so-called Golden Hollywood Musical. The finished result has very little to do with these films, I feel. Was it ever your intention to make it look like them?*

L v T : No, I was leaning much more towards the European traditions, like *The Umbrellas of Cherbourg*, which it resembles in its idea and concept and also in the social themes.

J L : *I feel it's quite close to Dennis Potter.*

L v T : I don't really like him that much. I've seen *Pennies from Heaven* in the television version and I feel it was too much parody, something I wanted to avoid at all costs in *Dancer in the Dark*. I didn't want it to turn into a Hollywood universe when the song-and-dance numbers commenced. I wanted to be as serious about everything the whole time, also when they burst into song.

JL: *But isn't the film so serious, so grave, so gruesome—*
LvT: Oh, thank you!

JL: *—and sad, that it almost turns into a great dark joke—parody, if you will—on your part?*
LvT: Well, humor and darkness are of course very closely related. Even in *The Element of Crime* there was a high degree of humorous content, although that film is regarded as very serious. But there was never any conscious intention on my part to include any dark humor in *Dancer in the Dark*. It's been a sad film that I have been telling myself. I prefer telling things to myself instead of other people because that's the only way to work—with yourself as audience. If the audience reacts the same way as I do, well, that will eventually be evident. What might seem comical in the film might be that we push the envelope quite a lot, extremely much so.

JL: *Like you've caught a couple of poor little flies in an airtight jar and then you stick needles in them and then pull off a leg and then pull off a wing and then another wing. . . .*
LvT: Precisely! But I've never enjoyed doing it with flies. I'd rather do it with actors because I feel sorry for the flies.

JL: *I detect a little fun-poking after all. But seriously, actors really seem to enjoy working in your films. Peter Stormare said he had a great time. Part of your faithful stock company returns: Stellan Skarsgård, Jean-Marc Barr and Udo Kier. . . .*
LvT: Yes, there is certainly a family bond there! And I'm so glad that they come back to me. They do rely on me to make something good.

JL: *So let's assume that you're not only the bad boy/actors-should-be-treated-as-cattle character that you've been portrayed as in the media through the years. Ernst-Hugo Järegård could never praise you enough as a director. . . .*
LvT: . . . and especially as a friend. We talked on the phone every week. It's totally incomprehensible that he just could disappear like that. But I

know—of course I hope that they enjoy working with me. I think, for example, that Emily liked doing *Breaking the Waves*.

JL: *There are some new faces in* Dancing in the Dark. *Björk and Deneuve have been very well documented lately, but what about Joel Grey?*

LvT: Vincent [Paterson, choreographer] got him. Our first idea was to get Donald O'Connor from *Singin' in the Rain*, but he's had a stroke so he can't dance anymore. It would have been a blast to have him. Then Vincent asked Joel if he wanted to come and he was delighted, and he was a blast, too. Actually, Joel told me that *Cabaret*, too, had been pure hell to work on, because Liza Minnelli was just as bothersome as Björk was. And you can't see that when you watch *Cabaret*, can you?

JL: *David Morse and Siobhan Fallon were both in a film called* The Negotiator. *Have you seen it?*

LvT: Never heard of it. That's a funny coincidence.

JL: *You printed a little note to the Cannes journalists, asking them not to reveal the ending of the story. But without giving too much away, we can say this much: Björk put in a song of her own—"New World"—at the end of the film, and you had nothing to do with it. In that song we are told that Selma can look forward to better days. I'm told that she insisted on that ending and that you had to relent. What was your own idea of the ending—just a black screen?*

LvT: Well, no. There had to be something, but I never made any decisions at all. She already had made her mind up about the song and the prospect of future hope. She'll have to stand by all that—I wouldn't have done anything like it.

JL: *There seems to be a movement "away from the basics"—in contrast to your "back-to-basics" philosophy of aesthetics. Several of the directors associated with Dogme and related schools of filmmaking seem to have developed a craving for a great wide screen, high-budget production values, and elaborate effects. Don't you feel like doing something like that at all?*

LvT: It's not a thing that I can navigate myself towards or away from. What's next in line for me is what's next in line for me and when you've done something, it turns into something else, almost by force. There's actually a connection between all these different states, at least for me, which prevents me from moving back and forth between the different phases of my career.

JL: *So we will never see you do anything like* Europa *again? Or* Medea?
LvT: It's very possible that you will, but right now I don't feel the slightest bit like that.

JL: *When you did* Medea *for Danish television in 1987, the Swedish director Vilgot Sjöman was working on a project over there, too. He recently said that he was shocked by the strictness of your working methods at the time. "What a dead end," he said that he thought. "How will he ever break free from that?" Today he and everyone else knows that you did manage to break free from it—with flying colors—and that you came out on the other side as a truly "liberated" man. Are you afraid that you couldn't handle "losing control" again?*
LvT: Well, as you say, I worked very hard to get as far as possible away from it. But, like I said, it's not really within my control.

JL: *Dogme95 really seems to have "cured" you and pointed you in a new direction:* Dancer in the Dark *certainly has more of an alleged Dogme look than a* Europa *look. But the movement, the rules and so forth, as such, is a closed chapter, right?*
LvT: Right. But I thought it was a very pleasant and fun experience.

JL: *Any thoughts on the* D-Dag *[D Day] project? Are you disappointed with the results?*
LvT: I've just been doing some editing on it. No, not really disappointed. I actually thought it was quite good, at least my part of the concept—the idea of sending actors out on the town with earphones is an exciting technique. You start out by developing a character and then you inject different sorts of input into the situation—I really liked that and I think you could develop it even further. On the other hand it wasn't a very good idea to have four different camera crews, we should have worked more collectively. But the idea of having each director responsible for one character and doing it more in sync, that I think would work. The problem was also that it was impossible for the television viewers to get a grip on the whole thing, as well as the fact that few viewers had access to all of the channels, and so forth. But we have

a DVD in the making now, with all four films plus an edited version of the story, and there you get it all.

JL: *In the beginning of the history of Dogme95 there were not four, but rather five directors. The fifth, Anne Wivel suddenly disappeared with little explanation. What happened?*
LvT: I don't think she had the courage to do a fiction film, quite simply— she's only made documentaries. But she was part of the society and all along the plan was that she would make a Dogme film. But she didn't want to, despite the fact that we kept on asking her. She probably felt too big a load, not only to make fiction, but fiction through rules and regulations. In my opinion it was a great loss—I've always liked her films very much.

JL: *Otherwise you've been known to be rather displeased with Danish cinema. Where, if at all, would you like to place yourself in the Danish tradition?*
LvT: I do like some Danish films, but they never come from what I would regard as a tradition or school. Dreyer never founded any school, no one in Denmark does. But there are some films that I like a lot, like *Weekend* [1962, dir. Palle Kjærulff-Schmidt], which is a damn good one. I recently saw *The Windmills* [*Balladen om Carl-Henning*, 1969, dir. Lene and Sven Grønlykke], which also really blew me away. *Ditte, Child of Man* [*Ditte Menneskebarn*, 1946, dir. Astrid Henning-Jensen] is great and Nils Malmros has made some really good films. So there are some good Danish films, but they are few and far between.

But the films they made when I went to film school were things I just couldn't stand. They were strange compromises and didn't succeed at any of the things they set out to achieve. Today I watch very little, but of course I like Vinterberg and the others. And I've seen the Dogme films. But at the moment I'm re-discovering the Swedish Golden Age from the '60s and the '70s. Troell and Widerberg mean more and more to me. And I have a very nice relationship with many Swedish actors. It was really such a pleasure to work in Trollhättan. I look forward to exploring Sweden a bit more—and Norway, too, by the way.

JL: *But couldn't we even call what you're doing a Danish school—you, Vinterberg and the others?*

LvT: Yes, maybe we could. In any case it's much more interesting today that it was ten years ago.

JL: *And the next film?*
LvT: Well, I don't know. I feel really tempted to do a film with a male cast right now. To be free of actresses for a while! But right now I'm just relaxing.

JL: *Relaxing or not, your name seems to be working around the clock. You have gradually become something of trademark these days. The Morten Korch television series is referred to as "Lars von Trier's new television series" and the porno films from the Puzzy Power label are called "the porno films of Lars von Trier." Aside from the fact that they're Zentropa productions, do you actually have anything to do with them?*
LvT: Definitely not, and it's really pushing it a bit too far. You'll have to talk to my associate Peter Aalbæk Jensen about those things.

JL: *You seem a little annoyed.*
LvT: Yes, I'm annoyed when I get exploited when I shouldn't be. I came up with the idea for the production of *Morten Korch*—other than that I haven't had anything to do with it. This is so stupid! Yeah, well—we just have to try to sort these things out in due time. He isn't that easy to control, that Aalbæk guy.

JL: *But you have to agree that the products get more attention with your name "on the cover," so to speak.*
LvT: Yes, but I think it's pure drivel. Stupid nonsense! I have nothing whatsoever to do with Puzzy Power, and I never had! Even though I have to say that I find the concept of women doing porno quite brilliant.

JL: *Around 1990, long before the discussion of pornography entered your world of topics, you had some serious plans of adapting two erotic classics for the screen: de Sade's* Justine *and Reage's* The Story of O. *What happened?*
LvT: Well, I had some contact with the son of "Pauline Reage"—who by the way amazed me in that she actually *was* a woman, I always thought that that novel had been written by a man—and I told him I was interested in the rights. But when he found out who I was, he said, "Never!" He had seen *The*

Element of Crime and he absolutely hated that film. And then I gave it up altogether.

J L : *Otherwise, the French seem to be some of your big fans, all the way back to your earliest work.*

L v T : Well, they're more serious about it than anywhere else in the world. When *Epidemic* was released they watched it very seriously, while maybe one or two Danes found it quite amusing.

J L : *Isn't* Epidemic—*a film you still seem very fond of—getting re-released quite soon?*

L v T : Yes, I am fond of it! And, yes, it is! Even in Sweden, as strange as that might sound. I think around thirteen people went to see it at the 1987 premiere in Denmark. I find that film humorous.

J L : *Maybe the Swedes can resurrect it for you—Sweden was quite nice to Dreyer when he was around.*

L v T : I know. Do you know that they found out about his Swedish father? His name was originally Nilsson or something like that.

9 A.M., Thursday, September 7, 2000: Lars von Trier

KJELD KOPLEV/2000

KJELD KOPLEV: *Director Lars von Trier's new film* Dancer in the Dark *opens tomorrow in forty-nine theaters around Denmark, and today we've headed out to the Zentropa film town on the outskirts of Hvidovre, and we're at the, if you will, office of Lars von Trier. So I'm away from the safe surroundings of my studio—my comfy chair, my Chinese amulet. Frankly, I'm a little nervous. How are you, Lars?*

LARS von TRIER: Never better. When people around me have it bad, I have it better than ever.

KK: *At this point you must have given a whole lot of interviews, and this one's your very last for a while. You're going fishing tomorrow, right?*

LvT: Yes, I'm going fishing very soon and it's going to be marvelous. Yes, I've given so many interviews lately—I hope that these two hours, or one hour and fifty minutes, will put me back on track again. Right now I'm in this state where there's always a microphone and you have to talk away all the time. It's not a decent place to be. So you—you're not allowed to say *you*, by the way, that's what my psychologist tells me. I'm supposed to say *I* and *me*—so *I* am really tired of talking about the same things over and over again. And it's the same questions again and again—I know we won't talk about those things today, but that's the situation, the starting point, all right? So I'm so tired of talking to anyone. But it's nice to talk to *you*—I really think so. And I've always thought that you were very pleasant and likeable.

From Danmarks Radio, 7 September 2000. Transcribed and translated by Jan Lumholdt.

KK: *That's a very good starting point.*

LvT: The very best there is. However, I'd like to talk about some other things, too, apart from the nice stuff. I might just as well make some important pronouncements now that I have 180,000 little old ladies sitting out there listening. Are there actually 180,000 little old ladies in Denmark? There really are, right?

KK: *I think you have a lot of younger listeners as well right now. A lot of construction workers.*

LvT: I'm really not that crazy about construction workers. I've had some repairs done at home, and they are really the so-and-so of the earth.

KK: *Now, let's not offend the listeners.*

LvT: No. OK, but if we go down from 180,000 to 170,000 it really doesn't matter to me—if it's OK with you.

KK: *That could be of vital importance, as obsessed as people are today with listener and viewer ratings.*

LvT: No, but what I wanted to talk about was all this talk about how unpleasant I've been towards Björk. I haven't talked about anything else lately: my atrocious behavior towards her. And the unpleasant thing has to do with the process of making fiction. But then there's the documentary part of it and that interests me more and more with age. As you grow older you get more interested in reality compared to fiction, right? That's why I'm interested in working with reality in relation to my work. So you could really take it one step further and make something in the documentary vein, or something like what you're doing—not exactly journalism, but bordering on it, right?

And all of a sudden you find out that this way of working is even more repulsive. Because these people who do all the interviews. . . . I'm sitting here with you, you're a nice guy, and that's all well and good. But you're not here because of me, and it could still be pleasant enough despite all, but all journalism is a little leech-like in character. It can be a nice leech and you really can enjoy yourself with that leech, but it isn't because of the interviewee that they show up and are nice. The same thing holds true if you were to go to some underdeveloped country and interview some down-and-out, oppressed family in Latin America: it's still some kind of parasitic operation, I can't change my view on that.

Granted, there are many positive things about it, you can change the world and all that, that's all well and good. But the relation between the interviewer and the interviewee, as nice as it may be on occasion, is basically false, because it's all about filling the tape or for the journalist to get what's in it for him. He's out to get a legend he can then put in print, and it's always at the expense of the interviewee. Always. They always take something from you. But I truly appreciate a good relation. I remember you coming out to me when I went to film school. Do you remember?

KK: *Sure, I remember.*

LvT: At that time I was really hurt—you really stabbed me in the back afterwards . . . which was what it was all about, but still it was really rough since we had had such a nice time. It was one of those exercises where I was supposed to interview you in front of a camera and I thought it had all gone very, very well. You were so nice and Jewish and it couldn't have gone better—man, a really sweet Jew! And afterwards at the evaluation you said, "Well, Lars could have done a lot better on this and that occasion." That really hurts.

And this is where the journalist rears his ugly head. The worst thing about journalism is when it starts to get critical afterwards. You should just have said that I was great! I wouldn't have learnt anything, but what the hell.

KK: *I was probably very unsure of myself in that situation.*

LvT: No you weren't! You were on the teachers' side. First you were on my side when we did the interview and we had a really nice time. Then you were on the teachers' side.

KK: *Come on, Lars, you know just as well as I do that that kind of arrogance and toughness hides a profound feeling of insecurity towards the situation. That's why it gets awkward at times.*

LvT: No, no, no. Despite the Jews having always been oppressed and all, they have their bad sides as well, just like other people.

KK: *You think so?*

LvT: You don't think so?

K K :   *I think so, yes. Not only do I think so, I know so.*
L v T :   You're not orthodox or anything, are you?

K K :   *No, I'm nothing at all. Not even a member of the congregation or anything.*
L v T :   But you're circumcised?

K K :   *Yes.*
L v T :   But you didn't ask for it?

K K :   *I didn't ask for it. And I also attended the Jewish School, because it's something your parents decide. But when I turned eighteen, I immediately withdrew.*
L v T :   And then you had your foreskin sewn back on?

K K :   *You can't do that. Or, I've read in some American magazine that they perform some operation where you can get it back.*
L v T :   Ah, yes! Just like with hymens.

K K :   *Anyway, I'm not considering that. I'm quite happy with things as they are.*
L v T :   OK. Furthermore, the saying is that there's much more sensitivity in the prickhead after a circumcision. Isn't that right?

K K :   *Well, I really don't have anything to compare it with.*
L v T :   No, of course, you don't. But I've heard that from people who get circumcised at a later point—it's a tremendously sensitive part of the anatomy, of course.

K K :   *I have no experience of that at all. I can't really tell you.*
L v T :   But you've been happy with it and it's all worked out for the best?

K K :   *It's all worked out. I've lived with it and I've had the wives and the children I was meant to have. In that respect things have all worked out. I have a good relation to the whole thing.*
L v T :   That sounds good. But it's a strange idea.

K K :   *Well, just like so many other religious ideas, it has its origin in basic hygiene. And it's also a way of branding you, making you a true member. In Hitler's Germany they just had to pull down your trousers and then there wasn't really any further discussion about whether you were Jewish or not, right? But this isn't about me, now is it?*

LvT: Well, I think it is. That's why you do these broadcasts, in order to show off a bit. Or—why do you do these broadcasts, may I ask you that? We have plenty of time left, we've only used up seven minutes or something. Why do you do them?

KK: *I do them because this is a form of conversation I enjoy. And because I have been tired—for many years—of doing quick things with instant pay-offs. You get the lowdown but never the background of the people you interview. I find it very exciting to travel the road that people choose to pave in order to reach their goals. That's much more exciting than their final statements.*

LvT: Definitely.

KK: *So when you say that I have a reason for being here that's not about you, I'm a little—well, one of the big reasons is that I've really wanted to meet you. I've really looked forward to this hour and fifty minutes. And also it's a wonderful opportunity to do it on the radio. And if I would have called you up and told you that I wanted to talk to you for almost two hours—then you probably wouldn't have—*

LvT: Then you would have been my very welcome guest, dammit!

KK: *Then you would have told me that you were busy and had to finish the film.*

LvT: No, it would have been much easier without all this around us. No, I'm not asking you because I don't know anything about this. I've just written a little text on documentary filmmaking called *DeFocus, about de-focusing* rather than focusing—and we need more of this. So everything is just so amiable. I just wanted to express that opinion of mine.

KK: *So what's the solution, then?*

LvT: Well, I'm just reflecting from an emotional point of view. I've been talking to all these journalists, right? And as soon as you have another person in front of you, you try to create a good relation with some mutual understanding and all—and it often turns out well, too. The fact that they then write some shit afterwards, to hell with that, but it's a very strange kind of parasitic operation, all this documentation. Then why do I do it, one might ask. And of course, why do I? For various economical reasons, of course. To sell the film, for example.

K K : *I just want to stress the point that I didn't choose this date, the day before the premiere.*
L v T : You didn't? I thought it was your idea all along.

K K : *No, it wasn't our idea from the start.*
L v T : All right. So, maybe I'll hum some songs from the film. Or maybe I'm not allowed to, due to copyright reasons. I'd better not. But, no— everything's OK with you and all this. But after sitting here all these months talking about how unpleasant I've been and how unpleasant it's been. Like, the difference compared to when you do fiction is that you normally work towards a common goal, unpleasant as that can be, whereas you don't do it like that in a documentary situation. The upper hand, the cynicism is always on the side of the journalist. Just for the record. Duly noted?

K K : *Duly noted. Tell me a little about this fishing thing. What's exciting about fishing? I've just tried it once, and I actually caught a little fish and that was reasonably exciting. But you really look forward to it—and you're leaving just after our broadcast.*
L v T : Well, first I have to suffer my way through that tunnel and then rejoice my way over the bridge and then I'm going fishing. It's just a few hours into Sweden. So that's just super! What do I like about this? Well, and this is hardly a surprise, I immensely enjoy my own company. To be alone out in nature, as it's so beautifully described. I like that very much. And the whole thing about fishing—I remember when I got my first fishing rod and my father sneered at me and asked me to consider the pain of the hook going through the mouth of the fish. And I have considered that.

But then again, and to make a comparison with the journalists, you can't do much in this world without hurting someone else. Every time you take a breath it's to the disadvantage of someone or something. And then you have to decide how and in which way you will hurt others. And I find it quite agreeable trying not to hurt anyone, but I have made this decision about the fish. It's a pity about them, but also, if I pull up a fish, then it makes space for another fish who will be so happy to get more space. And he will become a very happy little fish. You can rationalize it in a number of different ways—

maybe the fish that I pull up is depressed and wants to end his life, but he hasn't really been able to do it. It's not easy if you're a fish. I wouldn't know what a big salmon who's really tired of it all would do.

KK: *But it could also be a little happy fish who just got himself some space.*
LvT: You're absolutely right. That would be hard. But I've made up my mind about the fishing and it's very exciting.

KK: *What do you use?*
LvT: I try to use flies. I've done it for a while. Without much success, but still. It's also about biology and that thing about being able to catch something. We want to do that. We want to hunt. If there's some weak little animal who runs in front of you, especially if it's limping, then you run after it and bite it in the back of the head. That's the way it is, I think. That's why it's fun to fish. I also go hunting now and then, I must admit.

KK: *I see some cartridges over there on the window frame.*
LvT: Oh, but those are for the journalists. If things get too violent.

KK: *It's a consolation that they're at the other end of the room.*
LvT: And furthermore, you're only allowed to have two cartridges in a Danish gun, so if you get out of the room quickly enough it shouldn't be that bad.

KK: *What do you hunt?*
LvT: Well, I've attended battues as part of a hunting party and I don't like that very much, there's a limit to what I can stand with that sort of thing. With the line of beaters and all that.

KK: *You just shoot the prey as it leaps out of the brush in front of you?*
LvT: Yes, it has a lot in common with something your race has been subjected to on occasion—a little too much Theresienstadt for my taste. But duck hunting—that's nice. When you just sit there in the blind and wait for them in the morning or at night. But would the ducks be happier if they were shot under these circumstances rather than in the other way? Probably not. But if there wasn't any hunting going on in Denmark, then we'd only have a third of the wild animals we have. And most people appreciate wild

animals. They set loose a bunch of hens and pheasants and then you can plunk them. I'd rather be a pheasant than a hen, I think.

K K : *Anyway, I think it's a little weird, this thing about animals. Everyone wants them to grow up in good environments. Then, after they've grown up—Wham! Bam! Thank you, ma'am!*

L v T : Yes, that's right. It's the same with people, whether you get to be one minute or one thousand years old.

K K : *But we won't get eaten at the end of the day, hopefully.*

L v T : I don't know about that. Your race, for example, you all get fed to the worms. But you're not really into that. All right, I'm going to stop talking about the race thing. The reason for all these references to the race thing is of course my own unlucky relation to the Jewish genes—the fact that I found out that I didn't have any.

K K : *We'll get back to that a little later.*

L v T : OK? You have a plan?

K K : *There's a masterplan inside my head, don't worry. Nothing is left to chance— fate is not allowed to rule this show. Lars von Trier is our guest, in a live broadcast far from the nice and secure room up in the radio tower. We are at Avedøre and we're in Lars von Trier's at this point not very well-equipped study.*

L v T : So?

K K : *There's a new bathroom and a kitchen that's not quite finished. I said before that it's only Lars and I here, but that's not entirely true. There is actually a third person present and that bothers me. Over there on the wall is a giant picture of Baden-Powell. I've been a Boy Scout, so he's one of the people I hate the most. Why is there an enormous picture of Baden-Powell hanging there?*

L v T : It was actually a prop from this film and suddenly I saw it in the prop warehouse and asked for it and got it. He was also one of the people my father hated the most. Before Hitler and Mussolini it was Baden over there, so he's hanging around and getting some honor and dignity. My father's opinion was that nothing was worse than putting short trousers and Wellingtons on little boys, as well as putting military discipline in their heads.

And I basically agree, but I think he looks a tad pedophilic there on the wall—he amuses me.

K K : *But why?*

L v T : I feel oddly connected to him, I don't know. I don't know much about Baden-Powell, I think I was a Wolf Cub for three days. I managed to get permission, because everyone else was a Wolf Cub. The source of a certain amount group pressure. No, it's pretty strange all that scouting, I think so, too. I don't like it.

K K : *My great knowledge of Danish cinema I owe the to Boy Scouts. After finally having persuaded my parents to let me join the Boy Scouts, I soon found out that I didn't like it, but I didn't feel like going back and telling them that I didn't like it after all. So every Tuesday while the Boy Scout meeting was being held I went to the Roxy Theater, and that was the day they changed the repertoire, so I saw every Danish film during that period in the '40s and '50s—I acquired a great knowledge of cinema from that.*

L v T : OK. Well, here's to Baden, then. But seriously, I'm quite certain that we share the same opinion on him. I just find it quite funny to have him hanging around.

K K : *It's a funny picture. He's standing there with his arms folded looking like Big Brother—watching you.*

L v T : Yes, but it's only a reproduction, so it's not that scary. I'm fine with him. He watches all the different activities in this office and has never really changed the look on his face.

K K : *There's a picture of you as well.*

L v T : That's not me, I didn't put that up. Somebody else did—somebody who was cleaning up and thought that it should be there. It's me all right, but I haven't put it there. It would never occur to me.

K K : *Lars von Trier, if we could try to get back to something that might pass for a topic of conversation today—why did it turn out to be film for you?*

L v T : Well, it couldn't have been television—you put a stop to that when you flunked me that time!

K K : *Did you really want to do television?*
L v T : No.

K K : *As far as I see it, you've been doing film forever . . .*
L v T : Yes, that's right. Almost forever.

K K : *. . . and a long time before you knew that you were going to attend film school and all that.*
L v T : That's true. I started out making these—now I'm starting to be reminded of all these interviews again. I can't answer why it was like that and how it became all this. I never doubted it—ever.

K K : *But you could also have painted or written or chosen some other form for expression.*
L v T : I've tried it all and I wasn't very good. So things turned out the way they did.

K K : *You were sure of that?*
L v T : Yup.

K K : *Why did you think you were good at it? Today I know you are, but how did you know back then?*
L v T : I thought I was good from my own point of view, and I don't know if others agreed. They might have thought I was a better painter. But it made me feel satisfied. I had the feeling I had a good grip on it. I just saw Peter Schepelern's new book on me where he has included a lot of pictures from my 8-mm films. And they're really good, if you look at them like that, just as simple frames of film. Sometimes I can see that the young man who made all this has really worked with his material. He'll go far.

K K : *If you're tired of talking about it, we won't.*
L v T : Yes, I'm a little tired of it. I'd rather talk about everything else.

K K : *Let's drop it, then.*
L v T : I have a suggestion for this show: at some point, could we perhaps have one minute of silence?

KK: *Sure.*

LvT: You don't mind that.

KK: *Not one bit.*

LvT: But it shouldn't be such that people who just tuned in will think there's something wrong with their radio.

KK: *And then start to beat on their radio and call up the network.*

LvT: I think it would be a very beautiful thing to include.

KK: *Just tell me when you want it, all right?*

LvT: I think we'll do it at 10 o'clock.

KK: *So now we've warned people. That was a little stupid.*

LvT: No, I don't think so, because apart from some of the most senile old ladies, I think that a lot of our listeners will appreciate a minute of silence.

KK: *I still don't like it when you offend the old ladies just because they're old.*

LvT: I'm really not—I don't aim to offend anyone from the P1 demographic. I usually listen to pop music on P3, but I sometimes tune in to P1 and you really get happy when you hear it, I must admit. Just like you, I also happen to think that the state of media today sucks. It truly sucks! And that's why it's so nice that there's still a radio channel called P1. But that might be on its way to getting destroyed, too. But you know more about that.

KK: *We hope not. We—*

LvT: No, not we—*I*!

KK: *It's something we'll have to see about . . .*

LvT: No—you're not allowed to say *you* or *we*. It's *I* or *me*. How's your relation to the Danish broadcasting situation?

KK: *I think it could be the greatest working place in Denmark—I don't doubt that for a moment.*

LvT: But there's something really rotten somewhere, isn't there?

K K : *There's something really rotten in the way that the media are constructed today, just like you say. For many years I had an American colleague who traveled a lot and saw a lot of Danish television during the monopoly days. At that time, he said, everyone complained over the fact that there wasn't enough talent to maintain even one decent Danish television channel. Then when TV2 came around, he maliciously commented that now we had solved the problem by creating another channel! And that tale might be very telling of the situation. The original thought was that we would create a pluralistic situation of competition with a bit of variety instead of having a monopoly . . .*

L v T : And I agree with all that wholeheartedly! And now, with Internet and all, everyone can make anything and just post it on the web and that's really cool. But what TV2 introduced was this whole thing about surveys and ratings . . .

K K : *But that's commercial thinking . . .*

L v T : But that's what's totally insane about all these surveys. They should be prohibited, all those surveys and rating systems. It should be legislated! I'm not much for legislation, but here, when they adhere so strictly to it, and they use them as a reference for everything—that's very wrong. Don't do that! Is that the fault of your bosses?

K K : *No, I have nothing to do with them. All right—now we've offended my bosses and my listeners.*

L v T : Yes, but we need some spark in the show. You don't mind that, do you? When you're so egotistical as to come here and interview me?

K K : *Getting back to this race thing—*

L v T : Getting back to offending someone.

K K : *You talked about races—and you did it because you realized you weren't Jewish.*

L v T : I realized I wasn't a Trier, yes. And the Triers are one of these old Jewish families in Denmark. But then, of course, there's this smart thing that you're only Jewish if you have a Jewish mother. And then they have a reasonably good way of keeping track of things.

K K : *It's from the old nomad days, when the only thing they could be sure of was who the mother was.*

LvT: Well, I don't think it has that much to do with nomads . . .

KK: *I think it does—all these tribes who wandered around in the deserts.*
LvT: From my own experience, I happen to know that the origins of the father can be a little dubious . . .

KK: *Yes, and that's why I mention it.*
LvT: Yes, I know what you mean. The mother's always a sure thing. It's really smart. So I've never been a real Jew by definition, since it was my father . . . but the Trier name was of course something that . . . anyway, I've always felt very Jewish in some way or another.

KK: *Meaning what, exactly? It's exciting for me, since I'm a—*
LvT: —a real Jew! No, I've never been circumcised—the Trier family have been atheists for generations. Some of them have been politicians and they wanted to be Danish, of course. But I have had a feeling of being culturally connected to a Danish form of Judaism and that has given me a sense of community—with people like you, for example! Despite the fact that they may very well stab me in the back at a critical point while I'm attending film school!

Be that as it may—I have another back-stabbing story to tell you, by the way. A really, really nice guy—and another Jew!—came here from the *New York Times* to interview me when I had made some movie. And I invited him to visit Tivoli with me and treated him to some fjord shrimps—he wasn't orthodox, so he was fine with the shellfish—and we had the time of our lives. We went on one ride after another and he was the sweetest man. We exchanged phone numbers and all and he was so damn nice. Then I saw the article—it was the worst piece of mudslinging! He even emphasized the fact that I had dirty fingernails! I had just come from my house in the country where I had been planting potatoes and the first thing in his piece was that here we have this miserable guy—

KK: *How are you with things like that?*
LvT: I think it really sucks! It's exactly what we talked about, the whole problem with journalists.

KK: *What did you do about it, then?*
LvT: I didn't do anything. But you really get. . . . In some ways you mature

on account of events like these. You learn that you can have a nice time with someone for five minutes, but deep down inside we're all loners. I don't know what he had to gain from writing about this completely unknown Dane with dirty fingernails who was an obnoxious character, but when it all came from that situation when we enjoyed ourselves immensely, then it's not really—

K K : *How does that affect you in the long run? The next time you sit there with someone you'll probably—*
L v T : Then I'll get slightly anti-Semitic! Because it was really that Jewish thing that did it for me—he's my *bro'*, I thought. He wound up in the States and it's so nice that he should come here! And you get hurt. You open up and then you're vulnerable. That's the way things are. You get really hurt if someone stabs you in the back.

K K : *When you were Jewish, as it were—when you thought you were Jewish—what was that like?*
L v T : It was so cool!

K K : *You were Jewish from birth until—how old were you when you found out you weren't?*
L v T : It was twelve years ago.

K K : *How was it? It's really exciting to get a statement from someone who used to be a Jew.*
L v T : First of all it's really cool to be among the ones who were always perse-cuted. Say what you want, but you have to admit it's really cool and it has some kind of aura to it. Of course it's awkward that some Jews have become indisposed because of that—but I thought it was cool. I've always seen myself as something of an outsider and felt a little persecuted and then it's very nice to belong to a club of persecuted people. That's more a general thing, but I've also been going through all the family trees and the books and all—my God. Both my mother and my father—no, just my mother, my father never did that—my mother constantly encouraged me to—that stupid cow!—she encouraged me to look into all the family trees. "Look here, I've found all the family trees!"

Of course she must have felt guilty as shit! Fuck, man, that's really cold!

And I've been scouring the different families and looking and looking! What a rip-off! And I've been to every Jewish cemetery I could find and placed little stupid pebbles on top of the tombstones! And I've been going around with that miserable little handkerchief with knots on the corners on my head. All this out of respect for the great past. I feel a little cheated. And I've been to concentration camps and felt so locked in! This is huge, really huge!

Being Jewish is supposed to be something defined by the outside world. Obviously I defined it myself—to a large degree. But unconsciously I think I've had some feeling of something being wrong and that's why I've tried to prove something. But what do I know? It's anyone's guess.

KK: *But what forms did it take, apart from your visits to the camps and the pebble business? Did you also go around telling people you were Jewish? Did you boast about being Jewish? Were you proud?*

LvT: I was proud of the Family, yes. All Jews were Family. Even though I thought that Israel was really screwed up. I don't have an opinion today really, but breaking the arms of Palestinians and things like that, I'm not really in favor of it. It's not that orthodox thing, really, even though I've been to the synagogue on a few occasions and that was great fun. When I enter a Protestant church, or Catholic, for that matter, I don't really feel I belong, right? But when I'm in a synagogue—I sit with my feet up and all, and it's great fun! And I remember the Jewish shops. Man, they were always so grumpy. But I thought, "Hey, it's OK!" They looked at you with bleary eyes and you could hear them think, "What are you doing here? You don't have curls in your hair! You're probably only here because you think this is exotic!" and all that. I always had that feeling in the back of my head. But that was OK—the guy was just grumpy. I said "Hello." And "Give me some matzo balls, please." And things like that. And I was really comfortable with all this—I had the feeling I had a family, and that I belonged. And with families there are good things and bad things.

KK: *I'd better interject here, for those who are not familiar with your story: until your mother died, you thought you were Jewish.*

LvT: Yes, that I had Jewish genes at least, through my father who bore the family name of Trier.

KK: *And so she told you that you weren't. He wasn't your father because your father was someone else entirely.*

LvT: My father, I was informed, was someone called Hartmann. He was supposed to be a really sweet guy but when I met him he wasn't nice at all. But
I later met my siblings—on that side—and they seem to be tremendously
nice.

KK: *And very un-Jewish?*
LvT: I don't know. Hartmann could have some connection, at least I know
there are some Jews named Hartmann. Screw the Jew thing—you hopefully
mature enough with age to realize that there are other things that matter.
But when you're a young searching human being you have your thoughts
on things like that.

KK: *But did you at that time ever consider becoming religious? Orthodox?*
LvT: No, I never did. That's a very complicated process—for one, you have
get circumcised.

KK: *Really?*
LvT: You bet. But it's done much more gently than with the babies. You get
an anaesthetic, so it's not that hacking away business.

KK: *True. I've often thought about the current debate about female circumcision
and how everyone talks about how traumatic that is. It's probably just as traumatic
for little Jewish boys.*
LvT: Well, they cut into different parts, don't they?

KK: *Yes, but the thing about being cut while you're awake.*
LvT: Yes, that must be tremendously traumatic. Of course.

KK: *So in a way you've been spared from something.*
LvT: Yes, you're right about that. It must be really traumatic. But you can't
remember anything of it, can you?

KK: *No, but that's almost always the case with traumatic experiences. But they
leave their scars somewhere or other, I guess.*
LvT: I believe so.

KK: *That's probably why the guy from the* New York Times . . .
LvT: Oh yes, of course! The dirty fingernails and the shrimp and everything.

He was probably furious because I had a foreskin. I even think we took a piss together at some point! And then he thought, "This guy is really gonna fry!"

KK: *Is this something you experience a lot? That people are cruel to you?*
LvT: Yes—sob, I do! You won't charge me for this, will you?

KK: *No, this is a free session. And while we're at it, don't sit there on the couch— lie down.*
LvT: Do I often experience that people are cruel to me? Do I? I'm definitely one of the sensitive ones. And sometimes I feel that people are cruel to me. And that bothers me. More than anything, I'd rather have a good relation to everyone. And then I'd have it good.

KK: *How do you handle it? Do you always get by with a little irony, a crooked smile and a little satire?*
LvT: Yes, you can use those things for many purposes, and that's good. But usually, I see to it that everything is cleaned up after me. I'm good at that—I write letters of complaint and things like that. I do it immediately. So I think I'm quite good at cleaning house.

KK: *So you better complain about this broadcast before you go fishing.*
LvT: No, but here I'm pretty much responsible for what is said. But to return to this Björk character, whom I've done nothing but talk about for months.

KK: *I hardly dared mentioning it.*
LvT: No, but now I'm mentioning it. The thing that bothers me the most about that situation is that I've had to be so damn diplomatic. And maybe I shouldn't be so damn diplomatic—but I decided to be, right? I should be fair, I thought. And it's a struggle, so annoying. Because we really had the worst possible times together. All these things that I definitely won't get into here—but it's just not me! I normally always say exactly what I feel. Always have. And you might say that it's been a privilege for me and it's been uncomfortable for others, but that's the way it is. It's a luxury I've been able to afford. And that's why it's such a constricted, unpleasant situation to have to deal with all this. And also, I haven't really settled things with that shrew—we haven't been on speaking terms and probably never will be again. And it's much more like me to just sit down and then talk all this crap

through—you talk things through and then it's finished. Oh, this is so annoying!

KK: *Björk is your main protagonist in* Dancer in the Dark. *In theory there are a lot of people who haven't seen the film yet. It doesn't open until tomorrow, in forty-nine theaters all over the country.*

LvT: Forty-nine—all over the country! When I did my earlier films, we just used to say, "Coming to a film museum near you!" But now it's forty-nine theaters.

KK: *What's that little piece of cloth you're holding?*

LvT: I just got it "return to sender" in the mail. It's a little pillow I had made for Björk, since we already at an early stage had a communications problem—she's even more sensitive than I am and has the feeling that people are constantly stabbing her in the back, right? So I made her this pink pillow—I thought she might appreciate that color—with an Icelandic inscription. I don't know Icelandic of course, but someone translated it and it says: "If I always allow myself the time to feel my feelings, and then tell what I feel, then Lars can't manipulate me." I think it goes like that. I wanted her to sleep on it and remember it. The worst thing that can happen in the communications between two people, like when you're married or have some other similar kind of relation, the worst thing is when you think that the other one is a mind-reader. And it's so destructive—you get so angry when the other one can't read your mind. And that's dangerous ground.

KK: *Like, "You should have known that I wanted some diamonds."*

LvT: And not *those* diamonds you gave me, but some *other* diamonds. And in this case I think I gave in by writing this message in Icelandic—we're the old colonial power and all, so that's a sacrifice in itself. But she has clearly sent it back to me, thrown it back in my face. I don't know exactly what it means—if it's good or bad. If she already had mastered the lesson of the text and therefore doesn't need it, or if she simply didn't want it. I'm not sure.

KK: *She didn't include a letter or anything?*

LvT: No, nothing. But to heck with that—but I don't like leaving something behind that's unresolved. Regardless of who or what it's about. You want some closure, some point to it all.

KK: *But now that you're finished with the film—now that everything is finished and behind you, why do you still have to be diplomatic? You should be able to speak your mind to Björk today.*
LvT: But why the hell should I speak my mind to anyone but her?

KK: *Go to Iceland?*
LvT: That won't happen. We were about to meet in Hamburg. I drove down to Hamburg in my great new sports car, which you haven't seen yet because I just lent it to Peter Aalbæk while I'm away fishing . . .

KK: *Can't you go fishing with it?*
LvT: No, that would just be too much.

KK: *Can Peter Aalbæk really fit into a sports car?*
LvT: Oh, he'll do what he can to get into it. He'll cut off some toes and a heel to do it.

KK: *Back to Hamburg. You were going to meet Björk there, you said.*
LvT: Yes, I was. But we never even got to that stage. It's just like those aborted negotiations when they couldn't decide on the shape of the table, whether it should be round or square.

KK: *Some Vietnamese peace negotiations, yes.*
LvT: Just like that. From their side, it's been nothing but demands and more demands! I have another point of view, to put it mildly. I'm so fed up! But the lowdown is that if you have a problem with someone, then you should talk to that person about it and not to everyone else.

KK: *Everyone else?*
LvT: Yes, if I talk about it in interviews and things like that. And that's why I have to be indirect about the whole thing and go blah-blah-blah all the time. I should really abduct her and tie her down and put some gaffer tape over her mouth and speak my mind and then remove the tape and listen to what she has to say and then it would all be over with. But that's not how things work. Frustrating.

KK: *So, you didn't know her at all before this film?*
LvT: No, I'd never heard her music. I knew of her, and I saw one video of a

song, which turned out not to have been written by her. Screw this Björk talk. That's such a boring topic, and one that I obviously spend a lot of time talking about and thinking about.

K K : *Yes—just for the record—I did not bring this up. You did.*
L v T : I know! I know! But you would—sorry, *I*—would so much like to get myself out of the situation in a decent way, right? And you do that by talking to that person, right? That's the way it's supposed to be. You speak your mind.

K K : *And that's something you feel you'll never be able to do with Björk?*
L v T : No, I probably won't. And that goes for a lot of other people as well—but it's equally frustrating every time around. Especially when you have to deal with it by talking to others about it.

K K : *So, it's that guy at the* New York Times *and it's Björk.*
L v T : Yes, there are some people out there who've been out to get me.

K K : *Well, as the old saying goes, "Just because you're paranoid, it doesn't mean they're not out to get you." Let's leave Björk for a minute and have that minute of silence.*
L v T : No, I decide when. It's my stopwatch. OK, let's do it—now.

(One minute of silence passes.)

K K : *OK.*
L v T : OK, please carry on.

K K : *May I?*
L v T : You may. That was good, wasn't it? It makes you really feel like having another one. Your boss will be furious.

K K : *Let's take another one when we feel like it.*
L v T : Yes, let's take one now and then.

K K : *I'd like to ask you more about religion. If you're not Jewish, what are you? I ask you that as a leech, but also because I have some problems with it myself. So, from one derelict Jew to another—*

LvT: And I'm on my way to becoming a derelict Catholic as well. Since religion was so taboo in my childhood home, to the point that not having a religion was a religion in itself, then you start to wonder what there might be of value in such a forbidden area. It's always like that when something is forbidden, just like with the apple in the Garden of Eden. I was attracted to something spiritual that I was missing at home. And I immediately saw Catholicism as something with many interesting features, and much more sound than Protestantism, right? I only know Protestantism from the State Church of Denmark and that's so hopeless and boring and duty-ridden—I've never paid any church taxes, my father saw to that and that's very nice. And it's a lot of money—listen here, you 180,000 listeners of which there's probably 179,000 who pay church taxes, you pay a hell of a lot in church taxes. If I paid church taxes I would feel like a bit of a sucker, I have to admit that. And you, you're going to get buried anyway—it's not like I'm going to be left hanging around on some pole, rotting away—so don't worry about that. There are some rules. But it's a lot of money. Do you pay them?

KK: *No, for a good reason. Because of my religion.*
LvT: But every Danish citizen pays unless he or she specifically asks to be removed from the list.

KK: *But still, when I left the Mosaic community at the age of eighteen, I took care of that. Because those were the radical '60s—religion was opium and all that.*
LvT: Yes, but what attracted me to the Catholic Church—apart from the fact that I'm always drawn to groups of different sorts—was that it possessed qualities that were superior to those of Protestantism.

KK: *How old were you at this point? Because you said that religion was forbidden in your childhood home.*
LvT: I must have been sixteen or seventeen, I think, when these things started to interest me.

KK: *In other words, when you still thought you were of Jewish descent.*
LvT: Yes, that's probably true. I've never actually considered joining the Jewish community of faith—for some reason or another. Strangely enough.

KK: *That's very strange. You think you're Jewish, you're very proud of it—*
LvT: Yes, but I'm proud to be an atheistic Jew at this point. Because of the cultural background it includes.

KK: *But still you wore little handkerchiefs and visited cemeteries and you put little pebbles on tombstones and all.*
LvT: Yes, but my father did that, too. A part of the family was buried at one of these cemeteries, so we went there. That was a part of it that you respected, if someone had been connected to things like that, to religion, even though you yourself weren't. And I think he respected the Jewish religion more than Protestantism and the State Church and such—that was out of the question. There were some degrees there.

But going back to Catholicism—the things I saw as positive phenomena were the system with the saints. And the Virgin Mary was another thing—she is all but forgotten in the Protestant Church. And of course the practice of confession—that's psychoanalysis in a way and that's very sound on a social level. So there were some sound things there. At the same time I've talked to some young people who are born and bred Catholics and they hate it and see it as the most limiting and suppressive thing in the world.

There is probably something good in every religion, the important thing is how you practice it. And this is when I found out that the most beautiful thing is to be able to live with a religion. Not just by displaying it and going to church and all, but by really being able to live some of these thoughts in your everyday life. This is a good thought. My problem right now is—and I just went to a Catholic service in connection with my daughter's something-or-another—and I got so damn annoyed by the fact that every text was about humility in relation to God. That's annoying, and I keep on being annoyed by it. Granted, the texts were written by people and not by God, but it's still so annoying.

I don't see the meaning of you being humble just because you've been created by God and He has created all this. You can be humble toward life and toward other human beings and toward creativity and everything—and you are—but being humble toward the man who has created the whole circus? Of course, but you shouldn't have to prostrate yourself, and you do that in many religions—you crawl in the dust before these gods. Why? I can see why some king down here on earth might enjoy seeing people crawling before him, but if this guy is that great, then he shouldn't care whether I

bow down before him or whether I play around with my dick at night—he
shouldn't care a bit about anything like that. As long as I don't do anything
that will harm his creation, as long as I don't kill, say, too many fish—well,
he's OK with fish, they eat them in the Bible.

But this thing about throwing yourself to the floor and exclaiming,
"You're so great! You're so great!"—that's completely illogical. If you believe
in him, then he's the greatest anyhow. You look at a tiny leaf and you'll get
humble—everyone will—even some stupid redneck in an ugly car. You really
have to be stupid not to be able to appreciate a thing like that—a little leaf is
like looking into eternity. It's totally amazing! And you don't have to stand
around in church every day proclaiming that you're a little sinner and worth
nothing and that he is everything. That's annoying. Sorry, I must have made
my point by now.

K K : *And what have you done about it?*
L v T : I've done nothing! It's just annoying. I can't understand it. And that's
of course because I see God as a person and that's wrong. I can see that it
serves a pedagogical purpose in order to pacify people so that they don't go
around committing evil in society. But from a religious standpoint I think it
smells too much. The religions I know of smell too much and I know full
well that I'm returning to the standpoint of my parents, who taught me that
these things were made up in order to suppress people. Or in order to make
them behave, which is OK. But another thing is that they always get back on
their feet after every denouncement. Paradise, for example, wasn't really
there, now was it? That was just a symbol. And the generations mentioned
in the Bible, you couldn't really interpret it literally because that was such a
long time ago. I'm annoyed—I want stringency, dammit! And you don't get
that with a religion. OK.

K K : *But isn't it quite unimportant?*
L v T : It is—but I'm still annoyed. You asked me and that's what I think.
What do you want me to think? OK, we could go back and say, "All right,
there was a Paradise, those generations did exist" and do it all dogmatically.
I'd rather live with that, actually.

K K : *I think that would be easier—we probably need some kind of utopia, don't
we?*

LvT: Possibly.

KK: *But don't you think that people lose interest if they don't have something like that?*
LvT: What I do think is that people are losing interest in this broadcast. I hear radios being turned off all over Denmark.

KK: *Can you really hear that?*
LvT: Yes, I can.

KK: *Oh, then we'll just observe another minute of silence again and they'll return in a jiffy.*
LvT: Yes, then they'll return.

KK: *But don't we need these utopias in order to prevent spiritual dissolution?*
LvT: You could call it utopias. It doesn't have to be a beautiful dream as such, but we need a system. We need to battle chaos because our senses have so much more potential than we realize, I'm positive of that. We need a system in order not to have chaos falling down on us. And that system can be 117 different things, for example a religion.

KK: *What's the importance of a system, then?*
LvT: Well, with a system you're bound to get sucked into the cosmos eventually—by saying your Ave Maria's or having your party membership in order, by just getting up in the morning and going to work.

KK: *You don't mean that.*
LvT: Yes, I do. That's why things are the way they are.

KK: *Is that your vision of life? Your dream? All these rules?*
LvT: It's not a dream. Life is like that. You're dependent on these systems. You can exaggerate these systems, of course, to an absurd limit and beyond the limit of what's human, but you need the system. You have to accept that. This is getting increasingly philosophical and I really don't know anything about this—you're luring me into it all!

KK: *I wouldn't say that. The Virgin Mary—why is she so important? You said that she isn't that prominent in the Protestant Church. Why do you find her so appealing?*

LvT: Well, just the fact that there's a woman involved—I find that very positive. So there's not only men. That's sound. My ex-wife, who is a Catholic, pointed that out. She thought that was important and I agree. Not because there should be any gender quota or something like that—but I just have a problem envisioning a gathering where there are no women present. And God has always been a "he." Why is "he" a he?

KK: Well we don't know. May I ask about—
LvT: You may ask about anything!

KK: I see that you get some kind of expression on your face, now and then, when I ask about certain things. Although you're a friendly man. But, this thing with women, and this is what I tried to lead up to—women characters are present in your films and they play an enormously important part in your films.
LvT: And in my life!

KK: Of course. It's like that for everyone—especially if you're heterosexual.
LvT: And regardless of sexual preference, everyone's had a mother. And it's already tough going at that point. It's hard. Really hard.

KK: Why is it hard to have a mother, then? Does it become hard once you realize that she's cheated on you?
LvT: That she has been screwing away like mad at the Ministry of Health and Social Affairs? No, that hasn't bothered me. But this whole story of her keeping me in the dark about it—I find that totally abominable. Even though I'm spending a lot of time on a couch, spending a lot of money on someone who listens to my problems—still it's quite horrendous that I lack some crucial information that's supposed to be important.

KK: Did she ever explain to you why she kept it a secret?
LvT: Well, the man already had a family and no one was supposed to find out. It actually went against my mother's entire being and all her principles to have secrets. She's been crazy about him, that guy. I've read her diaries. And that's fine. But it's strange—she was a communist and very liberated in many ways, and at the same time she had to cover everything up. That's very strange. But in all probability it's because of his family and wife and children and social standing and all. So she had to take all that into account. But I

think it was a big thing at that time with all the freedom and being able to do what you felt like and to fuck around and all, and I sympathize with all that. But I don't sympathize with the secrecy, I must admit. But there are so many secrets in our lives. And as you gradually mature, you find out that some secrets can be blessings, too. This life is a difficult one. I happen to think so.

K K : *You'd rather she kept it a secret forever.*
L v T : No, I don't. Apart from the fact that it was reasonably pathetic to deliver the whole thing on her deathbed. But that's the way it went.

K K : *And your father, or the man you thought was your father?*
L v T : Well, he died many years ago. And I thought that was the hardest thing about it. It would be hard to discuss it with him. He died when I was eighteen. But some of the good that came out of all this has been that in the Hartmann family they have good arteries, whereas the Triers have had a tendency to drop off around fifty or sixty years of age from some blood clot or something. But the Hartmann's have good arteries. So I might get cancer instead. I heard that from my new siblings.

K K : *What did he say when you contacted him?*
L v T : He wanted nothing to do with me. We had to communicate through his lawyer and things like that. Hardly an amiable situation. "I never accepted that child," he said. But I've talked about that before. I understand everyone, even him, and he couldn't take it at that point of his life. But it was far from the picture my mother painted. She said, "I'm sure you'll love him. He's a fantastic person!" He wasn't at all. Oh, screw all that. I have two new siblings and that's nice. One of them plays the bass. I like that. He's sixty-three and he plays the bass.

K K : *Classical or jazz?*
L v T : Jazz. Like he says, "It's a really good vibe." And it moves me, all this.

K K : *Back to women. Apart from the fact that we've all come from a mother's womb, how great a part do they play, and how do you create your women characters in a film? How much do you think in terms of female or male? As far as plot, personality, et cetera?*

LvT: [Writer] Klaus Rifbjerg said a wise thing—it was about me and then I always think it's wise—he said that I divide my own person into different characters, like different sides. It's a technical way of working, and this is my way of doing it. Whether it's women or men might not be that important, but of course I decide somewhere whether it's going to be a woman or a man at the end of the day. I think that the women I portray in my films are more men than they are women because they originate from the head of little Lars. That's the way things are—you're not a Martian and you can't think like one. I think that women are hard to understand, I must admit. I think I'm getting better at understanding them, but still I'm so much more at ease with men. But then men are so much easier to unmask. Which gives women much more authority, because they certainly have much more of that. When a woman interviews me, I really try to polish my act. And they have always been so didactic, all these women. Even my mother who let me do everything was awfully domineering—a dominant hag is what my mother was— and they go on about what you ought to have read and this and that. And when I visited my new siblings, something turned up, something I hadn't read, and immediately my sister went, "Hmm, maybe you should brush up a little on your knowledge of history." Oh, yes. But I have a good thing going with women. What's your point? That they constantly go around sacrificing themselves in my films?

KK: *Yes. And if that's a part of your personality—if we could keep pursuing the same theme, from religion and humility on to sacrifice.*
LvT: In the Catholic religion women don't sacrifice themselves one bit! I just talked to some Italians and they went, "But the Virgin Mary sacrificed herself." She didn't sacrifice shit! Only if it's a sacrifice to have intercourse with God, then she might have sacrificed herself—maybe he had bad breath or something. But apart from that—yes, she lay there crying under the cross, but what else was there to do? Furthermore, she had loads of kids together with Josef later on. You really can't talk about a great sacrifice there. She didn't do shit—it was that Jesus guy who hung on the cross. So there's no sacrificial role as such that I want to attribute to women. That role has appeared later on, more from a social point of view than a religious one—but that's only my opinion, because I really don't know this. But I think it's like that. Because it's Jesus who should be regarded as the one who sacrifices himself.

KK: *But then again—women are regarded as the stronger sex and men as the weaker one. In so many contexts.*

LvT: That's probably right. But it's first and foremost our ignorance about them that makes them strong. Women are as stupid as men are, I strongly believe that's a fact. But it's hard to notice because they're hard to read, and that's why you think they're more clever and stronger and more beautiful than they really are.

KK: *But these women characters in your films—aren't they in some ways saviors?*

LvT: Oh, there's a big difference in my whole body of work. In the most recent ones, they're idealists. The big difference between the men and the women in my films lies in the fact that men fail like hell, while the women fail just as much—only the men don't go the whole nine yards. They abandon ship at the sixth or the eighth.

KK: *As a rule, don't women go the whole nine yards? In real life, aren't they more consistent?*

LvT: Maybe they are. They have a drive, their desire to give birth is enormous, that's my experience. It's a biological drive more than anything else, but it's quite amazing—what the women I've known will go through to give birth.

KK: *Let alone the pain—*

LvT: The delivery is one thing. But there's so much more to having children, but they'll go through it all.

KK: *Don't underestimate the pain.*

LvT: Oh, I think that's nothing but a myth—a tall tale.

KK: *I don't think so.*

LvT: You don't think so? Have you tried giving birth yourself?

KK: *No, I haven't, but I have a deep respect for it. I'm so squeamish when it comes to pain. If men could give birth, there would be a lot of one-child families around.*

LvT: I don't think there would be any children at all. I think it's a biological thing and that men want to spread their genes and then they couldn't care less. But I'm very fond of my children, we really get along well and they're so wonderful and pleasant. I don't really like to look after four kids all at once—then I'm just a policeman and that's no fun. Not that I think that women find it any more fun. Where's the fun in looking after a bunch of kids and constantly have to go, "Don't do this. Don't do that." That's not fun at all. It's more fun to enjoy each other's company and do something together—preferably one child at the time—but no one can possibly like that policeman role.

K K: *How do you handle your four kids?*
L v T: Well, you have to be the bad cop now and then, of course. But you hang on to them until they've learnt to fly—and that's the way the system works.

K K: *Are you a good father?*
L v T: My big problem is that I think I'm good at everything. And of course I've had the thought that "These kids must really be happy to have a father like me!" And that all comes from the fact that my mother always praised everything I did when I was a child. So I have this feeling that even if I only devote five minutes to them in a corner, they'll feel so grateful toward me—that it'll be a memory for life. Thirty years from now they'll think about the wonderful times with Father when they peeled potatoes, "Ooh, I remember that! He really gave me something great and important there."

K K: *Do you spend much time with them?*
L v T: I don't know—as much as I can. But sometimes I need some time on my own. I happen to have a tremendously wonderful wife and she spends more time with them than I do, all four of them, and that's beautiful and I'm very happy with that. But sometimes I need to get away and spend some time alone, like this fishing trip—I've looked forward to it for years! I think it's good for men to spend some time outdoors now and then. And then they should return—with a fish.

K K: *Lars von Trier—our guest this week—*
L v T: Why do you have to say that all the time?

K K: *Because otherwise the listeners will call in and complain that they don't know what they're listening to.*

L v T : Screw them! They don't decide on this! Is it your boss who tells you to do this?

K K : *No, he doesn't. It's just my ego. Maybe we should have two minutes of silence at this point. But seriously, when I ask about this father business, it's because I just saw an interview with your Swedish colleague Ingmar Bergman—*
L v T : The one where he's being interviewed together with Erland Josephson? That's a killer of an interview! May I deliver the punch line from it?

K K : *You may.*
L v T : Well, listeners, this is the punch line: both Erland Josephson and Ingmar Bergman—who have about ten kids each—are sitting there pouring out their hearts about their fathers who never were there for them. "He was never there" this and "he was never there" that. And then this woman just says—so brilliantly—"Have you ever thought about the fact that your own children also have fathers?" And not once had they mentioned their children during the whole interview! That's cold! And then Ingmar Bergman talks about one of his sons. At one point, Bergman has told one of his sons that he is aware of not having been a very good father. And then the son answers, "'Not a very good father'?—You haven't been a father at *all*!" I know. And for me, I think I'm a father. Bergman hasn't been shit to them. And I envy that sometimes—being able to face being an asshole, just like that—I see the advantage of that. But on the other hand—well, I happen to like these kids a hell of a lot. I don't think he had that in him. He couldn't care less about them.

K K : *But nowadays there's a new demand on fathers.*
L v T : In that they should be more involved, yes. But I'm not finished with the women—seriously, sometimes they're quite frightening, these women. . . . And they get displeased. And the feminists and all that comes with that. It's very strange that feminists regard *Breaking the Waves*—and *Dancer in the Dark*, too, in all probability—as one of the most repressive films imaginable, because it depicts a woman sacrificing herself. What they forget is—firstly— that it's a film with a female lead, which is quite uncommon. Very few films have female leads. And most important, it's a strong woman who takes her fate into her own hands. And she holds her own against all the men all the time—she calls all the shots! I think she should be seen as a role model, first

and foremost. That she then chooses to sacrifice herself for a man and a child, respectively, that's something between her and her conscience. But she goes the whole nine yards and she calls all the shots the whole time, right?

KK: *She also says something beautiful in* Dancer in the Dark. *Outside the factory where Björk works—I know her name is Selma in the film, but I have a hard time calling her anything other than Björk—every day outside the factory Jeff waits for her after work. Every day he offers her a ride home and every day he gets the cold shoulder—she'd rather walk or ride her bike, but he doesn't give up on her. And then one day she feels sorry for him and she says something like, "I don't have room for a boyfriend in my life. But if I did, Jeff, it would be you." It's incredibly beautiful to say something like that!*
LvT: I guess so. One can only hope she means it.

KK: *Well, it's something we men appreciate to be told.*
LvT: Of course. And then we go home happy. And then she says the same thing to the next one, right? That's the way these things work—and then she'll make many men happy at the end of the day. Simply on account of their sex, women have the ability to make many men happy.

KK: *But they can also, as you mentioned, make men insecure and nervous?*
LvT: Yes, they can. Because they're also power-obsessed assholes, all these women. Men are much more fair in all this, even the guy who has his dinner first and all that, because you can understand it. But then you have the Jewish-mother type who really pulls all the strings and runs it all, including the husband, because it's a part of her power apparatus that he's the one who gives the kids a whipping after school. Men tend to disguise their motives much less, even in their practice of power. I like that. It's the other thing, the below-the-belt way of dealing with things when one really knows who's actually calling all the shots—that I find uncouth. In that respect I find women uncouth, I have to admit that. I'll stand by that statement.

KK: *Are you speaking from your experiences with your mother, or—*
LvT: From my experiences with every woman.

K K : *It doesn't come from those bitter fights with Björk, then?*
L v T : No, it's a fundamental thought I have. But that's me—I find that trait uncouth. They have great success with that trait, there's no doubt about that.

K K : *Have you tried to talk about it? With your wife, for example?*
L v T : To let her know that she's uncouth? No, I think she understands.

K K : *How? By reading your mind?*
L v T : You're right. Maybe I should tell her that she has that bad characteristic but that she shares it with the rest. My opinion is that it's much more honorable to stand up and say, "I'm running things here," than to say, "No, I'm not running things" and then still run things at the end of the day. And this is not always the case—it certainly isn't like that at home—but there's an element of that in women, of withdrawing and then running the whole show anyway. I've experienced that many times.

K K : *Maybe we're more straightforward. We don't wear masks.*
L v T : Exactly—I think so, yes.

K K : *Are you going fishing straight after our conversation here?*
L v T : Yes, I am.

K K : *How do you deal with the tunnel to Sweden, then? Do you close your eyes?*
L v T : No, I've had a couple of chances to practice. I was given this cool sports car. It's really grotesque—a red sports car! It's a Spider, an Alfa Romeo, unbelievably beautiful! Originally I wanted a black one, like really posh, but they only had the red one at that time and when I saw it I just went—of course, it has to be the red one. And I've been zooming back and forth into Sweden with it just to practice—and now I'm fine with the tunnel.

K K : *Is it something like, if you just drive as fast as you can, it's OK?*
L v T : Well, they do have some speed limits, so you can't just drive as fast as you like. No, it doesn't bother me. It's strange, but in that tunnel you lose your sense of what's up and what's down. And it's a beautiful bridge, even if it's Swedish. They weren't that nice about receiving Jews during the war.

K K : *Well, they did receive some—at least after Stalingrad.*
L v T : I think that the Swedes, the Germans, and the French are alike—it's a

human thing. And humans aren't really that good. I'm working on a new script here and it's all about the question of giving a person power without that person using or abusing it. Can this be done? No, it can't. And that's the problem. God has a power that he doesn't benefit from. That's beautiful—and inhuman.

K K : *I thought we would talk more about film but since you showed some reluctance, I didn't want to bring it up. But now that you did, I'd like to talk to you a little about script writing. What do you need to get started when you write a new script? A character? An idea? A plot?*

L v T : I need to have a basic idea. And then I walk around and get a feel for it for a while, and now I've just started to write a little. And then I'll go fishing and then maybe I'll be able to write some more. But I have to admit that after these battles against Iceland—

K K : *We just beat their soccer team.*

L v T : Yes, I had the idea of sending Björk a little note saying, in Icelandic, "Iceland's team is a bunch of cartoon characters." That would have been beautiful. But after all this I've been more uninspired than ever, I think. It's been so hard and unpleasant and how dare she take three years out of my life like that? But that goes for me, too—I took three years from her. And she's probably given me more than I've given her and all that. But it's been annoying in that I haven't been able to shake it off. And it's given me a scar and for the first time in my life I'm not 100 percent sure about what I'm doing next. But it's OK—I can always get another job.

K K : *But you have already started the next project?*

L v T : I've done a little bit—but I'm lazy. I'd rather go fishing. I want to stay at home with my family and be lazy. But I feel guilty about it.

K K : *Are you very disciplined otherwise?*

L v T : Like mad. Unreasonably so. I have a high degree of self-discipline. Luckily I have a sweet wife who tells me that you have to enjoy yourself as well. And I'm trying to do that at the moment. And that's why I told myself that I had to have a sports car. It's fun. And you might ask why someone should have a sports car when the world is starving? But on the other hand it isn't more expensive than a station wagon. And you might ask why I should have only two seats when I have four kids? Yes, but I really put pressure on myself to be able to have a good time. And I have had such a hard time learning to enjoy myself. And I think many people feel that way.

K K : *That's a very Protestant thing—you're not allowed to have too much fun—*
L v T : —for if you do, it will come and bite you in the behind, yes. And that rule really, really sucks!

K K : *I went to Italy once and met with some of these Il Manifesto people—left-wingers—and at dinner we were served this enormous plate of virgin lobster. And I asked them, very self-righteously, "Is that really something for left-wing people to feast on?" and this guy looked up—the lobster running down his mouth—and said, "Yes, and that's what the revolution is all about. Everyone should have virgin lobster every day." And I got so quiet—because it's true.*
L v T : When I eat virgin lobster I only eat five out of six because I think the sixth is poisoned.

K K : *Getting back to the script. Will you refrain from using actresses this time around, because of Björk?*
L v T : No, I don't think so. I usually have fun when I make a film. This time around it was more of a lesson, perhaps.

K K : *You seem to have had some fun together with choreographer Vincent Paterson, at least.*
L v T : Yes I have. But there has been a shadow cast over the whole film. Granted, the film set out to be a clash from the start—a clash between genres and a clash between people. And we certainly got what we set out to get. But it was tiring. This time around I'll make a film without that many clashes—a film where we all do the same thing.

K K : *What's the idea behind the new film?*
L v T : Oh, I don't know yet. I change my mind all the time so there's nothing to talk about yet.

K K : *Do you constantly have to have a film in the making? So that everything is in order?*
L v T : No, I don't think so at all. On the contrary—take a man like Dreyer

who took ten years between films. Kubrick is another one. That's quite beautiful.

KK: *Woody Allen makes three films a year—*
LvT: —and most of them are crap. No, there's no reason to make films all the time. Again, it's my self-discipline that accounts for that. And, of course I have to put some food on the table and it would be good if Zentropa were to survive and things like that. No, I think those works that appear after many years—they're much more beautiful. But—and it's the fault of the bad media climate of today—if you're away for a while, then you're gone. It's so important for me right now—after the success at Cannes—to do something completely different. The most dangerous thing is to go in and try to milk more good fortune out of a previous success. You have to work against that success, in order to move on.

KK: *Thank you for your time and space.*
LvT: Are we finished?

KK: *Yes. Now you're free to go fishing.*
LvT: Yes, kill some animals. If you have a fear of dying then kill some animals. Just like Hemingway.

KK: *Rene Eriksen and Flemming Ljunge were the technicians for this program and Karen Dahlin did the research and produced. You can hear this broadcast again—*
LvT: —Oh God, who would want to do that?

KK: *—on the Internet at www.dr.dk/p1/koplev.*

Lars von Trier in Dogville

MARIT KAPLA/2001

THE LAST TIME LARS VON TRIER was in Trollhättan, he took on Björk. Now he is back for a match with Nicole Kidman. She plays a woman on the run who seeks shelter in the American town of Dogville. Lars von Trier draws parallels between the script and the new tougher Danish immigration policy.

His eyes are the first thing you notice when you meet the Danish director, Lars von Trier. They are deep-set and slightly asymmetrical. Consequently his glance is searching and a little deceptive. He is rather short, and when we met him he was wearing green huntsman's trousers and a green jacket. You can't help sneaking a look at his ears. If they had been hairy and pointed, it would have confirmed a suspicion that he was half gnome, half elf. His ears are, however, entirely human. The only supernatural aspect of Lars von Trier is his fantastic success as a director. After the North Sea drama *Breaking the Waves*, the remarkable Dogme 95 Manifesto, his Dogme film *The Idiots*, and the Golden Palm prize winner *Dancer in the Dark*, every new von Trier film is of great interest to film enthusiasts throughout the world.

In January 2002 he will start to shoot his next film, *Dogville*. Like *Dancer in the Dark*, it will be filmed in Trollhättan. It will be made in a gigantic hangar which is adjacent to the Film i Väst premises in the Nohab industrial area. The production company is Zentropa, which von Trier and Peter Aalbæk Jensen founded in 1992. Film i Väst is one of the co-producers. The producer is

From *Film Factory*, published by Film i Väst, 2001. Reprinted by permission of the author and Film i Väst.

Vibeke Windeløv, who also produced *Dancer in the Dark*. *Dogville* will have
its première at the beginning of 2003. We met Lars von Trier two weeks before
Christmas 2001. He had come to a winter-grey Trollhättan to supervise the
completion of the set and finalize technical details before the start of filming.
The most spectacular aspect of *Dogville*, apart from the superstar status of the
leading lady, is its bare, economical form. The film will have many affinities
to theatre. In the large studio, carpenters have built a stage floor which has
been covered with coarse black carpeting. On it, von Trier has drawn buildings with thick white lines. It looks like the floor of a school gymnasium.
Apart from these markings, there is not much scenery. Each building has
some symbolic feature of 1930s American film sets—a wall with shabby wall-
paper, an old iron-framed bed, a shop counter, and the top of a spire hanging
in the air represents the chapel. As filming is not yet underway, Lars von
Trier has had time to relax a little during his two weeks in southwestern
Sweden, and he has had a chance to go hunting here. This explains his forest
green clothes.

Q: *Was the hunting good?*
A: No. . . . It was fine, but there wasn't so much to shoot at. But I was able
to hunt on the Royal beat—the beat the King usually takes. We were at Hun-
neberg, it was really beautiful.

Q: *Do you get new ideas at this stage of the film process, or have you already
planned everything for the filming of* Dogville?
A: I take great pains not to decide too much beforehand. I want the work
with the actors to be as open as possible. While we are filming, I work all the
time, so now I'm relaxing a little. I took a drink at lunchtime, that's very
nice!

Q: *What came first in the new film, the story about the people in Dogville, or the
form?*
A: The story is based on a text by Bertold Brecht. It's a song, that I'm sure
you know, about a ship that comes to a harbor. It has fifty cannons and so
and so many masts. . . . [von Trier's cell phone—which seems to be packed
with many technical finesses—rings, playing a familiar tune. He answers but
there is no response.]

Q: *What a good tune!*
A: Yes it's the Internationale!

Q: *Tell us more about the Brecht song.*
A: It's about a servant girl at an inn. She sees the ship come in. It attacks the town and the only survivor is the girl. It's a story of revenge. Although she is the lowliest inhabitant of the town, the ship comes to wreak vengeance on its people because they've treated her badly. I wrote the manuscript before I decided on the form.

Q: *What prompted you to chose this bare symbolic form?*
A: I came upon it while I was fishing—I don't know why it happened just then. The story is about a town, and you can see a town as a map. So I thought why not make the film in that way? So I've painted the buildings on the ground. We found that this concept has many advantages. For example, as there are only symbolic walls, we can see through them and follow what the other townspeople are doing all the time. We concentrate on the characters completely, as there are so few other elements involved. When you have seen the film, you should know more about the town than if the film had been shot in a real town. The idea is that the town should take form in the audience's imagination.

Q: *When I saw the map of Dogville you had drawn, in Peter Aalbæk Jensen's office, I thought of Tolkien. In his books he was very particular about the maps of his fictitious countries.*
A: I've never read Tolkien. I know that many people are enthusiastic about him, but he was not a source of inspiration. However, there is another source, and that is the film of the Royal Shakespeare Company's production of Nicholas Nickleby. It was long performance that was very stylized and very interesting. It was a great experience for me in the '70s.

Q: *When I've talked about the stylized form of Dogville with friends, some of them have been reminded of the German expressionists, and the film The Cabinet of Dr. Caligari.*
A: Yes, that's also stylized, but this will be even more naked. It's really a theatrical form. You could say that over the years film has developed away from the theatre.

Q : *So you want to bring film back to the theatre?*
A : You might compare it to fashion. If long skirts are in fashion, we reject short skirts. One of my principles is to try to be open for what film can be, without worrying too much about what it is just now. There are obvious qualities in the stylized *Nicholas Nickleby* that filmmakers currently ignore. That's why I think it is fun to take up the form again.

Q : *What do the art directors say, now that they're unemployed?*
A : I think they can put up with it.

Q : *What about costumes?*
A : The few that we use are entirely realistic.

Q : Dogville *takes place in the U.S.A., like* Dancer in the Dark. *Why did you choose the U.S.A. again?*
A : I allow myself to be provoked. I was very provoked by lots of American journalists in Cannes. They were angry because I'd made a film about the U.S.A. although I hadn't been there. So I thought: that's fine . . . at last . . now I'm going to make lots of American films. I also thought that it might be interesting for the Americans, and for others, to find out how someone who's never been there sees America. If it were my country, Denmark, I would like to know what someone who hadn't been there thought. Perhaps they think only of the Little Mermaid, or that polar bears roam around there. How should I know? In any case it's interesting to have one's country illumi-nated. I didn't think it was such a great sin. Besides that is just what Ameri-can filmmakers have always done.

Q : *You mean, they've portrayed countries they've never visited?*
A : Yes, always. Of course, they never went to Casablanca. That's why I find it difficult to understand why we may not reciprocate.

Q : *Why did you choose to set the film in the '30s and not the present?*
A : There are elements in the Brecht song which need an isolated commu-nity and the depression was a good setting for this story. Also my experience has been that if you choose a time other than the present the film becomes more realistic. . . . "It was the sixth of January, eighteen-hundred and some-

thing." In some way it becomes more like a documentary and assumes greater authority.

Q: *You have moved from the '70s in* Breaking the Waves *to the '60s in* Dancer in the Dark, *and now to the '30s.*
A: Yes, what next?

Q: *The Middle Ages?*
A: No, the problem with going back too far in time is that it is difficult to convey feelings.

Q: *All of* Dogville *turns against Nicole Kidman's character, Grace, doesn't it?*
A: I'd rather not say too much about what happens in the film, but it's about someone who comes into town from outside. She is on the run, and that is a parallel to the immigration debate. She intrudes on them in their hometown, but at the same time she is vulnerable and has no other choice. I never thought the film would be a contribution to the immigration debate, but many parallels may be drawn. My parents were refugees in Sweden during the war. I think that the moral standing of a country can be measured by its attitude to refugees. It's not that Sweden was so special in that respect, but my parents were very happy that they could come here then, and I have always felt a bond with Sweden. Denmark is awful at the moment.

Q: *Yes, the Danish election was a success for those who want a tougher immigration policy.*
A: I think it's shameful, especially as we are one of the richest countries in the world. It is contemptible. The liberalism that they are all so proud of is based on the freedom to move to where the opportunities exist. When the poor people of the world see how we live, it's hardly surprising that they try to get here, it's only human nature. I think it is very dangerous to try to solve these problems merely by drawing boundaries. It is immoral and stupid. Of course, the problems get bigger and bigger and finally there's an eruption. These problems must be tackled with a humanitarian approach, it's the only way. [Lars von Trier, who has become deeply engaged in the discussion, takes a short break.] Yes, that was politically correct!

Q: *The subject is of immediate interest because of the European Union's boundaries policy.*
A: The biggest problem is the unfair distribution of wealth in the world. There have always been boundaries. In one way or another we will be forced to think internationally.

Q: *You said before that* Dogville *is a story about revenge. Is that the central theme?*
A: Brecht's song is about revenge. The film portrays what happens before vengeance is wreaked. This film has a theme similar to that in my other films, except that this woman doesn't turn the other cheek. The gender politics are different, if you want to use that terminology. I've been accused of being "cliché-macho," haven't I? Now perhaps this is a cliché in the other direction. What do I know? Of course that's not why I'm making the film. My mother was chairwoman of the Danish Women's Union. I've been very influenced by her. She was against positive discrimination in principle because she thought women won nothing by getting a job only because of their sex and not their qualifications. When you get older you realize that your opinions are becoming more and more like those of your parents. When you're young, you distance yourself from them, but slowly and inevitably. . . . My mother was a communist and my father was a social democrat, so it's quite clear where I will end up. I do have the Internationale on my cell phone.

Q: *Your three latest films,* Breaking the Waves, The Idiots, *and* Dancer in the Dark, *are about good women—a "hearts of gold trilogy." Is this the first film in a new trilogy?*
A: Well . . . I won't know that until I make film number two, but it's a possibility. I'll have to consider that later, I think. Maybe people will get tired of seeing the same film again and again. But then, most directors make virtually the same film again and again. We call it style rather than recycling!

Q: *Why did you choose Nicole Kidman for the main part?*
A: She wanted to be in one of my films. I said she could be in this one. I wrote the role largely for her, although I didn't know her. I believe she is right in the part, and I'm very pleased that she is with us.

Q: *I saw her recently in* Moulin Rouge.
A: Yes, dammit! It'll be interesting. I saw her in a music video she made with Robbie Williams.

Q: *She is incredibly beautiful.*
A: Yes, but other qualities are required for this film. We won't be working with controlled lighting like in a music video or *Moulin Rouge.* Our filming will be less controlled, but she knows that. It won't be glamorous, but I think she realizes that.

Q: *She played a tough weather forecaster in* To Die For. *Apart from being incredibly beautiful she can be a bit sharp.*
A: Yes, a bit cold. I shall try to work with that. I think it would be interesting to find another side of her personality.

Q: *That will be exciting to see.*
A: Yes, I am the director and I have huge confidence in my ability. We can discuss it afterwards, then we'll see if I've managed to change anything at all.

Q: *But Grace is a gentle character?*
A: Yes, I would like to see Nicole Kidman softer than she's been in the roles she has played so far. We've talked about it and she is also interested in that. But she does look wonderful—like a princess.

Q: *You've worked with some of the actors before, like Stellan Skarsgård in* Breaking the Waves *and Siobhan Fallon, the prison guard in* Dancer in the Dark.
A: Yes and Udo Kier and Jean-Marc Barr will play minor roles, and there's Katrin Cartlidge who played Bess's sister-in-law in *Breaking the Waves.*

Q: *And you have Chloë Sevigny from* Boys Don't Cry.
A: Yes, I don't know her, but her husband is Harmony Korine. I think that's fun. And I don't know if it's finalized yet, but I think we're going to get Lauren Bacall and Ben Gazzara. Gazzara was in John Cassavetes' films. When I was in film school, he was the greatest. He is a very, very good actor. It's going to be a really good team.

Q: *These are actors from Scandinavia, Britain, and the U.S.A.*
A: Yes, but we'll try to get them all to sound as if they come from the U.S.A.

Stellan mustn't be a Stockholmer—too Swedish. I'm pleased to be working with him again. I know him well and I like him very much. He is so sweet and kind and sensible—a good man and a good friend. He should be in everything I do. He is really one of the family.

Q: *Are there special demands on you now, compared with when you direct a Danish cast.*

A: This is something entirely different. In your own language you can use so many nuances. But the big experiment here—what is exceptional—is that the team of actors will be onstage all the time, because there are no walls between the buildings. We are going to live together, like a collective. It will be fun to see how it works out. It won't be like in *Dancer in the Dark*, when often I only worked with the main characters. This time all twenty actors will be working simultaneously.

Q: *Is it important for you to do something quite different from* Dancer in the Dark?

A: Well, it's not so different really. I can only say that I do those things which I find fascinating. This is such a project. I don't plan what kind of films I do, I do what amuses me. Perhaps that sounds self-indulgent, but that's how it is.

Q: *Was the place name, Dogville, your idea?*

A: Yes, with the help of some friends. They said it was not English. It should be Dogsville. I think that's interesting—another blunder by a non-American filmmaker. I believe in these small faults. They humanize the project and put things in perspective.

Q: *Is there any symbolism in the meaning of the title—dog town?*

A: It will probably become apparent, I'm afraid. In any case there is a dog in the town.

Q: *Is there a dog buried? (meaning: Is there a skeleton in the closet?)*

A: One might think so. But it's not buried so deep.

INDEX

Aalbæk Jensen, Peter, 114, 131, 141, 159–60, 168, 188, 205, 207
ABBA, 132
Allen, Woody, 91, 204
Altman, Robert, 131
Andersen, Hans Christian, 135
Arnfred, Morten, 92, 114
ASA Film, 107
Astaire, Fred, 163
August, Bille, xii, 14, 63, 128, 137
Aury, Dominique. *See* Reage, Pauline
Axel, Gabriel, 63

Babette's Feast, 63
Bacall, Lauren, 211
Baden-Powell, Robert, 177–78
"Bakerman," 76
Balladen om Carl-Henning. See Windmills, The
Barr, Jean-Marc, 78, 82, 85, 131, 139, 164, 211
Beatles, The, 91, 118
Bedroom Mazurka, xv
Bendtsen, Henning, 56, 62, 65–66, 70
Bergman, Ingmar, 44, 85, 101, 139, 142, 159, 199; *Fanny and Alexander*, 15, 55; *Persona*, 55, 75; *The Silence*, 55, 75; *Through a Glass Darkly*, 75; *Winter Light*, 55

Berkely, Busby, 163
Bertolucci, Bernardo, 7
Besson, Luc, 146
Billy Liar, 157
Bjerregaard, Ritt, 97
Björk, xvi; announced as lead for *Dancer in the Dark*, 131–32, 134, 145, 153; pre–*Dancer in the Dark* acting career of, 131; von Trier's conflicts with, 156, 161–63, 165, 172, 186–89, 200–03; winning the actress award at Cannes, 153, 162
Björkman, Stig, xiii, 160–61
Blade Runner, 74
Blow-Out, 127
Boman, Barbro, 3
Borg, Björn, 89
Borgen, Johan, 68
Bowie, David, 89, 140
Boys Don't Cry, 211
Brecht, Bertold, 206–08
Bremner, Ewen, 136

Cabaret, 165
Cabinet of Dr. Caligari, The, 207
Callas, Maria, 47
Cantor, Eddie, 163
Cartlidge, Katrin, xvi, xxiii, 105, 211

Cassavetes, John, 44, 211
Cassidy, Liz, 35–36
Celebration, The, 126, 138, 141
Chandler, Raymond, 75
Circus Casablanca, 23
Clarkson, Patricia, xiii
Clausen, Erik, 13, 21–23
Clockwork Orange, A, 26
Constantine, Eddie, 66–68, 83; "Lemmy Caution," 67
Corman, Roger, 74

De Palma, Brian, 76
Decalogue, 132
Defoe, Daniel, 57
Deneuve, Catherine, 131, 134, 145, 165
Ditte, Child of Man, xv, 112, 167
Dr. Kildare, 132
Dreamlife of Angels, The, 139
Dreyer, Carl Th. (Theodor), xii, xv, 16, 19, 75, 78, 111, 157, 160, 167, 169, 203; Gertrud, xv, 47, 57, 62, 66, 70, 101; Jeanne d'Arc, 57–58, 137, 140, 142, 150; Ordet, 66, 70, 110; The Word (see Ordet); They Caught the Ferry, 57; Vampyr, 101; von Trier getting Dreyer's tuxedo, 70
DRTV (Danish Broadcasting Corporation), 6, 89, 94, 113

Eco, Umberto, 105
Elementfilm, 77
Elephant Man, The, 26
Elling, Tom, 8, 27–30, 32, 36, 132
Elodie Bouchez, 139
Elphick, Michael, xii, 26–27, 34–36, 86
Ernst, Ole, 18
Escape from New York, 74
Europa, Europa, xiv, 86

Fallon, Siobhan, 165, 211
Family at War, A, 82
Fassbinder, Rainer Werner, 19, 23, 56, 67; Effi Briest, 108

Festen. See Celebration, The
Final Combat, The, 74
Fleming, Edward, 5, 10
Foucault's Pendulum, 105
Fredholm, Gert, 9
Frøge, Bente. See Trier, Bente von
Fruen fra Hamre, 107

"Gå i bad med Ekstra Bladet," 76
Gabin, Jean, 68
Gauguin, Lulu, 3
Gazarra, Ben, 211
Gislason, Tómas, 27–28, 30, 32, 91
Godard, Jean-Luc, 141
Goethe, Johann Wolfgang von, 56
Golden Heart, 109–10, 145
Greenaway, Peter, 54
Grey, Joel, 165
Grønlykke, Lene, 16
Grønlykke, Svend, 16
Guðmundsdottir, Björk. See Björk
Gummo, 136

Hammett, Dashiell, 75; Red Harvest, 33
Harris, Jerald, 36
Hartmann, Frits Michael (biological father), 184–85, 195
Heimat, 132
Help!, 91
Hemingway, Ernest, 204
Hemmelig sommer, 3–4, 71–72
Herrmann, Bernard, 78
Herzog, Werner, 7, 137; Fitzcarraldo, 15, 44; Kaspar Hauser, 44
Hitchcock, Alfred, 36, 44–45, 78–79, 82; Vertigo, 78, 82
Holbek Trier, Cæcilia (first wife), 194
Holland, Agnieszka, xiv
Holst, Per, 28–29, 40, 73
Holten, Bo, 18
Homicide: Life on the Street, 91, 127
Høst, Børge, 49

I Am Curious, Film, xiii
In Cold Blood, 157
Iversen, Jon, 107

Järegård, Ernst-Hugo, 67–68, 78, 90–92, 132, 164
Jarmusch, Jim, 55
Jørgensen, Bodil, 121
Josephson, Erland, 199
Joyce, James: *Finnegan's Wake*, 119; *Ulysses*, 119
Juniper Tree, The, 131
Justine, 110, 118, 168
Juul Hansen, Holger, 90

Kafka, Franz, 82–83; *Amerika*, 83
Kelly, Gene, 147
Kidman, Nicole, 205, 210–11
Kids, 136
Kier, Udo, 56, 67, 83, 90, 113–14, 131, 164
Kieslowski, Krzysztof, 132
King of the Moor. See Mosekongen
Knight, Esmond, 34–36
Korch, Morten, 107, 110–12, 128, 168
Korch, Morten A., 112
Korine, Harmony, 139, 211; *julien donkey-boy*, 134, 136
Kragh-Jacobsen, Søren, 130, 132, 139
Kubrick, Stanley, 140, 204
Kurosawa, Akira, 128–29, 139

Lady of Hamre, The. See Fruen fra Hamre
Laid Back, 76, 96
Lang, Fritz, 62; *M*, 39
Lawrence of Arabia, 83
Le Grand Mal, 61, 75
Leigh, Jennifer Jason, 139
Les Miserables, 128
Leth, Jørgen, 16, 32–33, 51, 63
Levinson, Barry, 91
Levring, Kristian, 130, 132, 139
Lie Kaas, Nikolaj, 121
Lovers, 139

Lynch, David, 94, 112–13; *Eraserhead*, 94; *Twin Peaks*, 90, 94, 104, 113, 132

Mad Max, 74
Mai, Thomas, 131
Malmros, Nils, 167
Matador, xv
McEnroe, John, 89
Metropolis, 85
Michelsen, Trine, 127
Mifune, 139
Minnelli, Liza, 165
Minnelli, Vincente, 73
Miracle in Milan, 110
Miserables, Les, 128
Monty, Stine, 24–25
Morrissey, Paul, 139
Morse, David, 131, 145, 165
Morten Korch. See Stillebækken
Mosekongen, 112
Moulin Rouge, 211
Müller, Robbie, 141
Munk, Kaj, 110

Nedergård, Niels, 38
Negotiator, The, 165
Nicholas Nickleby, 207–08
Nyman, Lena, xiii
Nørby, Cæcilie, 128
Nørby, Ghita, 90–91

O'Connor, Donald, 165
Oedipus Rex, 47
O'Fredericks, Alice, 107, 112
Okking, Jens, xv, 90
Olesen, Kirsten, 10
Olivier, Laurence, 36
Ophüls, Max, 73
Oppressed People Is Always Right, An, 3
Owe, Baard, xv

Pasolini, Pier Paolo, 15, 19; *Arabian Nights*, 47; *Canterbury Tales*, 47; *Oedipus Rex*, 47; *Salo, or The 120 Days of Sodom*, 47

Paterson, Vincent, 165, 203
Pennies from Heaven, 163
Percival, 30
Petersen, Leif Sylvester, 23
Piaf, Edith, 68
Picasso, Pablo, 68
Piil, Morten, 113
Pilmark, Søren, 90
Polanski, Roman, 81, 103
Potter, Dennis, 163
Prêt-à-Porter, 131
Private Schultz, 26, 35
Puzzy Power, 168

Reage, Pauline, 168–69
Rebel without a Cause, 52
Red Horses, The. See *Røde heste, De*
Renoir, Jean, 36
Rex, Jytte, 20
Rifbjerg, Klaus, 197
Rolffes, Kirsten, xv, 90
Royal Shakespeare Company, 207
Rukov, Mogens, 17, 44
Russell, Ken, 91
Røde heste, De, 107, 112
Røde Mor, 23

Sade, Marquis de, 110, 118, 168
Sauna. See "Gå i bad med *Ekstra Bladet*"
Schepelern, Peter, 160, 180
Schlesinger, John, 91, 157
Scorsese, Martin, 139
Secret Summer. See *Hemmelig sommer*
Sevigny, Chloë, 211
Seymour, Cara, 145
Shoah, 138
Sigurdsson, Sigurjon B. "Sjón," 134
Singin' in the Rain, 145, 147, 163, 165
Sirk, Douglas, 108
Skarsgård, Stellan, 131, 164, 211–12
Sound of Music, The, 145, 163
Spielberg, Steven, xii-xiii, 98, 139
Star Wars, 30

Sternberg, Josef von, 49, 140
Stillebækken, 107
Stormare, Peter, xvi, 131, 145, 164
Story of O, The, 168
Stroheim, Erich von, 49, 140
Sukowa, Barbara, 67
Sydow, Max von, 85, 148

"Take a Bath with *Ekstra Bladet*." See "Gå i bad med *Ekstra Bladet*"
Tarkovsky, Andrei, 7, 71, 74–75, 79; *Stalker*, 74; *The Mirror*, 55, 72; *The Sacrifice*, 55
Third Man, The, 26
Thomsen, Christian Braad, 40
Thomsen, Preben, 77–78
Thorsen, Jens Jørgen, 19
Thorvald and Linda, 16
To Die For, 211
Tolkien, J. R. R., 207
Tove, Birte, xv
Trainspotting, 136
Trier, Bente von (second wife), 114–15, 124, 134, 158, 201–02
Trier, Inger (mother), 49, 73, 75, 124, 138, 149, 158, 183–84, 194–96, 198, 200
Trier, Lars von: as actor in *Epidemic*, 51, 61; as actor in *Hemmelig sommer*, 3–4, 71–72; on actors, 8, 18, 27–29, 34–36, 66–68, 92–93, 100, 116, 119–20, 151, 154, 164, 211–12 (*see also* Björk); on assumed Jewish ancestry, 138, 181–86, 190–91; on back projections, 79, 82, 85, 87, 108; "beauty of ugliness," 5–6, 19–20, 30; on becoming a filmmaker, 178–79; on being in/out of control, 58, 109, 115–16, 117–18, 123, 126–27, 131, 134–35, 137–39, 166; on being interviewed, 48, 126, 160–61, 171–73, 182–83; on/at Cannes, 49, 63, 69, 81, 86, 88–89, 103, 114, 125–26, 128–29, 131, 134–35, 138, 140, 146, 153–54, 157, 160–62, 165, 204, 208; on Catholicism, 105, 108–09, 190–94; on childhood and upbringing, 54, 107, 109, 116, 118, 137–38, 190, 198; on commercials and/or music videos, 52, 57–58,

75–76, 96; on critics and reviews, 10, 14, 16, 82, 97, 113–14, 182–83; on Danish cinema, 5, 8, 10, 13–14, 16–23, 48, 55, 63, 74, 98, 167; on the Danish Film Institute and Danish film politics, 9, 11–12, 13–14, 17, 20, 28, 33, 39–40, 50, 58, 63, 73, 76; on documentary filmmaking, 123, 174; on Dogme95, 117–22, 126–29, 130, 133–43, 165–67; early short films of, 4, 49, 71, 180; on the "Epidemic" logo, 52–53; on "The Europa Trilogy," 50, 59–60, 65, 79–80, 86; on fatherhood, 198–99; on film school, 9, 48, 72, 172; on the French New Wave, 79, 118, 127, 131, 141; on "The Golden Heart Trilogy," 123, 131, 145, 210; on handheld camerawork, 90–91, 93–95, 127, 141, 151; on hypnosis, 57, 85, 101, 108, 137, 143, 148; on idealism of his protagonists, 53, 148–49, 197; on improvisation, 50, 56, 79, 119, 141–42, 150–51; on inspirations and influences, 7, 16, 26, 39, 43, 55–56, 62, 66–67, 72, 74, 101, 109–11, 118, 127, 141, 147–48, 157, 163, 167, 206–07 (see also Dreyer, Carl Th.); on life after death, 161; on location choices, 10, 24, 26, 28, 36; on making films abroad, 42, 55, 114; on non-Danish language choices, 6, 26, 35, 55, 211–12; on the 100 cameras in Dancer in the Dark, 131, 149–50, 155; on the 180-degree rule, 91–93, 96; on passion and fascination, 5, 8, 11–12, 15, 18–19, 21, 30–31, 41–45, 79; on phobias and anxieties, 113–16, 126, 134–35, 138, 158; political standpoint of, 54, 209–10; post-synchronization, 26–27, 29; provocativeness of, 10, 22–23, 72–73, 82, 84, 140; on religion, 11–12, 95, 107–11, 138, 143, 185, 189–93, 196; on revelations on real ancestry, 105, 138, 183–84, 194–95; on screenwriting and screenplays, 14–15, 25, 28, 32, 50, 53–54, 59–61, 64–66, 79, 82–83, 85, 94, 104, 111, 118–19, 127–28, 138, 140, 157, 202–03, 207, 210; on self-image, 49, 89–90; on shooting on video, 47–48, 78, 127, 152; on sound recording,

120–21, 130; on storyboards, 28, 61, 79, 82, 141, 154; on technical aspects of filmmaking, 10, 26, 33, 51, 54, 61–63, 64, 69, 71–73, 77–79, 81–82, 87, 100–01, 120–23, 130, 149–52, 155–56; on visual aestethics ("images and moods"), 5, 7–8, 14–15, 19–20, 29–30, 38, 52–54, 64, 83, 156; on "von," 9–10, 49, 84; on women in his films, 44, 148–49, 194–97, 199–200; on World War II, 5, 64, 73, 87

Television: D-Dag (see D Day); D Day, 132, 142, 166; Lærerværelset, 89, 96–97; Medea, 47–48, 77–78, 90, 97, 101, 111, 166; Riget (see The Kingdom); The Kingdom, 90–96, 98–99, 102–05, 112–13, 116, 127, 132, 142; The Teacher's Room (see Lærerværelset)

Works: Befrielsesbilleder (see Images of a Relief); Breaking the Waves, 94, 105, 106–11, 114, 116, 118, 123, 125, 131, 133–35, 137, 140–41, 144–45, 147–48, 153, 157, 165, 199, 209–11; Dancer in the Dark, 131–32, 134, 140–41, 143, 144–52, 153–57, 162–66, 171, 187–89, 199–200, 203, 208–10 (see also Björk); Den sidste detalje (see The Last Detail); Dimension, 83, 85; Dogville, 205–12; The Element of Crime, 13, 17–18, 24–31, 32–46, 49–52, 59–61, 65, 69, 73–75, 81, 84, 86, 90, 98–99, 102, 105, 106, 108, 125, 134, 144, 153, 164, 168–69; Epidemic, 48, 50–53, 55–58, 59–63, 65, 69, 76–77, 79–80, 86, 90–91, 95, 99, 108, 125, 134, 148, 169; Europa, 50, 59–61, 64–70, 71, 78–80, 81–83, 84–85, 86–87, 88, 90, 100, 102–03, 105, 106, 108, 122, 125, 134–35, 138, 144, 148, 153, 166; The Idiots, 117–24, 125–29, 133, 135–36, 140–42, 144–45, 161, 210; Images of a Relief, 5–11, 15, 17, 19–20, 22–23, 27, 30, 32, 34, 38–39, 56, 65, 72–74, 88, 108; The Last Detail, 27, 72; Nocturne, 27, 32, 72; Zentropa (see Europa)

Trier, Troels, 23

Trier, Ulf (father), 109–10, 113, 138, 175, 177, 182–84, 190–91, 195, 210

Trier Mørch, Dea, 23, 54

Tristan und Isolde, 78
Troell, Jan, 167
Truffaut, François, 44

Umbrellas of Cherbourg, The, 163

Vinterberg, Thomas, 126, 130, 132, 138–39, 167
Vørsel, Niels, 25, 28–29, 32–33, 50–53, 55–57, 59–62, 71, 74–77, 80, 94, 99, 104, 113–14

Wagner, Richard, xii, 26, 32, 42, 62, 78
Warhol, Andy: *Dracula*, 56; *Frankenstein*, 56
Watson, Emily, xv-xvi, 105, 135, 165
Weekend (1962), 127, 167
Welles, Orson: *Citizen Kane*, 81; *Mr. Arkadin*, 56; *The Lady from Shanghai*, 81; *Touch of Evil*, 56, 81
Wenders, Wim, 44; *Alice in the Cities*, 55; *Paris, Texas*, 55
West Side Story, 148
Whale, James, 54
Widerberg, Bo, 167
Wiedemann, Katrine, 107
Williams, Robbie, 211
Windeløv, Vibeke, 123, 141, 160, 206
Winding, Thomas, 3
Windmills, The, 167
Wivel, Anne, 167

Zappa, 14
Zentropa (production company), 88, 107, 131, 133, 136–37, 139, 141, 171, 204, 205

CONVERSATIONS WITH FILMMAKERS SERIES

PETER BRUNETTE, GENERAL EDITOR

The collected interviews with notable modern directors, including

Robert Altman • Theo Angelopolous • Bernardo Bertolucci • Jane Campion • George Cukor • Brian De Palma • Clint Eastwood • John Ford • Jean-Luc Godard • Peter Greenaway • John Huston • Jim Jarmusch • Elia Kazan • Stanley Kubrick • Spike Lee • Mike Leigh • George Lucas • Michael Powell • Martin Ritt • Carlos Saura • John Sayles • Martin Scorsese • Steven Soderbergh • Steven Spielberg • Oliver Stone • Quentin Tarantino • Orson Welles • Billy Wilder • Zhang Yimou

Printed in the United States
201323BV00005B/156/A